"This wise book is essential reading for anyone who recognizes that the world's problems demand spiritual solutions, because it is we who must change before we can expect to change the world. Rabbi Jaffe draws on deep and time-tested Jewish wisdom to guide us to become more effective activists by bringing our highest truth to bear on public issues. He shows us how to tap the wellsprings of motivation, channel emotions, and align our behavior with our highest values to make us more effective in serving the public good. *Changing the World from the Inside Out* is full of valuable lessons that will help ensure that your holy light shines like a beacon in these dark times, when we need it so much."

—Alan Morinis, author of *Everyday Holiness*

"David Jaffe offers an incisive investigation into the key questions that confront anyone who hopes to make individual or systemic change. He encourages us to understand our motivations and drives—and how to use these to move toward the change we want, to help others move with us, and to not burn out in the process."

—Ruth W. Messinger, former president of
the American Jewish World Service

"*Changing the World from the Inside Out* combines sweeping, idealistic visions to repair the planet with practical, realistic approaches that enable this to get done, one step at a time. It offers a path with directions how to repair one's self and grow into a kind, understanding, nurturing partner in progress."

—Rabbi Yitz Greenberg, president emeritus,
The National Jewish Center for Learning and Leadership

# CHANGING THE WORLD
# FROM THE INSIDE OUT

*A Jewish Approach to*
*Personal and Social Change*

## DAVID JAFFE

Trumpeter
BOULDER
2016

Trumpeter Books
An imprint of Shambhala Publications, Inc.
4720 Walnut Street
Boulder, Colorado 80301
www.shambhala.com

9 8 7 6 5 4 3 2 1

First Edition
Printed in the United States of America

♾ This edition is printed on acid-free paper that meets the
American National Standards Institute z39.48 Standard.
♻ This book was printed on 30% post-consumer recycled paper.
For more information please visit www.shambhala.com.

Distributed in the United States by Penguin Random House
LLC and in Canada by Random House of Canada Ltd

*Designed by Katrina Noble*

Library of Congress Cataloging-in-Publication Data

Names: Jaffe, David L., 1965– author.
Title: Changing the world from the inside out: a Jewish approach to personal and
social change / David Jaffe.
Description: First edition. | Boulder, Colorado: Shambhala, [2016] | ©2016 |
Includes bibliographical references and index.
Identifiers: LCCN 2015047917 | ISBN 9781611803358 (pbk.: alk. paper)
Subjects: LCSH: Spiritual life—Judaism. | Jewish way of life.
Classification: LCC BM723 .J34 2016 | DDC 296.7—dc23
LC record available at http://lccn.loc.gov/2015047917

# DEDICATION

*To my parents, Alan and Liz Jaffe, communal volunteers extraordinaire, who taught me the meaning of lifelong service.*

# CONTENTS

# NOTES TO THE READER

## About the Hebrew

I occasionally refer to the Hebrew spelling of a word to show its grammatical root. For some readers the Hebrew will offer additional meaning. If you do not know Hebrew, don't worry. You can skip over the Hebrew without losing any of the basic meaning of the word or sentence. Traditional Jewish terms are transliterated throughout the book. I decided to keep the traditional terms rather than use only contemporary English translations to give the reader the option of seeing the original language used by the Mussar and Hasidic masters.

## About the Stories

Most of the stories in this book use the actual names of the people and places involved. On several occasions I change the names to maintain anonymity. None of these changes compromise the underlying lessons of the story.

CHANGING THE WORLD FROM THE INSIDE OUT

# INTRODUCTION

The genesis for this book, and my personal drive to integrate the inner life with social change, dates back to two incidents toward the end of my time in college. I was raised in a warm, highly Jewishly identified, but not particularly religious, Jewish family. Like most of my peers my bar mitzvah was the end of my religious involvement. I lived out my adolescent years as a secular, assimilated Jew in the greater New York area.

This all changed when a close childhood friend died of leukemia during my junior year of college. I was shaken out of my spiritual sleep and began to question the set path I had been on—that is, college, graduate school, professional job, family, children. I knew there had to be more to life than the search for a high-paying job that occupied most of my peers just after college. I turned down law-school acceptances and headed out West. I needed physical and emotional space from everything I knew to explore this yearning for deep connection and transcendence that had only recently awakened in me.

I spent the next two years in spiritual turmoil traversing the landscape of popular Jewish mysticism and Buddhism until I found my way to observant Judaism and a disciplined relationship with God. By my mid-twenties spiritual practice was a central part of my life.

At the same time, I awoke politically. My parents and grandparents were wonderful role models of communal volunteers, both in the Jewish and general communities. I always knew I needed to be involved in and give back to the community and lived this out by volunteering consistently from the time I was sixteen. At the same time, I was asleep to the larger issues of social and institutional oppression around me.

My political awakening began during the last semester of my senior year when my fraternity was kicked off campus for four years due to sexual harassment. I joined this particular fraternity at age eighteen out of hope that it would give me the social status and popularity that I felt had eluded me in high school. I soon found out that the fraternity glorified the mistreatment of women. My friends and I would comment privately how wrong this behavior was, but none of us ever spoke publicly or did anything about it, in the meantime remaining members of the fraternity. During my senior year, a date rape case at the fraternity was a cause célèbre on campus all spring, culminating in the house being shut down for the next four years.

During the case I was dating a feminist woman who challenged me to speak out against my fraternity. I responded, "But in general they are good guys." I knew that mistreating women was wrong. I felt strongly about the mistreatment of individuals, but I couldn't make the connection to ending oppression in "the system"—in this case, the fraternity.

Shortly after the fraternity was kicked off campus, I sat down to eat in my favorite café wearing the fraternity baseball cap. The waitress rudely slammed down my food on the table. When I asked what was going on, she told me that wearing that hat in the café would be like her wearing a swastika into a Jew's restaurant. My first reaction was anger: how can you make that comparison! I huffed out not leaving a tip. By the time I got to my car, it hit me. If she could feel that strongly about what had happened, comparing us to Nazis, there really had to be something deeply wrong with my fraternity.

Something clicked: if I know mistreatment is happening in a system and I don't do something to end it, I am complicit in that mistreatment. This realization shook me. How could I have been part of that fraternity and not acted to stop all the wrong I knew was going on? Thus began my life as an activist.

In the span of eighteen months, I went from being a basically good, fairly asleep adolescent to being an on-fire activist and spiritual seeker. I found a cause in the movement to combat homelessness in the late 1980s and early 1990s and worked at a shelter in San Francisco. Finding jobs and organizing homeless people was hard, rewarding work. I could tell that dedicating to this work over the long term and doing it well would take being rooted and accessing spiritual resources.

However, I felt like my Jewish spiritual life was separate. People knew I was Jewish, but there were no outlets for me to consistently bring my worlds together. Occasionally I would bring one of the homeless clients to speak to a Hebrew school class. In those rare moments, I sensed the connection, but these were too few and far between to fill the great need for integration I felt on a daily basis. I envied the Catholic service providers for the way they seemed to live their faith in their daily work.

I began working in the Jewish community, as a way to integrate my life. For several years I worked in the community-relations field, bridging the Jewish and general communities around the work of justice. This was a wonderful opportunity to live out my values on a daily basis, while raising the profile of social justice in the Jewish community. After a number of years, I again found myself yearning for a deeper integration of my spiritual life and service. Again, my contact with Christian ministers, particularly those in the African American community, gave me a living example of this integrated faith.

Most of my actual work consisted of writing reports, attending and organizing meetings, and strategizing how to build relationships between synagogues and local inner-city communities. It was certainly meaningful, important work, but in some way it didn't feel that Jewish or spiritual to me on a day-to-day basis. Many of our Jewish communal organizations are structured after corporate models, with boards of directors, committees, and rigid hierarchies. While there is nothing inherently wrong with such structures, they can be challenging places to cultivate the vulnerability needed for spiritual experience.

After I had spent several years in community relations, an organizer friend asked in a one-to-one meeting what I thought was next for me. "I need to learn more Torah" was my immediate answer. "Well," my friend said, "what is stopping you?" This response changed my life.

Nothing was stopping me. I was newly married; we had no children; we had some money in the bank, and my wife indeed wanted to spend our first year married learning Torah in Israel. It was a bit scary leaving a good job and career path in Jewish communal leadership in my early thirties, but if I was to be true to the spiritual yearnings that ran so deep, I needed to learn Torah. I had become tired of the somewhat superficial way many of us in the Jewish social-justice movement applied verses of Torah to liberal ideas and was seeking more authentic and deep connections between Judaism and justice.

I had a sense that the way toward integration was through a deep engagement in Jewish sources of wisdom. Thus began a five-year journey far into the yeshiva world of Torah study in Jerusalem. Within the first few months of studying, I came upon the teachings that would form the bases of this integrated path. Jewish mystical theology gave me the words and an intellectual framework for what I had been growing to know more clearly in my heart.

Hiddenness was the big idea that spoke to me the most. *Olam* is the Hebrew word for "the universe." This word comes from the three-letter Hebrew root *ayin.lamed.mem.* (O.L.M.), meaning "hidden." Jewish spirituality is founded on the understanding that beyond the material world that we perceive with our five senses is hidden a completely different reality that connects everything together in a massive unity offering an ultimate perspective on the purpose and meaning of life. This reality is referred to in Jewish sources as "God" and is imperceptible to the human senses, although its presence, influence, and value can be felt. This reality of unity and presence is perceived or intuited through our "soul," the term used in Jewish sources for the human faculty to connect with this great unity. Every human being is endowed with a soul and thus has the ability to sense this hidden reality.

The spiritual life calls us to acknowledge and feel this hidden presence and channel this awareness as cocreators with God to build relationships, communities, and societies that reflect the reality of connectedness and the value of all creation. As ambitious as this task sounds, it would be relatively straightforward if it weren't for a great paradox built into the heart of creation. Jewish mysticism tells the story this way:

Before creation, God—the great unity and source of value—was everything. God desired to create the universe to bestow goodness and love on another, but how could there be anything separate from God to relate to if everything was one? God created a space vacated of presence and in that space placed vessels that would form the universe. God poured light into these vessels; the light was too great for the vessels to contain, and they shattered into tiny pieces. These shards make up everything that ever did and ever will exist in the universe, from molecules to animals to thoughts and emotions. Light, or God's presence, exists in all these shards, but the light is hidden within the shards. Our task—through our thought, speech, and action—is to perceive God's presence in all aspects of creation. This awareness releases sparks of light that make more manifest the real unity, love, and value that flows through creation.

The paradox is that everything is really one big unity, but existence, at its core, necessitates separation and otherness. We can get confused by this otherness and forget how all creation and particularly all human beings are connected to the ultimate source of all value. To live fully means to engage this paradox and be, at once, completely oneself—unique and distinct—and at the same time cognizant that separation is only an illusion and we are all really connected. While otherness is essential for anything to exist, it is the root of suffering, oppression, and cruelty. Recognizing and acting on an awareness of the hidden unity and value of all creation, while respecting the need for difference, is key to building a more just and peaceful world.

This mystical theology resonated with my intuitive sense of the world, particularly the invisible lines of connection obscured in daily life. At the same time, I learned that the Hasidic and Mussar movements offered wisdom and practices for living with this awareness on a daily basis, giving me the raw material needed for the deep integration that had sent me to study in the first place. Hasidism and Mussar are the two major spiritual revival movements that transformed the Ashkenazi Jewish world over the past three hundred years.

Hasidism takes its name from the Hebrew word for one who goes beyond the expected norms of piety and expresses extra love for God. The Hasidic revival was founded in mid-eighteenth-century Ukraine by Rabbi Israel ben Eliezer (d. 1760), better known as the Baal Shem Tov (master of the good name), or the Besht, for short. The Besht traveled the small towns of the Ukraine preaching a Judaism that emphasized joy, emotion, prayer, storytelling, song, and dance as equally powerful ways to connect with God as traditional Torah study. Building on the idea of the hidden sparks, the Besht taught that we can reveal God's hidden presence by bringing the right intentions to daily physical acts like eating and sleeping. The presence and light are accessible to all, no matter what your level of education. *Devekut*, or "cleaving to God," was the great religious goal. Hasidism spread quickly throughout the Ukraine and Poland, with communities centered around a rebbe, or holy man, who embodied certain unique spiritual qualities, giving each type of Hasidic community a different personality.

I was particularly attracted to the Hasidism founded by Rabbi Nachman of Breslov (d. 1810), the Besht's great-grandson. Rabbi Nachman was a unique character in that he never appointed a successor, while all other Hasidic groups function as dynasties with leadership usually passed on to one of the male children or leading disciples of the rebbe. Rabbi Nachman restored Torah learning and Jewish observance to their central place in Jewish spiritual practice and also emphasized joy, solitary conversation with God in one's native language, finding the good in oneself and others, yearning, spiritual community, storytelling, and the constant accessibility of the hidden presence no matter how distant one had become. This emphasis on finding the good and personal autonomy as essential components to drawing close to God spoke to my contemporary twenty-first-century sensibilities.

Contact with Breslov personalities gave me a living model for these teachings. The man who became my primary teacher, Rabbi Natan Greenberg of Bat Ayin Yeshiva, combined the profound openness and appreciation for pluralism of his uncle Rabbi Yitz Greenberg with the powerful devotion and spirituality of the more traditional Breslov masters. Rabbi Nachman Burstein, the scion of an important Breslov family, lived in my neighborhood, and I got to speak with him about learning Rabbi Nachman's teachings and, perhaps more importantly, got to see him dance on the tables in our synagogue with incredible joy on the Purim holiday. Rabbi Nachman and his disciples provide practical advice on how to see through the hiddenness and through one's own life experience grow in awareness of the oneness that binds all creation together.

While the fire of Breslov Hasidism spoke to my passion and yearning for God, I was also looking for teachings that provided step-by-step guidance for ethical and moral development. Mussar, the other major spiritual revival movement of the modern period, provided this guidance.

Being created in the image of God does not mean that we always live like we are images of the divine. One of Judaism's central goals is to help people actually live in the image of God, or, in the Torah's language, to "walk in God's ways." The underlying goal of dietary laws, holidays, and interpersonal commandments is to turn ordinary human beings into holy vessels capable of channeling God's presence into the world. The gap between this grand aspiration and the reality of most of our lives is a central theme of the Torah. Weeks after encountering God's presence on Mount Sinai, the Israelites build and worship a golden calf. King David commits adultery, and soon after dedicating the temple in Jerusalem, King Solomon oversees the spread of idol worship in the land resulting from his many foreign wives. The Torah is a continuing story of aspiration, imperfection, failure, and return. In this way it is so very human. Mussar is the branch of Jewish wisdom that addresses this gap, seeks to align values with behavior, and asks, "How do I actually walk in God's ways?"

The word *mussar* literally means "ethical instruction," and "discipline," and it can also refer to turning in a particular direction. While some parts of the Torah itself[1] and the rabbinic tradition[2] address this task of alignment, the specific genre of Mussar literature emerged in eleventh-century Spain with the publication of *The Duties of the Heart*, by Rabbi Bahya ibn Pequda. Rabbi Bahya recognized that the Torah asked us to love and trust God and live humbly, but it did not give specific instructions on how to develop these inner qualities. His classic is the first Jewish effort to provide meditations and specific exercises for this type of inner growth. For example, his book includes a guided meditation for imagining all the intricate physical processes that make our bodies work, as a way of developing awe for creation. Similar ethical-development literature emerged in every corner of the Jewish world over the next millennia, from the rationalists of twelfth-century Spain to the mystics of Tzfat in sixteenth-century Israel to Reform Jewish writers in late-twentieth-century North America.

In late-nineteenth-century Lithuania, Rabbi Yisrael Salanter founded the modern Mussar movement. In a similar way to how the Baal Shem Tov revolutionized religious life for the average Ukrainian Jew in the eighteenth century, Rabbi Salanter transformed the Lithuanian yeshiva world and through that most of Ashkenazi Jewry in the twentieth century. Rabbi Salanter's key insight was that we can't just use our intellect to change ourselves to align our behavior with our values. We must engage the heart and emotions. No matter how many times someone studies the verse "Love your neighbor as yourself," one will not love one's neighbor more unless one feels in one's heart what it means to love oneself and one's neighbor.

In the words of the Mussar leader Rabbi Eliyahu Lopian, the goal of Mussar is to make the heart feel what the head knows. Rabbi Salanter created a movement with systematic practices for opening the heart and aligning what we know is right with how we actually behave. This included rigorous study of Jewish ethical literature, fervent and emotional chanting of ethical teachings, meditation, daily practices to develop character traits (*middot*), and careful review and recording of daily behaviors to track growth. Rabbi Salanter was a pioneer in the exploration of the unconscious, and his program targeted mobilizing these hidden forces for growth.

If Hasidism aspires to a more direct experience of God in everyday life, Mussar aspires to *shleimut*/wholeness, or aligning thoughts, speech, and behavior with the highest desires of the soul. Like Hasidut, Mussar sees daily life as the fertile field for spiritual development. How we eat and how we conduct business transactions are among the ways we become holy and walk in God's ways. Rabbi Salanter was famous for his support of dignified work conditions for peasants and laborers. In this way Mussar is a practical discipline and highly accessible.

Rabbi Salanter was a traditional Orthodox Jew and his movement focused on building the inner spiritual life and ethical behavior of the traditional Ashkenazi Jewish community in Europe. His key disciples opened centers of Jewish study that emphasized Mussar and numbered over one hundred institutions before World War I. Unfortunately many Mussar practitioners, like many Hasidic leaders, perished in the Holocaust. A small number of teachers, Rabbi Shlomo Wolbe (d. 2005) being perhaps the most important among them, dedicated their lives to keeping Mussar teachings and practices alive by writing and passing them on during the mid to late twentieth century. The late twentieth century and first years of this millennium also saw a new interest in Mussar in liberal Jewish communities in North America. Through the work of Dr. Alan Morinis of the Mussar Institute and others, thousands of North American Jews are beginning to engage in Mussar as a practical spiritual discipline.

Over the next decade, I wove together Mussar and Breslov Hasidism into a meaningful and nurturing spiritual path. As my inner life became richer and more alive, I realized that the dual paths of social justice and Judaism that I'd been traveling since college were actually one. The vulnerability and mortality I'd felt after my friend had died and the brokenness I'd experienced and saw everywhere after the fraternity were also actually one. I had been trying to do *tikkun*/"repair" in an external way, by learning and teaching Judaism and by doing and promoting social justice. I was now getting clearer that repair on the outside could not be divorced from repair on the inside. Building the inner life informs and is informed by efforts to improve the world. Mussar and Hasidut gave me the tools for this inner exploration.

I now felt compelled to return to the original question that had led me to study in the first place: how do we walk a holy path that integrates deep spiritual awareness and righteous action in the world? I wanted this integration for myself and for the many other people looking to live integrated lives who refuse to separate inner experience and external action. I also wanted it to bring the deep wisdom of these spiritual traditions to the actual work of making change. Forming this path would mean bringing together the inner teachings of Mussar and Hasidut with the external work of political and social change.

Social change is the effort to shape the ways we live, work, and play together in institutions, communities, and nations to reflect the inherent value of all people and the truth of the deep connectedness of all things. Just as we grow as individuals by noticing and owning our imperfections and making choices to align our behavior with our ideals, so too do institutions and societies grow when enough people notice and own the imperfections in the social arrangements and decide to challenge these imperfections and change these arrangements to align with values like fairness, dignity, and freedom. Just as an individual becomes holy by walking in the ways of God, so too does a society become holy by reflecting the ways of God in its social arrangements.

The Hasidic and Mussar masters targeted the individual and, at times, the Jewish community as the locus of spiritual development. This book applies that wisdom to both the individual change maker and the broader society. Since societies are a collection of individuals, the wisdom that applies to the individual also influences interpersonal relations, groups, and collectives. Rabbi Lisa Goldstein, executive director of the Institute for Jewish Spirituality, compares these different levels to a fractal. A fractal is a natural phenomenon that contains the whole in each of its parts. Similarly what is true in someone's inner life gets reflected in that person's relationships. What is true in people's relationships gets reflected in families or workplaces, and what is true in families and workplaces gets reflected in the broader society. This dynamic works in the other direction as well. The quality of our societal arrangements affects our workplaces and families, and ultimately our inner lives are deeply affected by the societies we live in and our relationships. This book shows how to integrate Hasidic and Mussar wisdom with practical social change work, giving this work deep roots and transforming it into a sustainable spiritual practice.

# PART ONE

# The Compass

The book is divided into four parts, using hiking as the organizing metaphor: "The Compass," "Signposts," "Walking the Path," and "Rest." Part one, "The Compass," includes two chapters that explore two fundamental topics in Jewish spiritual life: motivation (*ratzon*) and unconscious drives (*yetzer harah*). These forces are foundational to the inner life, and many Jewish rituals, teachings, and practices are designed to channel these forces in a positive direction. The change maker needs to understand how to recognize and mobilize these forces in oneself, one's organization, and society at large to channel them for positive change rather than to undermine efforts to do good. Like a compass gives direction to the hiker, our deep motivation and unconscious forces direct our lives in more ways than we often know. These chapters help the reader build greater awareness of how these forces function in her life and give tools for directing these forces for good.

# 1

# MOTIVATIONS FOR CHANGE

## What Do You Yearn For?

In February 2014, the National Football League made the Super Bowl the largest event of its kind to go green. The venue, MetLife Stadium in New Jersey, brought all two hundred restaurants in its facility up to rigorous environmental standards. Composting close to eight tons of food waste, converting cooking oil to biofuel, installing over four thousand LED lightbulbs, and removing all Styrofoam constituted a huge investment in sustainability. Guiding all this effort was the Green Restaurant Association (GRA), a pioneer in the green business movement. The GRA got its start back in 1990, before most people had ever heard the term "climate change" and environmental activism meant protests and industry regulation. GRA founder Michael Oshman was a teenager when he saw a news story about photographs of the growing hole in the ozone layer, the thin layer of gas that protects the earth from the sun's harmful radiation. Human production of certain chemicals found in aerosol cans, Styrofoam, air conditioning, refrigerators, and other products were the clear cause of this ozone depletion. Stunned by this concrete evidence of our role as humans in environmental destruction, Oshman decided he could not go on with his regular life while this damaging behavior continued. At nineteen years old, he founded the GRA to help the food industry reduce its negative impact on the environment.

For its first twelve years, the GRA was a local San Diego–based nonprofit encouraging restaurants to adopt best environmental practices. Throughout the 1990s Oshman spoke at conferences and to anyone who would listen about how business could be part of the solution to environmental degradation. This was before Al Gore's *An Inconvenient Truth* and the consensus of climate scientists about global warming. His impact remained local and with the few forward-thinking restaurants around the country who understood his message. Relatively alone in his belief that business and market forces were key to making real change in the growing environmental crisis, Oshman needed to be patient as the movement slowly grew.

During this period, relationships with other change makers and his ongoing visceral reaction to humans' damaging behavior toward the environment renewed his commitment. By the time market forces started to side with sustainable practices and worldwide consensus began to emerge about climate change, the GRA was well positioned to take leadership in the environmental business movement. Oshman and his team had more than fifteen years' experience developing high standards and identifying best practices to help restaurants and the food industry as a whole reduce their environmental impact. Oshman began getting invitations to speak not only at environmental conferences, but also at gatherings of the country's largest food-industry groups. Eventually the vision became a reality, and market forces started driving sustainable business practices, like the use of renewable energy sources and composting. Oshman's motivation to keep acting on his initial vision that humans can indeed live in a sustainable way with our natural resources made a significant impact in the green business movement. In Jewish sources, this type of determined motivation to action is called ratzon and forms a key building block of our inner life and for making change in the world.

One of the great things about the Hebrew language is that words are related to each other through a system of grammatical roots.

*Ratzon*, which can be translated literally as "desire" or "will," is related to the word *ratz*—"run." We run after that which we desire.[1] Thus, ratzon is the force that motivates us to act. For Oshman, this ratzon was a deep desire to do good and prevent harm to the environment.

Ratzon is deeper than intellect. If I have a strong ratzon for something, I will do almost anything to attain it. For example, you can know intellectually it is a good thing to exercise regularly. You've heard the arguments from researchers and doctors about the value of exercise and agree. However, none of these arguments actually get you into your running shoes and to the gym. You will only get to the gym consistently when you actually feel the desire to be healthier. This is the power of ratzon. Ratzon is a deeply felt desire that has more power than our thoughts do to make us act.

Ratzon operates on many levels. We have desires for basic physical needs like food, physical comfort, and security. We have desires for human connection and community. We also have desires for things that seem closer to our core identity—desires for self-actualization, meaning, contribution to the world, and for some, spiritual connection and closeness with God. In Oshman's case, his ratzon motivated him to help build a movement that could significantly influence life on this planet.

Any of these desires can be life affirming or harmful, depending on the person or the circumstance. For example, the ratzon for human connection can motivate someone to build community and develop healthy, lifelong nourishing relationships. The ratzon for human connection, when distorted, can lead to a misuse of sexual energy and the objectification of other people. A desire for closeness to God can motivate incredibly selfless service on behalf of others while it can also motivate the religious violence we all know too well. The practices described in this book are designed to help us clarify our ratzon and work with and minimize the distortions so we are motivated to live lives that align with our highest values.

As humans we are created in the divine image. This means that despite the fact that we are physical beings, our essence is something other than just a purely physical potion of chemicals, neurons, bones, and flesh. What makes us unique is a spiritual quality, sometimes referred to as the "higher self" or "soul." From a traditional Jewish perspective, one of our core desires as humans is to know and connect with our source and with other unique souls. This desire for connection is part of who we are.

Rabbi Shlomo Wolbe writes that the essential state of the universe is connection and closeness—between races and ethnic groups, between human and animal life, and between humans and the environment, and with God.[2] For example, this intuitive connection and care for all people was a primary source of Oshman's motivation to found the GRA. Why then, Rabbi Wolbe asks, is there so much division, violence, and oppression in the world?

He answers by explaining that the Hebrew word for "cruel," *akzar*, can be understood to mean *k.zar*, "like a stranger." When we treat others like strangers, we open the door to oppression and cruelty. But why would we ever treat people like strangers when our essence is connection? Rabbi Wolbe explains that we have a destructive inclination inside us that makes us forget.[3] We forget who we really are and what we are doing on this earth. When we forget that we are connected souls, we open ourselves to treat others as less than human. Life is a constant cycle of forgetting and remembering. Our work in this world is to keep remembering how connected we really are—to each other, to all life, to the environment, and to God—so that we couldn't think of causing harm.

When we remember that we are souls and connected to all life, a desire to experience this connection awakens. It is this desire that can motivate the most prosocial, constructive action to create a world that reflects the reality of this level of connection. Being awake to this reality and having the ratzon to act on it is what the

Torah means when it says, "Be holy."[4] Holiness is living in connection and alignment with what it means to be a soul in relationship with all life.

## YEARNING FOR GOOD

Ratzon is closely related to yearning. What do we really yearn for? What we yearn for is in some ways who we really are.[5] Or, as some of the Hasidic masters put it, we are where we put our minds. During the High Holidays, the Gerer Rebbe urged his followers not to overly focus on their mistakes and shortcomings, but rather to focus on how much they wanted to be good and connected to God.[6]

I find this idea very encouraging. I may not have everything I want at the moment, but at least I can want—at least I can choose where to put my mind. What we yearn for develops over time. As prosaic as it sounds, my spiritual life came alive as a thirteen-year-old baseball fan who cried when his beloved team lost in the playoffs. During this same era, I prayed with passion for certain girls to like me and for my travel soccer team to win its games. Do you remember what you used to yearn for as a young person? These were real yearnings and can give us access to what it means to want, a skill that many of us lose as we enter adulthood. So many of us are cut off from knowing what we want because others—teachers, parents, friends, siblings, advertisers, society in general—put so many of their own expectations on us that we confuse what we want with what others want for us.[7] The spiritual practice of ratzon is recovering our sense of what we deeply want.[8]

Yearning is closely related to experiencing a need or lack in our own lives, or in the world around us. Abraham Maslow, in *Motivation and Personality* (1954), described six levels of needs, which he put into a hierarchy, arguing that the fulfillment of each level gave rise to yearning for the next. The most basic needs are for food and shelter, and the highest, for spirituality and meaning. While subsequent research challenged the exact order of the hierarchy, the existence of these needs is unquestioned.

Experiencing a need is the most direct way to cultivate ratzon. I want what I don't have. While marketers exploit this simple truth all the time, we can use it for spiritual growth. The key is actually letting ourselves experience and notice the lack. Once we move past basic needs for food, shelter, and physical security, there are at least two challenges to building ratzon based on these needs. I may feel a need for the latest iPhone and actually have a ratzon to upgrade, but should I really invest energy in this type of yearning? The reason I feel this need most likely has to do with how I and my peers are manipulated regularly by Apple's marketing department. Not every sense of lack should be cultivated as an active ratzon.

At the same time as we in Western societies are bombarded with messages that we lack this or that product, there is also a subtle message that we should be rugged individualists who do not need anything. This pretense of independence is particularly acute in the United States. If I show I need help or that my life is lacking in some way, I haven't "made it." On the one hand, our lives lack fulfilment because we don't have the latest product, and on the other, we are not supposed to need anything. How is one to develop healthy ratzon?

Maslow's hierarchy of needs can be a useful tool. Go through each step and ask yourself if you are lacking anything in that area. Most people reading this book will not be lacking food to eat or shelter, but in what ways is your body unhealthy and needing different self-care? In what ways is your housing situation—be it unpleasant roommates or actual living conditions—leaving you lacking? In what ways are you needing something different in your relationship with your friends, life partner, family members, or work colleagues? Moving to the top of the hierarchy, can you feel something missing in your spiritual life, in your awareness of God or the hidden connection between all things? Can you really feel the brokenness in the world and the lack of security and dignity experienced, for example, by refugees fleeing war? Can you feel the impact of environmental degradation on fellow humans living in coastal areas and the many species on this planet?

The practice of ratzon calls on us to open our hearts to actually experience and feel these places where our lives and the world are not functioning as we would want. This takes courage and discernment. While it may sound depressing at first to notice lack, when we can notice our needs, a feeling of ratzon arises automatically. It is this feeling of ratzon that energizes our efforts to change our lives and the world for the better.

Spiritual growth is often thought of as leading to greater feelings of well-being, transcendence, and connection. Another, seemingly opposite goal of spiritual growth is increased yearning. Cultivating the awareness of the distance between the world as it is and the world as it could be leads to a deep yearning for the ideal. This yearning is a form of spirituality. Depending on who you are and what your theology is, these ideals can include anything from a world at peace to a close connection with God. At our most refined, Jewish spiritual teachers claim that we would instinctually yearn to bring healing, goodness, and closeness into the world. A common metaphor for this is that we become like iron drawn to a magnet. The magnet is holiness and we are iron.

To be like iron drawn after a magnet doesn't require looking outside of oneself. Like the Torah tells us, "It is not over the sea . . . but rather in your mouth and heart to do it."[9] It is our inheritance as humans to have a strong yearning for good and for love of God and other people. How to connect with and manifest that in our lives will be our focus throughout the rest of this chapter.

CLARIFYING RATZON

When I managed a citywide volunteer social-justice program, we often spoke about the importance of motivation. We brought together affluent, white, suburban Jews with working- and middle-class people of color from low-income urban neighborhoods to work together on joint projects like literacy tutoring and violence prevention. Feelings of guilt or pity by the folks from the suburbs could be experienced by the urban partners as a kind of disrespect that sometimes bordered on racism.

Have you ever felt pitied by someone? My family was going through some hard times many years ago due to a chronic illness my wife suffered from for six years. My wife and I used to hate the tone of pity and sorrow that some of our well-meaning friends had when they tried to help us. Our friends felt bad. We were suffering, and they didn't know what to do to help. In some conscious or unconscious way, they thought it would at least be helpful to show us how bad they felt for us. Instead, this show of pity felt to us like there was something wrong with us, as if we weren't the whole, capable, full human beings we were when our family was healthy. Thus, a well-intentioned show of pity was experienced as disability oppression.

The same dynamic happens in the social-justice arena because we are often dealing with a power differential between people working on a project or campaign. If a person in a more powerful societal position expresses pity for someone in a weaker societal position, this pity is often felt as an expression that something is wrong or broken with the individual or community. If the person or group is from a community of color, this sense that something is wrong may be experienced as racism.

This is why clarifying ratzon is so important. We need to identify the source of our yearning to get involved and make change. Why are you working on an organic farm and advocating for food justice? Why are you organizing your fellow teachers or nurses to improve work conditions in your institution? Why are you organizing in a predominantly low-income Latino community for better schools or organizing white, middle-class folks to advocate for affordable housing? Why are you volunteering in a development town in the south in Israel? Why are you applying business and market forces to create sustainable agriculture in Africa? What is it you really yearn for? Expressions of pity come from a ratzon to want to help, but why do you want to help? Our friends wanted to help us because they loved us dearly. If they could have just expressed their love without the pity, it actually could have lifted us up.

I learned this lesson just before the beginning of the second Palestinian uprising, or Intifada, when I helped start a peer-counseling community with Palestinians in Bethlehem in 2000. My original motivation for doing this was because I knew this particular counseling method very well and wanted to help two beginning Palestinian students get their own community going in their hometown. My first instinct was for them to recruit students and I would teach the class. Little did I realize that this desire to help by taking the lead was experienced as domination and racism. Everyone knew I meant well. However, the implicit message in my actions was, "You guys are so lame you haven't developed any local leaders in this method, so I will come in and teach you." Once this was pointed out to me by a close friend, I stepped back and reexamined my motivation.

What I learned when I sought greater clarity for my motivations was the following: I spent several hours every week coaching these young women and traveling to the Palestinian territories to recruit for the class because I wanted to be seen as a hero for social justice. I wanted to be the good Jewish man who helped start a Palestinian counseling community. At a slightly deeper level, I wanted to help. I knew I had more power, resources, and information than my Palestinian colleagues and wanted to do something to improve their lives. However, I was using others who were in a less powerful position to satisfy my need to feel useful.

I kept digging deeper in order to find the motivation that aligned with the dignity I wanted to bring to this project. I realized that I yearn for my Jewish state of Israel to live in peace with her Arab neighbors, and one way to help that to happen is help develop a well-functioning Palestinian society in what would become a Palestinian state alongside Israel. And I believed that this counseling method could help Palestinians, as well as all people, function better. Understanding my yearning more clearly allowed me to see that I could be effective by playing a behind-the-scenes supporting role, coaching the beginner Palestinian counselors to teach their Arab peers.

As change makers, our deepest yearnings for justice, peace, and wholeness are generally less about us helping others and more about creating something together that is central to our own identity. Knowing clearly what motivates us to act is what makes things real. When we are intimately familiar with our deep yearning, our involvement takes on a different quality than when we simply know intellectually that something is a good idea. When we have clarity about what drives us, we are present, and this makes all the difference. We need to drill down into our souls and identify that core ratzon that really speaks of who we are.

## THE DANGERS OF BLIND RATZON AND A CORRECTIVE

By now it is clear that ratzon is a powerful inner force. As we mentioned above, our ratzon and our intellect are two different inner faculties. Contemporary neuroscience locates what we call the intellect in the prefrontal cortex, and it is our faculty of analysis. Ratzon is located in the limbic system, which is made up of more primitive parts of the brain that involve urges and emotion. Ratzon motivates us to act. It is what makes things seem real to us. If we just live in our intellects, we are not really in life. We must touch and activate our ratzon.

The danger is that our ratzon doesn't have the power of analysis. It just gets up and goes without necessarily thinking about the particular direction. As mentioned above, pure motivated action is not necessarily good for the world. Islamic State fighters are highly motivated, as were Bernie Maddoff and the executives at Enron, and any other business that steals money from customers. It is easy to fool ourselves that the ratzon we act on is just and good for the world.

As unlikely as it sounds, seeking to know God's will and aligning ourselves with that will can be an important corrective to potentially misguided individual desires. Personally, I believe in God and that seeking God's will means trying to understand something essential about the universe. At the same time, I realize that many people reading this book either do not believe in God or are uncertain that God actually influences this world in any active way. I ask that you consider how this idea of God's will might translate into how you understand the world. An ancient Jewish teaching challenges us to not only understand God's will but make this will into our own will. It seems pretty elusive to even understand what God wants.

I propose three ways to identify God's will. One is classic Jewish religious literature and law. The three-thousand-year-old oral tradition is an ongoing effort to discern the divine will in each generation. This literature includes the Talmud and legal codes. So, if your ratzon is telling you to steal something, it is probably off base. We also can identify God's will by getting familiar with our intuition. This is the still, small voice of our soul that whispers more than shouts. We need to cultivate deep listening to hear it. The third way comes from awareness of our life situation and personal gifts. What skills do we have, and what is the need of our particular time and place that we are well positioned to meet?[10]

Taken together, these three are like data points that give us some sense of what God wants at any particular time. I say "some sense" because it is impossible for our limited consciousness to know God's will with any certainty. These points also balance each other. Jewish law on its own can crush the individual spirit, while pure intuition can easily be mistaken or narcissistic. The needs of this particular era keep us grounded in the here and now rather than drifting off into the past or into our own little internal worlds. Seeking and aligning ourselves with God's will is an important corrective to getting lost in our own minds. Of course people still fool themselves into thinking God wants all the infidels killed. This three-point method of discernment increases the chances that our sense of the divine will honor both tradition and the uniqueness of each individual, keeping our desire on track to improve the world.

### GROWING RATZON

Jewish tradition recognizes that we have competing prosocial and destructive desires, and urges us to develop our yearning for good.[11] Despite the messages of our cynical and competitive culture, most of us do have yearnings for relationship and for things to go well for others. How do we grow our desire for connection and goodness? Rabbi Nachman suggests two paths—engaging barriers and speaking one's desire.

### Engaging Barriers

In modern Hebrew a "barrier" is called a *meniya* and usually refers to pylons or wood horses used by police or construction companies to block access. For Rabbi Nachman, a meniya is a spiritual opportunity. The Hasidic master teaches that a spiritual barrier is something that keeps you from feeling close to God or behaving in ways that align with your values. A spiritual barrier could be anything from an inability to concentrate to a roommate who plays music too loud to memories of an overly critical rabbi when you were a child. The Hebrew root for barrier is *mem.nun.ayin.*, meaning "to withhold." A meniya withholds access to some place or something that we want. If we engage skillfully with the barrier, it can be a teacher and motivator. How does this work?

Let's take an example from the physical world. If I want to build my biceps, I will do arm curls with ten- or fifteen-pound barbells. In trying to raise my arm, the weight of the barbell acts as a barrier, keeping my fist from reaching my shoulder. The weight, or barrier, creates a tension against which I must struggle. If the tension is too great, I will not be able to raise my arm, or I will hurt myself. If the tension is just right, the effort to lift my arm will tear some of the muscle fibers, and they will grow back stronger. This is how we build muscle. The barrier is there to help me grow.

The key move is not giving up on what you want in the face of the barrier. Just like the weight of the barbell provides a counterforce to help build muscle, so too does the barrier provide a counterforce against which you can feel how much you want something. When we lean into that barrier, we can feel how much we care. It is challenging to let ourselves feel this level of caring for or wanting something.

Many of us, myself included, were humiliated as young people when we showed our enthusiasm. Think back to something you really wanted or cared about as a child. Were you met with equal enthusiasm by the adults around you, or were your desires denied? Worse yet, were you made fun of for what you wanted? This fear of humiliation or disappointment leads many of us to shrink back at the first sign of a barrier to getting what we want. We shy away from the barrier so as not to feel the discomfort. For example, we may avoid certain types of people or not take on certain challenges.

The practice of engaging barriers asks us to move in a different direction. Instead of retreating, this practice calls on us to get to know the barrier, feel its contours, and know how it looks and smells. This practice calls on us to really feel how much we care and communicate to others what we really want.

How does leaning into barriers work in a social-change context? Here are two examples from related campaigns for worker justice. My colleague Rabbi Barbara Penzner of Boston played a leading role in a national campaign fighting for justice for hotel housecleaners. One day three locations of a major hotel chain in Boston fired one hundred housecleaners on one day's notice; many of them had been employees for over twenty years. The hotel chain's new policy was to outsource housecleaning to temporary workers, who received significantly lower wages and benefits than the former housekeepers. To add insult to injury, months earlier the housecleaners had been asked to train their replacements, not knowing that they would soon be losing their jobs to these trainees. This was not an isolated incident but was part of a nationwide cost-saving strategy for that company. Rabbi Penzner organized the local Jewish community and, together with other faith communities, called on this hotel to reinstate their original workers. After several years of ongoing organizing efforts, the national hotel-workers union was allowed to organize workers at this hotel chain's key locations, and the company provided financial compensation to the workers fired in Boston.

What obstacles did Rabbi Penzner and others face? The hotel corporation saw the move to contract workers as a business decision. As a multibillion-dollar profit-maximizing company, it saw no economic benefit to stopping the outsourcing of housecleaning. In a weak economy, there are plenty of people willing to work for close to minimum wage with few benefits.

There are many reasons for Rabbi Penzner and others like her to give up on these types of efforts, especially after years of work. But time and again, activists stay committed against tremendous odds and occasionally achieve stunning victories. How was Rabbi Penzner able to maintain her drive despite daunting barriers to success? Her artful engagement with the barriers erected by the hotel corporation strengthened her pursuit of justice. Rabbi Penzner spoke about the workers' plight often and broadly to anyone who would listen within the Jewish community. Whenever a synagogue or school violated the hotel boycott, she spoke to them directly about the workers, showing how much this campaign meant to her. By showing her caring over and over again, Rabbi Penzner won allies for the campaign. Other rabbis were moved to join the boycott and to educate their communities about the larger issues of worker justice. Gaining allies in the face of opposition gave Rabbi Penzner an even stronger desire to achieve a just resolution for the workers.

Relationships with workers also boosted motivation. When we show how much we care about something, people of goodwill sense our vulnerability and trust us. As Rabbi Penzner put her reputation increasingly at risk for the sake of the workers, the housecleaners and organizers themselves came to see that she was an ally and opened themselves up to her. Real relationships began to form. Once we laugh, cry, and share life stories with people whose lives are affected by oppression, real solidarity is possible. Solidarity is a much higher level of engagement than pity or sympathy.[12] When I feel solidarity with another, I have a connection and can't just back away. I care deeply for his or her well-being and will extend myself outside my comfort zone to make sure things go well for my friend. In classic Jewish terms, this is called *noseh b'ol,* or "carrying the burden with the other." By showing how much she cared, Rabbi Penzner built real relationships with the workers, and this strengthened her motivation to win the campaign.

In this case, the hotel's resistance afforded those seeking change an opportunity to lean into the barrier. If they wanted to achieve results, the campaign activists had to shed certain aspects of their personality, perhaps shyness, self-doubt, or the illusion of independence. As people made themselves vulnerable in this way, they took risks for the sake of others and pushed themselves beyond what they knew was possible. As a result, their sense of connection and solidarity with each other increased. As discussed above, most of us live an illusion that we are independent actors who can function just fine without any help—that is, until we get injured or sick or lose a job or get divorced. In some cases, people will fight on, on their own, and make it. However, for many people, the stress put on us by these types of challenges will reveal the truth of our connection and interdependence with others. We need each other. If we manage these challenges well, the ensuing relationships can be new sources of strength and resilience.

I had a similar experience with engaging barriers in my own work setting. At the time, I served as the spiritual advisor at Gann Academy, a pluralistic Jewish high school in Waltham, Massachusetts. The school had several full-time workers on its maintenance team but also contracted out nighttime cleaning services. This subcontractor hired four crew members and a foreman to clean the building each night. The crew were all immigrants from Central American countries who did not speak English. I often worked late and was still in my office when the crew members came through to vacuum and empty the trash cans. One crew member, Juan, and I developed a nice relationship over the years trying to speak to each other—me in my limited Spanish and him in his limited English. One night I bumped into the foreman on the stairs and asked how his employer, the contractor, was treating them. "Not so good," he said. He went on to explain how they didn't get holidays or benefits, as he had expected. I chose to get involved and found out that our contractor was actually bound by a statewide contract with the union to provide these benefits. The union opened an investigation and also found that the company had not enrolled any of the crew as members of the union as they were supposed to have done. At the same time, I approached the head of the school and argued that we needed to take responsibility for the treatment of all workers in our building, even if they are not direct employees. He agreed and charged me and our chief financial officer with creating an "ethical contractor policy" that would ensure that we applied the same Jewish values that governed how we treated direct employees to contractors.

Creating this ethical contractor policy with our CFO was a rewarding and challenging experience. We started by deciding on the values that should govern the policy. This was fairly easy as we were in agreement about the importance of dignity and safety, as well as practices such as fair wages, transparent promotions, and grievance procedures. Things got tricky when it came to the issue of unions. The CFO was a deeply ethical, highly competent woman who was negatively disposed toward unions. Both her father and grandfather had had bad experiences with unions in their respective workplaces. I, on the other hand, favored unions as a default, particularly for low-income workers. Unsatisfied with our current contractor, the CFO had opened a bidding process to find a new cleaning company. The only bids we received, in addition to our current cleaners, were from nonunion contractors. A nonunion contractor posed at least two problems: they paid hourly wages considerably lower than the prevailing wage in the statewide contract (ten dollars versus thirteen), and they did not have to hire our existing crew members, who had been working for us for five years. Here was my obstacle.

First, I let myself feel despair and being overwhelmed. I was not the decision maker and my intervention might have in fact resulted in the crew members losing their jobs. Part of me felt like being small and slinking away from the whole affair. But with support from the New England Jewish Labor Committee, I remembered what had motivated me to get involved in the first place.[13] I remembered how much I cared that my Jewish community (in this case, the school) acted on Jewish and universal values of dignity for all.

I also remembered my relationship with Juan and how much I cared that his life should go well and that he would be treated with dignity. The depth with which I could feel my caring was directly related to how much I felt pushed up against the obstacle. If the CFO's resistance to unions had not been there, I would not have needed to dig down as deep and find what I really cared about.

Once I was able to feel how much I cared, it was easy for me to decide to speak about these issues in private meetings with our CFO and in meetings with nonunion contractors. Even though she and I continued to disagree about unions, I kept communicating with the CFO about Jewish values and concern for our crew. In meetings with contractors, she started asking how much they paid their crew per hour, a question that always startled them. I felt pride when she confronted one contactor during a tour of the building, telling him that it was not acceptable to pay our crew members ten dollars per hour. After doing more research into the field, she decided to hire back the original union contractor, primarily because only the union contractors would guarantee a dignified wage. We got this contractor to agree to abide by all the regulations in the statewide contract, and within several weeks all the crew members willingly joined the union.

---

### REFLECTION

What is one barrier you are dealing with to achieving a goal in your personal life, work, or social change?

What is being "withheld" from you by this barrier?

What does the barrier feel like? Look like?

What are some of the things you feel when you confront the barrier?

If you could communicate what you really care about regarding this goal, what would you say? What do you feel when saying this?

Imagine repeating what you care about to people involved in creating the barrier. How does that feel?

### FOCUS PHRASE

Create a statement that captures what you care about regarding this goal, and make a time every day to repeat it out loud to yourself for at least one minute. Do this for the duration of the time you are working on achieving this goal, or at least when you are consciously confronting the barrier. For example, I repeated the phrase, "This is my community!" to myself every day during the campaign for the cleaning crew at my school.

---

## Speaking One's Desire

The practice questions above lead in to Rabbi Nachman's next piece of advice about strengthening desire, a practice called *hitbodedut*. Hitbodedut literally means "solitude" or "being by oneself," but it is generally used in Jewish literature to refer to any meditative or contemplative practice that is done on one's own. Rabbi Shlomo Wolbe warns that without some time for hitbodedut—contemplative reflection—life is just a stream of activities. For Rabbi Nachman, hitbodedut refers to the specific practice of speaking spontaneously, out loud in one's own language to God. It is a form of spontaneous prayer. For change agents who primarily focus on making a difference in the world through our activities, cultivating a habit of self-reflection in combination with speaking our desire is crucial for ensuring that those activities continue to serve our higher goals.

How does hitbodedut work? In the practice section above, you were asked to create and repeat a phrase or sentence that described something you really cared about that was being withheld by a barrier. This could be a relationship you want to work out but is stuck because the other person can't commit, or a new role at work that is blocked by budget limitations, or a piece of legislation you want to pass that is being held up by a committee chairperson. Speaking one's desire is the practice of turning what we deeply care about and yearn for into a prayer. And as such, it is a marvelous vehicle for deepening our desire, our connection to what we most care about. Unlike formal prayer, the conversation is in the language most comfortable for the speaker and can take place for any amount of time, anywhere, although somewhere in nature is ideal.

I like to think of hitbodedut as a date with someone special to me. Like a good date, there is talking and listening. We speak our desire and also listen for what God may be communicating to us. Also, like a date, I plan time for it, choose the place to do it, and make sure I am not interrupted. Many couples have a regular date night. It is less important whether they go to a movie, music performance, or dinner than that they have committed to make this time for each other. Hitbodedut is similar. The commitment to practice regularly and dedicate time for the practice can be as important as the content of the conversation.

Before we proceed, it is worth saying a word about the role of God here. For some, this idea is nothing new; you've been talking with God informally for years. For others, it is a strange and challenging practice. I've taught this practice for over ten years with people who have very diverse attitudes and beliefs about God, and its usefulness is not limited to those who are devout theists. I've had students talk with their "higher wisdom" or "ideal support." God can be a complex, confusing, and, for some, problematic concept. Don't let that limit your use of this practice. Conversations can begin, "I don't know who I am talking to, and this feels really awkward, but here I go." If you wish you could relate to God but feel blocked, you can say that as well: "God, I have no idea if you exist, but I really wish I could sense you." You can even talk to yourself. Anything goes in this practice of speaking one's desire, and you get to start exactly where you are with no pretense.

Hitbodedut increases desire by creating an opening for the heart. Throughout the day we often need to put up a hard front to make our opinion heard in a meeting, around the dinner table, or to achieve a goal at work or in school. Our ego competes with all the egos around us, and success often depends on the firmness of the stands we take. At times taking firm stands or positions and fighting for ourselves is exactly what is needed to achieve what we want. The emotional danger in taking such stands is that we may confuse our essential selves and that for which we deeply yearn with the stands themselves.

In my example above, I originally took a position that we should commit to only hiring union contractors. This put me at odds with the CFO and probably was not the right approach for the organization. We were at a standstill. That is where hitbodedut came in.

I don't have to take a stand in my hitbodedut. When alone, at night, with just God and me, the ego gets to melt away. In this safe, intimate space, I get to say exactly what is on my mind. I also get to ask God what God wants of me. Sometimes it takes a few minutes of speaking around an issue until my heart opens. This is a space where I can lean into softness and vulnerability and not worry about winning or being heard. From the midst of this vulnerability, the quiet voice of the soul can be heard. This voice reminds me who I really am and what I care about.

In this example, I remembered that what I really wanted was for the Jewish community to act on its values. A union contractor might have been a vehicle for this, but this position was not the essence. Once I tapped into this desire, I felt renewed energy to fight for what I wanted without needing to hold so tightly onto my stand about unions. This combination of determined drive and flexibility enabled our process to move forward.

When we tap into what really motivates us, as I did with my desire for the Jewish community to act on its values, great energy is released. This energy is the motivation that drives our renewed efforts to make change. Speaking our desire is an important part of the back-and-forth between advocating for public positions and reconnecting with deep motivation.

Hitbodedut is also a space where we can mobilize unconscious resources by clearly and passionately articulating a vision. Psychological research shows the impact of stating a vision of where we want to be that is different than where we or the world is right now. Our unconscious minds start working to figure out how to narrow the gap between what is and what can be.[14] When we state what we deeply care about, day after day in a regular practice, different parts of our consciousness get to work to achieve this desire. I've heard from people who are committed to this practice describe amazing accomplishments that they attribute to developing clear desire.

For example, Rabbi Gedalia Fleer was the first Westerner to cross the Iron Curtain in the early 1960s to make a pilgrimage to the gravesite of Rabbi Nachman at risk of imprisonment. He credits the ability to overcome tremendous obstacles put up by the Soviet government on this quest to his rock-solid motivation to achieve his goal.[15] In a vivid biblical example of speaking one's desire, Hannah expresses how deeply she wants to have a child: "She prayed to God, weeping all the while. . . . Now Hannah was praying in her heart; only her lips moved but her voice could not be heard."[16] This description of a hitbodedut session became one of the Jewish tradition's models for authentic prayer. It was only when Hannah spoke openly from her heart that change began to happen.

We don't understand exactly how this change process happens, but it is clear that words spoken from the heart are heard clearly by both the speaker and others in a way that can mobilize change. Whether your goal is to pass legislation, organize a town composting program, create justice for low-income workers, raise children, or cross the Iron Curtain, using the practice of speaking one's desire to clarify and strengthen your motivation can move you toward your goal in surprising ways.

## REFLECTION

When you contemplate doing the practice of speaking your desire, what thoughts and feelings arise? What thoughts and feelings might you need to put aside temporarily to try out this practice?

## SPEAKING DESIRE PRACTICE

Hitbodedut[17] works when you commit to doing it at roughly the same time every day. Make a commitment to set aside a certain amount of time each day for a week. This can be anything from two minutes to an hour. The main thing is to be able to do it regularly, so don't commit to more than is realistic for you. Find a private place for your session where you will not be interrupted or concerned that people will hear you. I recommend setting a timer.

Some people start the session with a ritual like washing hands or saying a greeting to God. I start with, "Thank you, God, for this opportunity to talk with you." Do what makes sense for you. Once you've committed the time and gotten to your private space, just start talking. As mentioned above, you can say whatever is on your mind, no matter how irreverent it might sound. It doesn't matter; it is just you and God. This is your time. If "God" language doesn't make sense to you, you can talk to "the universe" or "higher wisdom" or anything that makes sense to you. You can also talk about the fact that you don't know if God exists.

The main thing is to start talking about whatever is on your mind and what you really care about. It is important to speak out loud, even in a whisper. If you just think and do not talk, I guarantee that before long, you will be thinking about your bills and the to-do list for the next day. This has happened to me more than a few times. Hearing your own voice keeps you on track.

If you stick with the practice at roughly the same time every day, after a period of several weeks you will find that a habit forms. Even on days when you really don't feel like taking the time, the force of habit can get you to the private place and speaking with God.[18]

---

## SUMMARY

The beginning of this path is also its end. This world never ultimately reaches perfection. We engage based on what we deeply care about, hopefully achieving victories along the way. Ratzon is the marrow, the juicy life source that keeps us going. We can become dry bones trying to make things better. There is so much push back that we may feel, to protect ourselves, we need to be hard and inflexible. There may be moments for rigidity, but not too many. Rigidity is the enemy of growth and change. To connect to and articulate our ratzon, we must decide to open ourselves up just a crack and really feel. This is not easy because many of us have a lot of scar tissue around places we opened in the past and got hurt. But opening to the softer places of yearning connects us to core parts of our identity that renew our commitment to heal and transform this world.

# SERVING WITH OUR FULL SELVES

## The Yetzer Harah

One of my first jobs out of college was working as an employment counselor at a men's homeless shelter in the Tenderloin district of San Francisco. In addition to helping the men get day-labor and longer-term jobs, I worked together with other advocates around the city to create more employment and housing opportunities for homeless people. The San Francisco Community Collective (SFCC) was one of the many groups in this loose and colorful network of advocates, homeless people, hippies, planners, and local politicians.

For at least a dozen years, the SFCC published a quarterly newspaper, *The Sheet,* with events, stories, psychedelic sixties-era illustrations, and job listings. *The Sheet* was one of the things that tied together this community and, in the pre-Internet era, homeless people looked to it for job listings. Several months after I started at the shelter, the SFCC stopped publishing *The Sheet.* My colleague at the SFCC told me they were having financial problems and couldn't afford it any longer.

As a new person on the homelessness and housing scene in San Francisco, I saw this as a great opportunity for me to make an impact. I knew the program director at a major San Francisco foundation from my work on a homelessness roundtable and thought he might be interested. Indeed he was, and I found myself writing my first ever grant proposal to fund *The Sheet* under the auspices of my shelter. Several weeks later we got the grant, and word got out that we would be publishing *The Sheet.*

My colleague at the SFCC went ballistic. He yelled at me so loudly that I had to hold the phone away from my ear. He accused me of stealing *The Sheet* from the SFCC and said I had no right to approach a foundation about it without his approval. I assured him that I planned on working with the SFCC to publish *The Sheet,* but this did not appease him at all. This was their product and they wanted control. In the end I realized he was right, and, with the foundation's permission, we transferred all of the grant money to the SFCC to run the project.

What happened here? What was the urgency that propelled me into action without thinking about the SFCC? I saw an opportunity to prove my worth to my boss and to the advocate community and jumped at it. My desire for recognition and approval overwhelmed my strategic thinking about relationships and the homelessness-advocacy ecosystem. With hindsight, of course I know that the SFCC should have been the lead on a grant about their newspaper. But in the heat of the moment, when my heart was pounding with an opportunity to "make it" and get recognized for doing something good, all I could think of was me getting the grant.

The rush of energy I felt is called, in Jewish sources, the *yetzer harah,* or just the *yetzer.* A literal translation of *yetzer harah* is "evil/ bad inclination," although the "evil/bad" part is not exactly accurate because it is a morally neutral force. It is simply the drive for instant gratification. Depending how we direct this drive, it can build and create or tear down and destroy. Jewish sources are filled with wisdom about how to understand and channel this energy. In my case, I wanted recognition and I was going to get it, no matter what the consequences.

In this way the yetzer is similar to how neuroscientists describe the limbic system, the integrative system for emotions, emotional behavior, and motivation that we mentioned and that is also the location of ratzon.[1] The yetzer wants to maximize pleasure, avoid pain, and achieve instant gratification.[2] I was new in my job and feeling somewhat insecure. I was also aware of friends who had prestigious fellowships or jobs. I come from a family and societal culture that emphasized high levels of success. I felt bad about not having achieved more, and this was an opportunity to not feel the pain of failure. The yetzer is all about "me" and what I need, in isolation of anyone or anything else.

In Jewish sources the yetzer harah lives in tension with the *yetzer tov*, the "good inclination." The yetzer tov functions in a similar way to what neuroscientists call the "prefrontal cortex," the part of the brain that weighs priorities, make decisions, and engages in rational thought. Again, "good" is a bit of a misnomer because too much yetzer tov can also be destructive. The ideal is a balance where both inclinations work together toward prosocial goals. Achieving such a balance is the art of living well. If the yetzer harah is all about "me," the yetzer tov is other focused and puts the "me" in a context of relationships and the world at large. The yetzer harah is like a single wall of an A-frame. Since it is only concerned with "me," it has nothing to lean against and falls over easily. By bringing the "me" into relationship, the yetzer tov helps create something sustainable.

Just based on yetzer harah energy, my drive for recognition might have torn apart the homelessness-advocacy community. It is not hard to imagine the backstabbing and organizational intrigue that could have followed had I insisted on holding onto the grant. It was yetzer tov–style thought that got me to back down, see the big picture of the community, and turn over the grant. Much of Jewish spiritual growth involves channeling the "me" energy of the yetzer harah into the greater context of relationship and community to build the world rather than tear it down.

## REFLECTION

What kind of urgent drives compel you to act in ways that may not be aligned with your best thinking?

Do you have a drive for recognition? For escape or hiding? For pleasing people?

When have you noticed an urgent drive to do something in your activism that may not be the best thing to do from a social or community perspective? What were some of the factors driving this urgency?

## ASPECTS OF THE YETZER

It is tempting to think of the yetzer harah as the little devil that sits on one shoulder and the yetzer tov as the little angel with a halo on its head that sits on the other. As simple and as popular as that image is, it does an injustice to the complexity of our inner lives. The yetzer and life in general do not lend themselves to simple moralizing between good and bad. The yetzer is a complex drive that can be either good or bad. In fact, an ancient Jewish teaching asks what the Torah meant when God looked at the world at the end of creation and saw that it was "very good."[3] What was *very* good? The ancient rabbis answer, "The yetzer harah was very good."[4] How can that little red devil be very good? We need to explore how various Jewish teachers throughout the millennia understood the yetzer to see how this vital, me-focused energy source that pulses through our veins can be a force for sustainable development and creativity.

First of all, this me-oriented drive for instant gratification is essential for our survival. This point is illustrated by a classic

Jewish teaching about when a person acquires the yetzer.[5] Rabbi Yehuda Hanassi, the leader of the Jewish community in Israel at the beginning of the third century, debated the topic with his Roman counterpart, Antinonus. Rabbi Yehuda proposed that we acquire the yetzer at conception. Antinonus countered that it had to be at birth because if it was at conception, the fetus would never have the equanimity to stay in the womb. Rather, it would abort itself. Rabbi Yehuda ended up agreeing that the yetzer had to appear at birth.

We can understand this teaching from a physical and emotional perspective. While in the womb, there is no need for this drive for instant gratification. Everything a fetus needs to grow is provided automatically by the mother. However, once we exit the womb, our nourishment and protection is no longer guaranteed. Once the umbilical cord is cut, we are physically on our own. This is a metaphor for the spiritual reality that our soul in this world is contained in a body that is physically separated from other beings.

The yetzer is a useful survival tool for ensuring that we get the nurturing we need to grow. The newborn cries and creates a sense of urgency in his or her caretakers when he or she needs food, warmth, and connection. A tiny baby is almost pure instant-gratification energy. If the baby's essential needs are met in a consistent and reliable way, the child will learn to trust others and have a good chance at managing the drive for instant gratification later in life. However, when the child experiences scarcity on a regular basis, the yetzer will work in overdrive to get these needs for nurturing met.

This experience of unmet needs will leave a residue of feelings that will be felt again in the future whenever an experience of need arises that somewhat resembles these early experiences of scarcity. These can be feelings of urgency and terror or that something is wrong with oneself, or they can manifest as a desperate desire for attention. You can be standing in line for ice cream and find out the flavor you want just ran out and get ambushed by intense sadness. It makes no sense to feel so sad about ice cream, but the ice cream is just a trigger of an old experience of not getting an essential need met. Since no one I ever heard of got all their needs met right away all the time when they were babies, we are all left with some residue of feelings around our essential needs for food, shelter, and connection. This is our life challenge: in moments where we feel urgency or terror, can we bring perspective to our yetzer, or do we impulsively grab what we can despite the consequences? In my story, old feelings of desperation for recognition overwhelmed my clear thinking, and I grabbed the grant from my fellow advocate.

The goal is not to banish yetzer energy. We need it. A colorful rabbinic story describes a time that the rabbis actually captured the yetzer harah and put it in jail.[6] They were going to destroy it and then noticed that hens stopped laying eggs and creativity and birth seemed to come to a standstill. In another place the rabbis teach that absent the yetzer people would not start businesses, build homes, or marry and have children.[7] In short, the world would stop functioning. The rabbis are teaching that the yetzer is essential to the human task of growing and developing the world. Our human task in this world is not to sit peacefully and meditate on the beauty of creation. That is one of our soul tasks, and we have Shabbat for that. Our role here is to be partners with God in creation, to build up the world and invite God's presence into the physical. This takes drive, ambition, creativity, and passion.

These are positive aspects of the yetzer. When we can use our drive to manifest our deep ratzon, we create and add to the development of the world in a sustainable way. On the one hand, the yetzer is energy we use for survival, to get our essential needs met and to achieve our ambitions. On the other hand, it is an unstable, irrational force that will potentially destroy whatever stands in the way of achieving self-satisfaction. The key is bringing the me-oriented yetzer into the other-oriented context of relationships and community. What did the rabbis do when they saw that all creativity ceased with the yetzer jailed? They released it but blinded it. The metaphor is that the yetzer must be not be squashed, but also must not function on its own. The rabbis compare the yetzer to a horse and the mind, or yetzer tov, to the rider. Without the horse, the rider cannot go anywhere. Without the rider, the horse will run wild. Rabbi Nachman compares the yetzer harah to a blind man in a forest and the yetzer tov/mind to a man who can't walk. The man who can't walk goes on the back of the blind man and directs him out of the forest. In both metaphors the yetzer needs to function in relationship with something or someone with a broader perspective.

When we can release our drive for gratification in the context of relationship and in service of a higher social purpose, we become effective partners with God in creating a sustainable world. According to the medieval Torah commentator Nachmanides, the very definition of the word "tov/good" in the Torah refers to sustainability. The trees are the first thing that God acknowledges are tov/good. Nachmanides explains that *tov* means that the Creation will sustain into the future.[8] Sustainability is the essence of goodness. When I act, even for a good cause, from a place of desperation or jealousy, I will be less likely to sustain my involvement. Desperation and jealousy are powerful and animating emotions, but they are ultimately unsustainable because they are based on the illusion of scarcity and lack of trust.

If tov/good is sustainability, then rah/bad is the opposite. As described above, the yetzer harah unchecked and unexamined will ultimately lead to destruction. The Hebrew root for *rah* is also a root for the word *r'u'ah*, which means "shaky" or "unstable." A flimsy door is a *r'u'ah door*, and a crumbling wall is a *r'u'ah wall*. This is the opposite of sustainability. The yetzer harah is most activated and hard to channel when one feels unstable and disconnected.

In my case as a new homelessness advocate, I felt unsure of my value, and given my emotional need to prove my worth, I was vulnerable to acting on feelings of urgency. Imagine if I could have taken all that yetzer energy and remembered that I was actually connected to lots of good people and organizations all trying to solve homelessness. I would have channeled my energy into working in partnership with the SFCC to see what we could do together to bring *The Sheet* back. Such a partnership between my organization, the SFCC, and the foundation would certainly have been more sustainable than going it alone and creating a wake of resentment behind my personal success.

Unchecked, our yetzer energy can do more damage than just creating enmity between social-service organizations. Real cruelty, domination, and oppression of one human over another can flow from this drive for instant gratification. The thirteenth-century rabbi Avraham ibn Ezra points out that the root of the word for "cruel," *akhzar*, is *k.zar*—"like a stranger" (as mentioned in the last chapter). One can only be cruel when one feels alienated from others or sees others as alien and distant from oneself.[9] *Zar* is "a stranger," someone distant from you. I can only oppress someone if I think of him or her as a stranger or I internally distance myself from his or her humanity. The rabbis of the Talmud ask, "Who is the *el zar*/strange god that is in the human heart? The yetzer harah."[10]

Our me-oriented drive for instant gratification can distance us from the humanity of the other since these others exist only as instruments to fulfill our needs. Once we see other people or other forms of life simply as instruments of our own gratification, cruelty and oppression are not far behind. Dominated by a drive for instant self-gratification, we can become separated from our deeper ratzon for connection and service. Disconnected from our essential selves, we can easily be manipulated to engage in oppressive practices that seem to offer the promise of feeling better about ourselves. We have in us the capacity to build sustainable relationships and societies and also the capacity for disconnection and distance.

The stakes are high. In a dramatic description of the result of the yetzer gone wild, the great flood that wiped out the world at the beginning of the book of Genesis is partially attributed to the fact that "every thought-inclination (yetzer) of the human heart was only bad (rah) all day."[11] The yetzer was "only bad," and not balanced with the yetzer tov, the broader perspective that notices and takes into consideration relationships and context.

The story of Cain and Abel at the beginning of the book of Genesis further illustrates the dangers of the yetzer unchecked and highlights our potential for choice. Cain, the farmer and older brother, is extremely upset when God seems more pleased with his younger brother Abel's sacrifice. God sees how upset he is and says to him, "The yetzer crouches at your door, and you have the power to master it."[12] In other words, God is telling Cain—and all of us—that we can't control many of the events that happen to us in life, but we have the power to decide our response.

We have drives in us that urge us to respond to stimuli as wounded young children, still hurting from unmet needs for recognition or love. Are we going to shrink back into the wounded self, or are we going to notice and value the relationships in which our lives are embedded and see that we are part of a larger system? Noticing the value of these relationships and our role in something greater than ourselves can calm the ferment of the yetzer. The Torah uses the term *chatat* for the yetzer in this verse, which literally means "missing the mark." In a way, God is telling Cain, if you don't master it, the yetzer will lead you to miss the mark, but you can master it and direct it toward the good.

We can sense what is at stake here. Left unchecked, our yetzer will lead us to grab what we can and avoid feelings of emotional discomfort. Greed, emotional distance, feeling bad, and domination are the result of otherwise highly capable adults acting on irrational feelings of urgency. This all stems from the yetzer. As God tells Cain, the outcome is not determined. The great human drama revolves around how we manage the yetzer.

---

**REFLECTION**

How does your drive for instant gratification serve you well?

In what circumstances do you feel most unstable and urgent?

In what circumstances do you most easily notice you are connected to others and live within a web of relationships?

What is an example of where you noticed the drives of the yetzer getting in the way of effective social change?

What is an example of where you noticed the drives of the yetzer producing effective social change?

## TRANSFORMING THE YETZER

How do we channel this me-oriented energy so it functions in service of manifesting our deepest motivations for creating positive social change? Rabbi Yisrael Salanter proposed three steps for doing the core spiritual growth needed to transform our yetzer into a prosocial force. Elements of these steps can be found in Hasidic sources as well, but for the sake of simplicity, we will focus on Rabbi Yisrael's formula.[13] The three steps are cultivating sensitivity to our inner life (*hergesh*), cultivating the power of decision (*kibbush hayetzer*), and transformation (*tikkun hayetzer*).[14]

### Cultivating Sensitivity to Our Inner Life: Hergesh

To grow we need to be aware of our inner life—our feelings, thoughts, and motivations. How do we build greater sensitivity and open our hearts? As a person who wants to make change, your heart was opened at some point to suffering. You felt this suffering deep enough to want to do something about it, even if your heart has been dulled by metaphoric scar tissue over the years. We know how to feel the pain of others and even get angry about this pain. To transform our instant-gratification energy into a prosocial force, we need to be sensitive to our own pain and other emotions. What triggers us and why? What happened to you when you were young that leaves you vulnerable to craving recognition? To being overcome with rage when a car cuts you off in traffic? We develop sensitivity to our inner life not just by noticing when we explode, but by looking for little signs of when we get triggered.

In my story above, practicing sensitivity would have meant slowing down enough to notice my feelings of insecurity in my job. These feelings were subtle because I wanted to think of myself as confident. However, by taking a few minutes on a regular basis to check in and examine my inner life, I would have found my urgent desire for recognition and could have tracked it back to my own expectations, my parents' expectations, and messages from teachers and society. This process brings the inner dynamic to the level of consciousness, thus making it less likely to undermine my longer-term goals. In this step of sensitivity, we are just noticing the dynamics, not actually making changes. Cultivating this type of sensitivity is central to Mussar practice, which Rabbi Yisrael claimed was the discipline to awaken "hearts [that] are unfeeling and hard as stone."[15]

---

### PRACTICE: *Cultivating Sensitivity*

A key practice for cultivating sensitivity to our inner lives is *cheshbon hanefesh*, literally, "soul accounting." We make a soul accounting by setting aside time every day, ideally the same time, to review our thoughts, feelings, and behaviors of that day. Try to notice when you were triggered during the day. Let your mind trace the event that triggered you back to its origin. Why did you get so triggered? What emotions and thoughts came up during the event? Are they similar to thoughts and feelings you have had before? Where do these thoughts and feelings come from? How does getting triggered in this way affect your social-change work? Soul accounting can be done as a form of hitbodedut, spoken out loud (as described in the last chapter). You can also write your cheshbon hanefesh in a journal, keeping a narrative record of your inner life.[16] A regular soul-accounting practice will produce a wealth of information about your inner life. This practice will be described at length in chapter 5.

---

## Cultivating the Power of Decision: Kibbush Hayetzer

Once we are aware of our vulnerabilities and triggers, we can make a conscious decision whether to follow our inclinations. This step is called *kibbush,* which literally means, "conquer." In this step we "conquer" our drive for instant gratification by using our will-power. For example, when I feel an urge to get up from the computer and raid the pantry for cookies or chips but decide by sheer force of will to keep my rear end in the chair and keep writing, I am practicing kibbush. Kibbush mobilizes what we know in our minds to dominate the urges of our yetzer.

In my story, I didn't use kibbush when I jumped on the opportunity to write a grant proposal. Using my power of decision would have meant slowing down and deciding to work in a collegial way with the SFCC rather than acting alone, even though I really wanted to get all the credit myself. It would have meant letting myself feel how much I craved the recognition rather than soothing this urge by jumping into action.

Kibbush is a muscle that gets stronger with use. In the grips of the yetzer—whether for a piece of cake, a sexual encounter, or acting out rage—being able to mobilize our power of decision to stop a behavior can be literally life-saving. The danger of kibbush is that it can crush the yetzer, which is our source of passion and creativity. Kibbush is a blunt instrument. While we need it and must develop it, kibbush is not the ultimate goal of Mussar practice.

---

### PRACTICE: *Decision*

Choose a drive or inclination that you want to act on less impulsively.

Make a "policy" decision that you will not act on this feeling when it comes up today.

Make a point of noticing the other feelings you feel when you do not act on the urge.

Repeat out loud or in your head your commitment to not act on the feeling. It is helpful to phrase the commitment in the positive. Rather than saying, "I am not going to eat that cookie," say, "I am going to stay focused on writing" or "I am going to keep my commitment to eating well."

Keep repeating your commitment and letting yourself feel whatever feelings come up until the urge subsides.

If the feelings are particularly strong, find a listening partner whom you can talk to for a few minutes about what you are feeling. Write or speak about the experience of using your power of decision in your soul-accounting practice.

---

### Transformation: Tikkun Hayetzer

Transformation is the most refined level of practice. In Rabbi Yisrael's system, it is the highest level and goal of Mussar practice. It is highly individual and involves channeling or riding the wild waves of our drives to fulfilling our deepest ratzon for goodness and service. It involves feeling the joy of service so deeply that our yetzer has almost no choice but to serve. In psychological terms *tikkun* is called "sublimation," or transforming a potentially destructive desire into something prosocial and life giving. The classic Talmudic example is the bloodthirsty person who channels his rage and bloodlust into being a kosher butcher.[17]

In my story, my yetzer energy came from a need for recognition, a desire to give to society, and a fear of being a failure. How could I have practiced transformation? Based on this Talmudic example, I would notice my yetzer for recognition (sensitivity) and set up my life in a way that would raise the odds that I would behave in a collaborative way that puts me in relationship with others working on similar goals. Choosing to work in a homeless shelter as part of a network of advocates was a good step.

But I also needed to make a decision (kibbush) to work collaboratively whenever possible. To go beyond just kibbush, I would also need to reconnect to my deep ratzon for doing this work. I wanted our wealthy American society to be able to take care of all of its citizens, especially those most wounded and struggling to make it. This desire came from a strong sense of fairness and aversion to the mistreatment of anyone. At the same time, I wanted to become aligned with my sense of God's will for all people to live with dignity.

Transformation would mean meditating periodically on bringing my drive for recognition into the service of these ratzons. Together with a decision to act collaboratively, this meditation on ratzon is the kind of practice that, when done consistently over time, could make my drive for recognition into a powerful engine for positive social change. Transformation enables us to take potentially destructive inner forces, like the desire for recognition, and use them for prosocial purposes. Each of us needs to construct our own program for transformation (tikkun) based on our individual desires, drives, and life circumstances.

## PRACTICE: *Transforming Drives for Good*

While you can do this practice on your own, it will most likely work best to do it with a partner or with a small group of people all committed to trying the practice together.

Choose a drive, feeling, or inclination that gets in the way of you functioning as effectively as possible in your social-change work. This could be a drive for recognition, a fear of failure or criticism, or a need to please people, for example.

What is at least one deep desire you have that brings you to this kind of social-change work? Use at least half of your soul-accounting time to meditate on or speak about this desire/motivation. Why do you care so much? If you relate to the idea of God's will, is this a motivating factor in any way?

In your mind bring this drive/inclination into relationship with the people or organizations around you in your social-change work. Let yourself feel the feeling, but now remind yourself that you are not alone. For example, how can your fear of failure be useful to the collective effort? How can you bring this feeling as an offering to the group project of social change? Let yourself feel how this drive transforms as, in your mind, you bring it into the service of the collective.

For example, your fear of failure may be commonly experienced by others, and talking about it can create more of a sense of unity and collective purpose among your group. It is common at this point for the drive to give off energy in the form of shaking, crying, or yawning as it transforms into a prosocial force. Let your body release this energy. Repeat this practice until you get a firm sense in your mind of how this inclination can be mobilized in a positive way.

In addition to the soul-accounting practice, you may need to set up your life in such a way that maximizes the chances for you to bring your yetzer/drive into the context of relationship and community. This could mean joining a coalition of people working on similar issues if you are working alone, or taking on a project that pushes you out front, if you tend to hide behind others.

The soul-accounting practice is typically done alone. In part three, where we go more in depth into middot, we will describe how you can bring this practice into a relationship with a partner.

---

## THE YETZER AND OPPRESSION

What is the role of me-oriented drives in the social oppressions we seek to end? Any social oppression—be it anti-Semitism, racism, or the cycle of poverty—is acted out on individuals and groups through social systems, like company hiring policies, the prison system, and immigration laws. These systems are created and sustained by humans. These humans all have a yetzer harah that pulls at them to act based on a sense of scarcity and fear. Decisions guided only by the yetzer keep the oppression in place while decisions that break with the yetzer can move the system toward liberation. Let's play out an example of how this works.

Immokalee is a town in southern central Florida that is the center of the tomato-growing industry in the United States. Picking tomatoes is a very labor-intensive task, and the industry relies on migrant laborers, most of whom are from Central America, do not speak English, and may be undocumented. Large corporations like Taco Bell and supermarket chains like Stop and Shop purchase their tomatoes from large industrial farmers who hire contractors who hire the workers who pick the tomatoes off the vine. These workers get fifty cents for every thirty-two-pound bucket they fill with tomatoes. To make the minimum wage of eight dollars per hour for an eight-hour day, a worker needs to pick 3,584 pounds of tomatoes, or nearly two tons of tomatoes, a day! Some of these contractors are quite unscrupulous and will keep their workers in virtual slavery by confiscating their passports or other documents.

In addition to fighting for the rights of the pickers, the Coalition for Immokalee Workers (CIW) has a campaign to get the large supermarket chains and purchasers to raise the price of their tomatoes and tomato products ten cents and to pass this increase directly to the workers in the fields. As of this writing, Taco Bell, McDonald's, and Burger King have signed on, but other major fast-food and grocery chains have not. Even when large companies have agreed to raise the price of tomatoes, the growers have refused to pass on the increase to the pickers.

What is the role of the yetzer in all this? At the risk of oversimplifying, in most profit-making situations, a strong yetzer is at work to grab what it can despite any ethical considerations. Capitalism is such a powerful force for wealth creation because it mobilizes the me-oriented drive for acquisition and security. This use of the yetzer was most boldly expressed by financier Ivan Boesky in his famous graduation address to the University of California–Berkeley Business School in the 1980s when he declared, "Greed is healthy . . . You can be greedy and still feel good about yourself." Boesky was only partially correct. Greed is healthy as an engine of productivity only when balanced with a prosocial vision that accounts for the well-being of all people and the planet.

As we know, the yetzer is an unstable force, and if it is not watched carefully, it will cause chaos and destruction. The managers of Taco Bell want to provide a high-quality product for the lowest cost possible to increase their profit. The growers want to offer a high-quality product to the corporations for the lowest cost to themselves as possible. The contractors want to deliver high-quality tomatoes for the lowest cost. The yetzer to acquire more and more, which is usually seen as greed, gets acted out most harshly on the pickers. The pickers have to do the hard physical labor. They want to make as much money for themselves as possible. Because there are many available migrant workers, the contractors can offer the lowest possible wages and demand as much work as they want without concern for issues of fairness or dignity. This is the yetzer at work—why not squeeze the pickers a little bit to make some more money? The contractor, and every other employer throughout the system, is faced with moments of decision: What do I set as wages? How long a break do I allow? How much independence do I give to the pickers? Similarly, at the top of the chain, the managers at Taco Bell decide how much to charge for a taco and how much to pay for tomatoes. The yetzer is at work in each of these decisions. If they just follow their yetzer and act on old feelings of scarcity and need for more, employers will pay workers less and give less independence simply because they have the power to do so. This is the spiritual anatomy of oppression.

The opposite is also true with the yetzer. The grower can face the yetzer and decide not to act on scarcity. The grower can act on trust that by paying workers a little more and treating them with more dignity, they will produce as much or more of a quality product. Taco Bell can decide to take pride in the working conditions of the folks at the bottom of the chain and pay a higher price for its tomatoes. However, because of the strength of the drive for acquisition and security, in addition to competition and market forces, it is very difficult to make such a decision. In spiritual terms, the role of CIW and most activists in these situations is to help people in power do tikkun hayetzer—to channel their drive for profit in a prosocial direction. In this case CIW used boycotts, hunger strikes, and sit-ins outside of corporate headquarters to create pressure on corporations to realize that they could only successfully fulfill their drive for profit if they also considered workers' rights as an important part of their business. Organizing and mobilizing power is an effective strategy for challenging the unchecked yetzer on a societal level.

The activists do not squash the yetzer. They use the drive for profit to encourage the growers and corporations to expand their prosocial vision by making yetzer-based practices less profitable. Activists also mobilize the yetzer tov, people's sense of caring and good thinking about the broader society and planet, by bringing the hard realities of injustice into the full vision of people with power. We will discuss this aspect of activism more in the chapter on free choice, chapter four. At times, people with power will respond positively to these promptings, but mobilizing the yetzer for prosocial purposes is often a more effective approach to achieving change.

CIW's relationship with Florida-based Pacific Tomato Growers, one of the largest producers in the United States, offers a good example of this dynamic. As CIW achieved more and more success getting big-name fast-food chains and supermarkets on board with the Fair Food Program, growers remained obstinate in their opposition to passing on the penny-per-pound increase. According to an article in *The Nation*, "The Florida Tomato Growers Exchange (FTGE), representing 90 percent of the state's growers, went so far as to declare that any members who implemented the pay raise would be fined $100,000 for *every worker* who benefited."[18]

This united opposition continued until 2010 when Jon Esformes, operating partner of Pacific Tomato Growers, broke with his peers and signed on to the legally binding Fair Food Agreement drafted by the Fair Food Program. What changed for Esformes? He risked the wrath of his fellow growers to actually meet with the leaders of the CIW. He explains, "The natural assumption by businesses is that anytime someone is approaching them from a labor perspective, it is somehow not congruent with the direction of the business . . . What I found in the coalition was a group of people who believed in the same things we did—good working relationships and having a sustainable business. That's the basis for a partnership."[19]

Put in the language of Jewish spirituality, Esformes was motivated by a yetzer tov concern to encourage other growers to deal with human rights abuses in their industry, but also by a yetzer harah concern to build his business. The tomato industry was suffering from a bad reputation because of the labor abuses and facing stiff global competition. Transparency regarding labor conditions and increased wages would help this reputation.[20] Esformes and the CIW leadership travel the country now promoting the Fair Food Agreement and modeling that there is no inherent contradiction between a drive for profit and commitment to workers' rights. CIW successfully influenced market conditions to channel the yetzer harah for profit in a prosocial direction.

Michael Oshman describes a similar use of yetzer-oriented market forces in battling climate change. The Green Restaurant Association's approach is based on making it easier for restaurants and distributers to attract customers by becoming environmentally friendly. According to Oshman, "We make it easier for business to identify as a 'green business.' Customers reinforce this behavior which creates competitive pressure to keep doing the right thing." As the price of LED lightbulbs and solar power continues to decrease, market forces increasingly are on the side of slowing climate change. These developments are promising for the GRA and others who seek to continue channeling the yetzer for profit toward prosocial outcomes.

The yetzer also plays a role within social-change organizations themselves. Many of us know that despite the grand mission of our organizations—to fight for workers' rights, to end racism, and so forth—discrimination against women, gays, or people of color, for example, is alive and well within the organizations. Activists have a yetzer. We know the high-profile examples of CEOs of major social-welfare agencies caught embezzling funds or heads of youth organizations mistreating young people. However, our yetzer is at work on a more mundane level in our organizations. The yetzer may tell me that I am not getting enough recognition or that my cause is hopeless. Unaware of these feelings, I cut off a female colleague in a staff meeting to ensure that my point is recognized by the executive director. This is an act of sexism rooted in my yetzer harah for recognition. I experience myself as the victim—the yetzer always does. I am not getting enough recognition for my work. Why do I never get any awards or trophies? If I choose to dominate another person, particularly a woman or person of color, to feel like I am getting more recognition, this is an act of oppression. Exactly what I am trying to eradicate through my activism I am acting out with my colleagues. I am sure you can think of examples from your own experience of when you acted this way or were acted upon in this way. This is the yetzer at work.

---

### REFLECTION

What yetzer, or me-oriented drive, do you feel you are up against in a social-change effort?

How does your organization or a social-change effort you are involved with try to bring the yetzer in a prosocial direction?

How is this me-oriented drive for instant gratification at work in your own group or organization? For example, how do you and your colleagues manage competition for recognition?

---

## SUMMARY

Our deep motivation and drive for instant gratification are foundations of our inner life. While they often function under the radar of our awareness, their potency makes them a central concern of spiritual teachings throughout the ages. Motivation, or ratzon, orients us, and our drives, or yetzer, give us the energy to act on this motivation. Together they are powerful forces for building a sustainable world in partnership with God. The challenge for us is to understand these forces and bring them into the service of prosocial goals. The next section offers two different perspectives for harnessing ratzon and the yetzer for personal growth and positive social change.

# PART TWO

# *Signposts*

While the compass points the hiker in a general direction, it is easy to get off course. Signposts and trail markers indicate which way to go when the path is unclear. This section explores two signposts for making effective, sustainable change. The first is Rabbi Nachman of Breslov's practice of finding good points, and the second is Rabbi Eliyahu Dessler's concept of the choice point.

Given the conflict and opposing forces that accompany any efforts to make social change, the way forward often is not clear. Any move is liable to undermine relationships and make situations worse. Like signposts, these two points guide us to where to make the next step toward sustainable social change.

# 3

## A LITTLE LIGHT OVERCOMES
## MUCH DARKNESS

### *Seeking Good Points*

Readers of this book probably are aware of what a broken world we live in.[1] In the United States, for example, we have a justice system that incarcerates black men at a rate seven times higher than white men.[2] Worldwide over fifty million human beings live as refugees, fleeing from harm or for economic opportunity and living in limbo in countries that refuse to integrate them.[3] Carbon monoxide levels in our air continue to rise, as do the sea levels, with major flooding predicted worldwide in many of the poorest regions on the planet. In the first decade of the new millennium, over fifty thousand people in the United States suffered hate crimes because of their race, sexual orientation, or religion.[4] On a personal level, who does not know people suffering in toxic relationships or unable to find meaningful employment or haunted by the internal demons of depression and anxiety?

Seeing brokenness is essential for making change, but it can quickly become overwhelming, especially if we can't fix the problems right away. On the one hand, we need to see how bad things are to motivate change, and on the other, this awareness can grind us down. How are we to engage with the suffering in the world in a way that does not lead to bitterness and despair, but generates hope and light?

SEEKING THE GOOD POINTS

> One needs to seek and find a little bit of good.
> —*Rabbi Nachman of Breslov*

Our brains are hardwired to notice what is wrong in the environment around us, as a survival mechanism. We take for granted that on most days we get to work without any accidents or that our plumbing systems pump water on most days without stoppage. Our brain sees patterns, and those patterns become what we expect to see. We are hyperaware of deviations from the patterns, especially those that are threatening, like a car accident on the highway or an insult from a family member or colleague. While I don't like to admit it to myself, my brain is vigilantly on the lookout for any indications of displeasure or upset directed at me by my colleagues.

The Breslov masters understand our mind's inclination to see what is wrong and, thus, instruct us to seek out good points, both in ourselves and others.[5] This is the practice. In Rabbi Nachman's words:

> When one begins to look at oneself and can't find good, and sees all of one's mistakes, and the [yetzer] wants to make one fall into deep sadness because of these . . . [one] needs to search and find some little good in oneself because it is impossible that one hasn't done some good.[6]

A good point is a positive, prosocial deed, thought, or state of being. It can be a simple action like greeting another person kindly, an intention like wanting to help your roommate find a life partner, or a state such as being created in the divine image. It does not need to be a specifically religious act, although many religious acts, like lighting Shabbat candles, can also be good points. The starting point is reflection and introspection.

Rabbi Nachman is talking above about a person who decides to reflect on his or her life: because it is easier to see what is wrong, the first thing he or she sees is all the imperfections. Once we see these imperfections, we are vulnerable to exaggerating them and making negative generalizations about ourselves. The search for good begins with an assumption. I must have done something positive, or there must be something positive about who I am. As obvious as this sounds, I assure you from my personal experience it is not easy. It takes a real decision to direct our minds to look with persistence through all the muck and negative inner voices to see and hold onto a success or positive contribution.

To give an example of how the practice works, I was feeling unconfident this morning about my writing. I had just read a fabulous article by a colleague that nailed the topic I was also writing about. It was well researched and persuasive. "I'm just a fake and could never write something that good," the voice said in my head. I felt intimidated and slothful. I started searching for a good point. My mind resisted the work it takes to search inside. Something was comfortable and familiar about these slothful feelings. With a little willpower, I remembered that I got an appreciative e-mail about a recent sermon from a woman the night before, which commented on the impact my writing had on her life. I could notice that the effort I put into writing that sermon actually positively influenced another human being. That's great! My attention immediately shifted and I felt more present, confident, and joyous. That is the power of finding a good point.

The practice is to search until you find a good point that really makes a difference to you. Rabbi Chaim Kramer, the founder of the Breslov Research Institute, describes the process. In classic Hasidic custom, Rabbi Kramer was at the ritual bath before a Jewish holiday. He stood at the edge of the bath and couldn't get himself to go in. He felt empty of any good deeds and unworthy of the spiritual purification promised by the immersion. Then he remembered a story:

There was this poor guy in nineteenth-century eastern Europe who really wanted his own *etrog*, the special fruit used for ritual purposes on the Sukkoth holiday. He was marrying off two daughters that year, so he was going to have dowry money. He would have enough for a beautiful etrog, which in eastern Europe was quite rare. The day before Sukkoth, he was on his way to buy the etrog when two guys walked by in the street and asked if they could come to him for the holiday because they were from out of town. He knew that if he hosted them, he wouldn't have enough money for the etrog. He decided to host them and invited them over and spent all the money on extra food. At the table in the sukkah, the guests noticed that he looked sad. They asked him why, and he explained that he was happy to have them as guests, but he couldn't buy his etrog. He really wanted an etrog, so he felt sad. The guests said to him, "First of all, you can have our etrog. It is yours, so you now have an etrog. Second, when your actions are weighed in heaven, two burly guys you hosted for the holiday are going to weigh much more than a tiny etrog."

Rabbi Kramer explains that once he remembered that story, he thought about all the pounds of paper the Breslov Research Institute had used over the years to print Rabbi Nachman's teachings. That is a lot of weight. He felt joyous about this and was able to immerse with a full heart. There was something about the physicality of this image that was able to penetrate.

Sometimes we need to flip through several good points until we find one that breaks through to our heart. The key is that we can actually feel our goodness and this feeling moves us. The most basic good point in all of us is that we are created in the divine image. Imagine deciding to bring awareness of this fact into your consciousness multiple times a day. This good point would certainly make a difference in the way you thought about yourself. The power of good points is that they remind us of our own essential goodness. Through this we get a deeper sense of connectivity among ourselves, others, and God, which produces a deep feeling of joy. From a Jewish mystical perspective, our goodness is our essential self, which is the manifestation of the divine within us. This goodness is always there, but our visceral awareness of it depends on the alignment of our thoughts and actions with this higher self.

## GOOD POINTS AND SOCIAL CHANGE

How do good points apply to social change? As mentioned in the last chapter, humans create oppressive systems and humans undo those systems. As an advocate for change, it is in your interest to understand the motivations of decision makers. Most people think of themselves as trying to do good even when their actions cause suffering. Seeing the good points in a bank president or politician is a good strategic move because it can help you understand how this person wants to see him- or herself. We all want to be known by our good points. We may need to use pressure to get the decision maker to change, but knowing his or her good points will provide valuable guidance in how to apply this pressure.

For example, a hospital president refuses to raise wages for nurses. One of this person's good points is that he or she has prioritized opening health clinics in underserved parts of the city. You can make it part of your strategy to demonstrate how raising wages for nurses, especially in the health clinics, will bring more highly qualified nurses to those clinics and increase usage of health care in those areas. According to an experienced organizer, the more a decision maker can feel like a negotiated solution expresses his or her own values and desires, the more likely it will be that the solution is implemented well.[7]

Later in the chapter, we will look more in depth at how to use the good-points practice as part of a social-change strategy. Finding good points is also useful for change makers themselves. As one organizer told me, having occasional wins is essential to keeping up motivation. In between these wins though, there are plenty of failures and mistakes. These failures can wear down self-confidence. In addition, difficult personalities and character flaws among organizational colleagues and leaders can drain the motivation from team members. Finding good points in oneself and in one's colleagues can be a source of renewal. Later we will also explore in depth using good points to stay committed to our big goals.

JUDGING FAVORABLY

A companion practice to finding good points is judging people favorably. A classic Jewish teaching instructs us, "One should make it a practice to judge all people favorably."[8] Another version of this teaching is translated, "One should judge the whole person favorably,"[9] meaning that when we take the whole person's life—all his or her qualities and circumstances—into account, we will see that people are generally trying to do their best. It is interesting to note that the teaching does not say, "Do not judge another person." It accepts that we will judge. Just like our brains are wired to notice what is wrong, we are wired to judge. Our ability to identify what we like and don't like develops much earlier than our ability to simply observe reality.[10] As with all human traits, the rabbis try to raise up judgment, directing us to use it to build up rather than tear down. As with finding good points, Breslov teachings apply this practice to the self and to others. The explanations here will focus on judging others favorably.

Judging others favorably was seen as so important to healthy interpersonal and communal life that it shows up in several different places in ancient Jewish literature. The most complete picture of the practice describes a man in ancient times who left his home and family in northern Israel and traveled to the south to work for several years to earn money.

At the end of the three years the man requested his payment from the land owner. The owner told him he had no money. The man asked if he could pay him in property and he answered that he had no property he could give him. The man asked if he could pay him in material goods or food. The owner answered that he had no material goods or food that he could give him. The man walked away dejected and returned to his home empty handed. Several months later that owner travelled north to the man's home. He asked him, "When I said I had no money to pay you, what did you think?" The man answered, "I thought you must have invested all your money in goods for your business." "You are correct," the owner answered and then asked, "When I said I had no property to give you, what did you think?" The man answered, "I assumed you must have dedicated your property to the holy Temple in Jerusalem." "Yes," answered the owner and then asked, "When I said I had no materials goods or food to give you, what did you think?" The man answered, "I also thought that you must have pledged them to the priests." "Correct again," answered the owner. "Because you judged me favorably when you had every right to suspect me I will give you double your wages for the three years."[11]

The Talmud will sometimes teach a lesson by giving an extreme example of a practice to make the point that under less extreme circumstances we can certainly succeed. The man in the story is highly unusual in that he can be so generous of spirit even after working for three years for no wages. There are at least two things we can learn about the practice from this story.

We only do the practice if there is doubt about the motives behind the action. This is a limit on the practice. If we have good reason to believe that someone is acting to cause harm, we do not ignore the evidence and judge that person favorably. For example, if a certain company has a history in other cities of dumping toxic waste into the river, when this same company comes to town, we don't need to judge them favorably and wait to see if they dump. Rather, we would assume they will continue their practice and put in place safeguards against dumping waste. But if a different company comes to town with no track record, the company's executives deserve to be judge favorably regarding their environmental practices.

Another lesson is that it takes creativity to judge favorably. You need to play out a number of reasonable scenarios why the person may have done this seemingly bad thing. This takes thinking about the whole person, his or her life circumstances and how this particular action makes sense to him or her. This is not an easy practice, but your heart will open as you do it.

Seeking good points and judging favorably are both based on an assumption of goodness. This may ring hollow to seasoned change makers who know from firsthand experience the brutality of oppressive systems. There are some truly evil people out there who are so disconnected that they willingly harm others. Unfortunately, we may occasionally encounter such people, but they are not the norm. As a politician once told me regarding his opponents on city council, "There are not so many Darth Vaders out there."[12] In most cases applying these practices will open up possibilities for connection and change.

## JOY AND RETURN

The power of the good point is its ability to generate joy and facilitate a return to alignment with oneself, others, and God. *Simcha,* or "joy," is not to be confused with a fleeting feeling of lightheartedness that comes with hearing a good joke. Joy is a deep emotion that arises from a sense of connectedness. What greater joy is there than to actually feel connected to another human being, to oneself, or to God? The Jewish wedding is such a joyous affair because it marks the potential for a lifetime of deepening connection between two people. Yom Kippur is seen as one of the most joyous days in the Jewish calendar because it marks the reconnection of each person with his or her highest self and with God. A feeling of joy gives us energy. Research shows that people who experience joy are generally healthier and more effective.[13]

The good point generates joy because it awakens reconnection with our best selves. When I see a good point in myself, I remember who I am, which grounds me in my center. Grounded, centered, and joyful, we are potent agents for growth and change.

"It is a great mitzvah to always be happy" is one of Rabbi Nachman's most well-known teachings.[14] Why is simcha so important to the Breslov spiritual system? First let's understand what Rabbi Nachman means and does not mean by this statement.[15] As we explained above, simcha is not a fleeting feeling, but a deep emotional state that results from an awareness of being connected. "Always being happy" does not mean walking around with a fake smile on your face. Judaism acknowledges that there are times for sadness and grief.

Rabbi Nachman refers to these emotions as *lev shavor*/brokenheartedness and *tza'ar*/pain. These are important feelings that accompany loss and should be encouraged at the appropriate time. The danger is when brokenheartedness becomes an emotional state of sadness and depression. Depression is marked by a sense of gloom and lack of any hope that things will get better. This is the despair that Rabbi Nachman's teachings address. "It is a great mitzvah to always be happy" means that it is a great mitzvah to cultivate a deep sense of connectedness that creates an underlying state of happiness that is present even when one feels brokenhearted over a loss. Just like the sun is always shining behind the clouds, the reality of connection is always there, even when it is obscured by temporary feelings of emotional pain. This underlying, subtle, quiet joy is crucial for getting us emotionally unstuck when the broken heart slips into deeper sadness.

When Rabbi Nachman said, "There is no despair in the world,"[16] he was talking about at an objective level. Objectively, because God is always with us and the potential for change always exists, there is no real despair. On a subjective level, many of us will forget this reality and feel deep despair. Simcha returns us to a proper perspective that God is there and nothing is ever static in this world.

Simcha is a key tool for change makers. Despair is a partner of oppression. People or systems that promote exploitation consciously and unconsciously try to get people to feel powerless and bad about themselves, so they won't challenge the exploitation. Someone in despair is not going to put up much of a fight against oppression.

For example, racist ideas are usually resisted at first by young people when they initially hear them from adults. Racism is founded on separation between humans, and most young people instinctively sense the deep connection between all people. The adults will then communicate directly or indirectly how naive and stupid the young person is for not understanding the "realities" of race. If you are a young person and you have your intelligence questioned enough times by your caretakers, you will doubt your own thinking about all people being equal and connected. These seeds of doubt may grow into despair cultivated by the sense of separation promoted by the adults who "know better." Based in despair about racism and separation, this person will have a hard time finding firm footing from which to battle racism or other oppressions. Cultivating simcha will enable this person to reclaim an inherent sense of connectedness and be a more potent advocate for ending racism.

As change makers ourselves, we will be much more effective approaching the tasks of organizing and communicating a vision for a different world from a place of simcha, versus bitterness and anger. Most people yearn to feel more connected and will respond more enthusiastically to a message of building up and joy rather than a vision of tearing down and despair. Simcha restores our ability to perceive the reality that change is always possible.

Finding good points also helps us realign our lives and relationships with others and with God. This realignment is the Jewish practice of *teshuva*, or "return." The idea and practice of teshuva are based on the principle that, through our own actions or circumstance, we get separated from our highest values, others, and God and always have the ability to come back. In spiritual life, as in relationships, we are constantly moving on an axis of closeness and distance. One moment we may feel deeply connected, and another we feel lost and adrift. Sometimes we cause this distance by our actions—a thoughtless comment, indulging in an unhealthy behavior, neglecting commitments—and other times we cannot identify the reason for feeling far away.

As described above, the yetzer can take this distance and make it seem like returning is impossible. "I really messed up this time, and they will never accept me back into the group again." "I haven't prayed in ten years. Who am I kidding that I can develop a prayer practice?" These are some of the ways the yetzer can sound.

Enter the good point practice. Rabbi Nachman understood how feeling stuck can get in the way of teshuva. Finding good points, which activate feelings of joy, will make you unstuck and open up the possibility of return. In the coming sections, we will apply these practices of seeking good points, judging favorably, simcha, and teshuva to the different aspects of social-change practice.

### FINDING GOOD IN OURSELVES

Seeking good points in ourselves as change agents helps counter the despair and attacks that we inevitably meet at some point in our efforts. At a certain point in the campaign to create an ethical contractor policy at my school it looked like the existing crew would lose their jobs partially as a result of my intervention. I was distraught. Had I not opened my mouth in the first place at least the crew would still have their jobs. The law of unintended consequences was at work. I had not thought through that I could make the situation worse. I felt guilty and wanted to avoid the crew members during that period. I noticed my enthusiasm for the campaign waning as I wanted to put my attention elsewhere and not feel the guilt and discomfort associated with the cleaning crew. I began to despair that anything positive would come out of all this effort.

Rabbi Natan of Breslov, Rabbi Nachman's primary disciple, describes this despair as a type of spiritual sleep.[17] Just like sleeping too much is a physical symptom of depression, lack of motivation and distraction are a form of spiritual sleep. Seeking and finding good points is the Breslov prescription for waking up from spiritual sleep. I needed to wake up and rededicate myself to my school doing the right thing by our contract workers even if it felt terribly uncomfortable. In the first section we spoke about ratzon. Ratzon can also be a good point.[18] I returned to my ratzon. What did I really want? As described in chapter 1, I sincerely wanted my community to live its values and I wanted the best for these particular workers and anyone who works for us. I imagined the faces of the crew members and created the affirmation that I repeated regularly during this period, "This is my community." This motivation was a good point. I could have let myself not notice the immigrants who service our building but instead I chose to push our community to do the right thing. Over time this reminder woke me up to my original motivation. Now awake, I was able to choose to keep advocating despite the emotional discomfort.

---

### REFLECTION

What is a time you lost confidence or motivation in the midst of an effort to make change?

What was the cause of this loss of enthusiasm?

Put your mind back to that time and seek a good point. This can be something positive you did in this change effort or simply a positive intention.

How might finding the good point make a difference for you?

---

Personal attacks are the other way we can get diverted from our change efforts. If you are trying to make change to a system or institution, or if you are helping people change, and your efforts are having success, you will most likely be on the receiving end of criticism or attacks. Every system has people in it who do not want change, and you are a threat. If these other parties are thoughtful, they will engage in principled argument. If they feel threatened and anxious, they may try to undermine you or even publicly lash out at you in ways that hurt. In chapter 8, which focuses on *kavod*/dignity, we will deal more in depth with handling attacks. For now suffice it to say that criticism and attacks can evoke two very different responses. Some people move into battle mode and feel a rush of getting ready for a fight. Others retreat and feel the attack personally in a way that can lead to despair. Both responses are fertile ground for the good-points practice.

David Hoffman is a lawyer and founder of the Boston Law Collaborative (BLC), a firm dedicated to resolving disputes in ways that build relationships and peace. Hoffman is a national leader in the field of mediation. He uses internal family systems (IFS) theory to make his mediation practice not only more effective, but also more spiritual.[19] In IFS, asserting self energy is the way to be our most grounded, centered selves.

Hoffman describes a difficult family mediation in which one of the parties was a driven New York City litigator known for being competitive, tough, and ruthless. His orientation was the opposite of BLC's collaborative approach. At one point he said privately, "Hoffman, you've done something I never thought was possible. You've made a really bad situation even worse!" David describes feeling terrible. In IFS terms, his defender parts were activated, as was his wounded-child part, which wanted to retreat. Hoffman called on self energy to come into the center. He felt more grounded and asked the attorney, "What was it I did that made things worse? I do want to help." Expecting an attack in return, the attorney was caught off guard. His defenses lowered, and he spoke candidly for the first time during the mediation.

While Hoffman doesn't use the term "good point," his search for self energy is a very similar process to that described by the Breslov masters. When under attack and on the edge of despair, he searched for his source of goodness, self energy. Viscerally feeling this goodness, he had the spaciousness of heart to respond with curiosity. Grounded in our goodness, which connects us to our source, we can skillfully manage the attacks that are sure to come our way as we make change.

Social-change efforts can also threaten those in power. Rachel Keller started an initiative to publicize the extent of childhood hunger in her state and coordinate food security efforts. The governor was furious and insisted that her effort would damage the state's reputation. He even publicly criticized her in the highest circulation newspaper for exaggerating the extent of the problem for personal gain. Rachel was distraught. She respected that the governor did not want to do anything that would hurt the state. But she knew childhood hunger was a serious issue that needed addressing. A colleague pointed out that getting attacked like this was actually a good point in itself. An influential person like the governor would not bother attacking something if it was not important. The criticism was a sign that she was actually succeeding in mobilizing attention to child hunger. Reframing attacks as an affirmation of our significance can also be a good point that keeps us going in our social-change efforts.

---

### REFLECTION

When is a time you were attacked or criticized in your change efforts?

Why were you attacked? What was your first reaction?

Did you get defensive and attack back, or did you try to hide?

How did you end up dealing with the attack or criticism?

How would finding a good point in yourself in the midst of this attack have made a difference for you?

---

## FINDING GOOD IN OTHERS, INCLUDING OUR ADVERSARIES

Finding good points not only wakes us up but also has the power to effect changes in others. Rabbi Nachman opens his teaching on good points with a description of the unlikely power our perception can have on other people.

> Know that one needs to judge all people favorably. Even regarding someone who is completely wicked one needs to seek and find in him some little good. In this little good he is not wicked. By finding this little good and judging him favorably you truly elevate him to the side of merit and are able to bring him to Teshuva.[20]

How can perceiving some good in a person who has done a lot of bad possibly change that person? Rabbi Nachman says that our perception actually elevates him or her. The key metaphor in the teaching is the scale of justice. There is an arm that holds liability for wrongdoing and an arm that holds innocence or merit for good intentions and behavior. The medieval philosopher Maimonides teaches that a wicked person is someone who has more liability than merit and most of us should think of ourselves as having the scales evenly balanced.[21] Imagine Rabbi Nachman's completely wicked person. This person's scale is quite lopsided with the arm of merit way in the air above the arm of liability, which scrapes the ground with its weight. When this person sees the huge imbalance in his or her own scale, feelings of despair may set in. "How can I ever change enough to get out of this hole?" The patterns of negative behavior are deeply ingrained.

It is this sense of being stuck that the good-points practice comes to open. The first step is to find something positive, no matter how insignificant, about this person. We metaphorically add this good point to the arm of merit on the person's scale. If he or she does something and the motive is in doubt, we similarly judge that also for merit. As we metaphorically add points to the side of merit, the scale shakes with movement. What seemed completely stuck now shows it can move. Perhaps it is this little movement that wakes up the wicked person to the fact that change is possible. Such a person is not a victim to his or her destructive patterns of behavior. Remember that we have not said anything to this person yet but just exerted effort to see something good. From a spiritual perspective, perception is one of the invisible lines of connection between all things.

How we perceive can make real change in another's self-perception. Seeing good can also change the way we talk about and approach a person. Our body language softens and our heart opens, even as we stay guarded because of his or her miserable track record. We are now out of the realm of pure spirit and into the realm of perceptible interaction. According to a classic Jewish teaching, "Just like water reflects the face, so the heart of one person is reflected in the heart of the other," meaning that, as humans, how we feel about someone has a deep impact on that person.[22] The wicked person may pick up on the new tone or body language and be struck just enough to wake up to the possibility of change. The path of return is now possible.

How can we apply this teaching to social change? First let's explore the limitations of the teaching to our context. Who is this completely wicked person? For Rabbi Nachman, most likely, it is a fellow Jew who has abandoned spiritually and ethically appropriate behavior. Could this person be someone like Hitler, surely the contemporary symbol of the completely wicked person? It is not clear that Rabbi Nachman would have applied this teaching to violent oppressors of Jews or even to Jewish oppressors. It is also not clear that we can expect a less powerful party in a dynamic to seek good points in an oppressor. If we are going to apply this teaching to situations of oppression, it may be the role of a third party to use the good-points practice to encourage change.

Within these limitations there may be ample room to use seeking good points as part of a social-change strategy. Rabbi Nachman does not limit the practice to the completely wicked. Rather, this is the extreme case used to teach us that we can certainly find good points in most people. In our activism we rarely encounter completely wicked people. Most people who benefit from and enforce oppression in one way or another are just like you and me, basically good people who are complex and stuck within certain destructive patterns of behavior.

Let's think of social change as a teshuva process. Where oppression and injustice exist, there is distance and imbalance regarding core values like human dignity being expressed in the oppressive situation. Other values, like expediency or profit or comfort or security, overshadow dignity or fairness. Teshuva would represent a return to a healthy balance of values. By seeking and finding good points in those who have decision-making power, we can shake up patterns of behavior and rigidities that lead to the imbalance and open the way for change. The following example demonstrates a strategic use of good points.

Meir Lakein, a veteran community organizer with Join for Justice, tells of a campaign in a suburban school district to address a spate of teen suicide attempts. In this one school district, sixty young people attempted suicide over the course of a year. Parents were distraught and wanted help from the school system. The superintendent said it was the parents' responsibility. There was a strong temptation on the part of the parent leaders to publicly attack the superintendent. However, according to Lakein, "People had a sense that this was not him." In other words, the parent leaders could see a good point in the superintendent. Despite his position not to take action, they could tell that he cared about this issue. Seeing this good point informed their strategy. They applied significant communal pressure on him to recognize their demands and attend a public meeting. Once at the meeting, they did not feel they needed to pressure him more. Rather, since they saw that he cared, they structured the meeting to build on this good point. They broke up into small groups to tell stories about pressures their children experienced. This was actually all for him, so he would be in a group. When he got up to speak, he put away his remarks and said he could only think of stories from when he was a child. One peer of his had committed suicide, and another had overdosed on drugs. He said, "We need to do something about this, but I don't know what." The next year he made social-emotional learning one of the top priorities for the school system.

Lakein explains that this type of outcome results from opening people up and not just forcing them to do what you want. By subtly projecting back to the superintendent through the story-based meeting structure that they knew he cared, the parent leaders shook him out of his rigid defensive position and opened the way for a solution. While the end result was not perfect, many young people's lives were made better as a result of this nuanced approach to social change.

---

### PRACTICE: *Finding Good Points in a Campaign*

Choose a campaign or change effort you are engaged in or worked on in the past. Identify a decision maker that you need to influence or a particular person who stands in the way of the change you want to make. This doesn't need to be the key leader; it can also be someone in the chain of decision making. What is something good about this person or something good he or she has done in this role? You may need to look hard if this person is putting up a lot of resistance to your change efforts. Once you find one good point, try to find a second. After you clearly see these good points, reconsider your change strategy. How can your strategy build on these good points?

If finding good points in a political opponent seems like too much of a stretch, try this practice with your colleagues and teammates. Finding good points in your team can build the cohesion crucial for sticking together under pressure during a campaign or a difficult negotiation. Find a good point in each team member and then a second. How might your strategy and approach change based on knowing these good points?

---

## A COMMUNITY IN SONG

The spontaneous response to finding a good point in oneself and feeling joy is often some form of exuberant sound. Melodies, shouts of joy, humming, and whistling are some of the sounds that burst forth from the human heart when it overflows with appreciation. Breslov tradition teaches that the essence of song comes from finding and collecting the good from within darkness. In Breslov, the prayer leader, or cantor, looks at the people gathered for prayer and sees good points in each of them. The leader joins all those good points together and makes song from them as a communal offering to God. This communal song is a manifestation of the good that exists in each member. Rabbi Nachman teaches that Moses, the archetypical Jewish leader, built the Tabernacle, the dwelling place for God on earth, out of the good points of all the community members. Song and the structure of the Tabernacle are metaphors for what we can do together when we raise up and join together the good points in each of us.

Social change is a communal endeavor. While one person may need to take the lead or initiate efforts for change, success will only come by enlisting plenty of allies. The best social-change leaders are those who can see the strengths in others and mobilize those strengths on behalf of the group project. Metaphorically, the change work of such a group is a form of song and communal offering. Song is not just a metaphor, but is itself an important aspect of social-change activism.

Many social movements have theme songs they use to create a sense of community and raise spirits. In the early days of the Greater Boston Interfaith Organization, Reverend Burns Stanfield wrote "Working Together for the City of God," which was sung at the end of large gatherings, almost as a form of prayer. Pete

Seeger's adaptation of the traditional African American folk song "We Shall Overcome" is probably the most famous of all protest songs because of its use during the civil-rights movement of the 1950s and 1960s. Referring to traditional African American and civil-rights freedom songs, Reverend Martin Luther King Jr. said, "They invigorate the movement in a most significant way . . . These freedom songs serve to give unity to a movement."[23]

Research shows the power song has to lift spirits and strengthen bonds among people. According to the journalist Stacey Horn,

> The benefits of singing regularly seem to be cumulative. In one study, singers were found to have lower levels of cortisol, indicating lower stress. A very preliminary investigation suggesting that our heart rates may sync up during group singing could also explain why singing together sometimes feels like a guided group meditation. Study after study has found that singing relieves anxiety and contributes to quality of life.[24]

Peter Yarrow, of the folk band Peter, Paul, and Mary, has played music at thousands of human rights gatherings over the past sixty years. He describes singing together for social change in terms similar to prayer. According to Yarrow, "These songs give us courage to keep going even when victory seems far away."[25] Real social change takes long-term commitment on behalf of many people working together. Finding good points and creating joyous community builds the determination and social cohesion needed to face the brokenness of the world over and over again until light overcomes the darkness.

---

**REFLECTION**

What songs or other creative expressions have you used in your change efforts? What impact did these have on you and your group in creating social cohesion?

How might you bring song or creativity into your change efforts?

What else can you do to build community among people working for change?

## PRACTICE: *Seeking Good Points in Yourself and Your Team*

Try making a commitment to seeking and finding a good point in yourself each day for a week. Then seek and find good points in other people for a second week. Then seek and find good points in the team or group with whom you work for a third week. Make this a daily practice for three weeks, and see if looking for good points becomes more habitual over time.

---

## SUMMARY

Seeking good points is a practice that you can bring to any aspect of your life. It is a perspective as much as it is a practice. When Rabbi Nachman advised his followers to go with this teaching their whole lives, he meant for us to make looking for good points a regular part of how we are in the world. We can train our minds to look for the good in ourselves, in others, and in any situation we encounter. This does not mean adopting a Pollyannaish attitude that everything is good. Seeking good points starts with seeing the brokenness and feeling how bad the situation really is. Only then do we search out and find the good that exists in the darkness and use this good as leverage for growth and change. Adopting a good-points perspective helps us bring more joy, creativity, and energy to our personal lives and our social-change leadership.

# 4

## THE POWER OF CHOICE

Some years ago the City of San Francisco implemented a fraud-detection program to ensure that women receiving family welfare grants were actually single parents and did not have a male partner living with them. To implement this policy, Department of Social Services (DSS) social workers would enter recipients' apartments unannounced and even check clothing drawers for male underwear. Low-income and homeless people and advocates were outraged by this violation of the privacy and dignity of recipients. I was among a group organizing on this issue, and our goal was to convince the DSS to eliminate this policy and figure out a more respectful way to deter fraud.

We needed to first get the attention of the DSS director and then get her to agree to negotiate with our team of recipients and advocates. Until this point she was unwilling to meet with our coalition to discuss the issue. A major social-policy conference was scheduled for the next month at San Francisco State University, and the DSS director was moderating one of the sessions. Our strategy was to disrupt her session at the conference and pressure her to agree to negotiations. The action involved having six women on public assistance sit in various places among the audience in the conference hall. At a predetermined moment in the conference, one of the women would stand up and ask a question about the policy. At that point the other five women would also stand up, briefly describe their humiliating experience with the home searches, and all demand that the director negotiate with our team to change the policy.

The day of the conference, we rented buses so a large number of advocates, recipients, and supporters could fill the hall. The women took their places among the audience, and the rest of us sat around the edges of the crowded room, waiting for the moment. The DSS director got the session under way, and it was soon time for questions from the audience. Wanda, the woman assigned to start off the action, had a choice. I am sure she felt scared. Was she going to let her fear keep her quiet, or was she going to stand up as planned, despite the fear? The fear was too much for her, and she didn't stand up. We all looked around at each other in panic. What should we do now? We whispered to each other, and the five other women looked for guidance from the organizers. The conference was moving on since there were no questions, and we were losing our opportunity to make a difference. I, too, felt frozen and unsure of what to do.

At that moment the lead organizer, a powerful female lawyer named Gail, bounded down the center aisle and grabbed the microphone that was standing there for public comment. She interrupted the panel member who was talking and presented our demands. The DSS director and the panel were shocked. They listened to Gail and, after some public back-and-forth, actually agreed to a meeting with our representatives later that week. I shuddered in my seat, watching Gail. She also had a choice. Was she going to let the action fail and develop a different strategy later, or was she going to take full charge of the situation despite any fear or risk of humiliation? The DSS director also had to choose between a protracted and embarrassing confrontation in front of her colleagues or an agreement to negotiate. The next week we did, indeed, meet with her team at DSS and succeeded in creating a policy that preserved the dignity of welfare recipients.

Social-change activism pushes us to make significant choices, and these choices are keys to our spiritual growth and the health of our communities. How were all the moments of choice in the story above potent moments of spiritual growth? Rabbi Eliyahu Dessler, one of the great twentieth-century Mussar teachers, explains that free choice only really exists at one point in any particular situation. For Rabbi Dessler, the choice point is that place that lies just between reality, or truth, as we know it and self-deception, or falsehood. He uses smoking as an example. The smoker lies awake at night unable to sleep because he is coughing so much. He vows that he will not smoke the next day because he knows that smoking hurts his lungs and causes him to stay awake at night. The next morning his addiction kicks in, and he tells himself, "Just one won't hurt." The reality, or truth, is that he knows he can't have just one. "Just one won't hurt" is the confusion about reality, or falsehood. He has that first cigarette and then another and another until he smokes the whole pack and stays awake coughing the next night.[1] Rabbi Dessler explains:

> Everyone has free choice—at the point where truth meets falsehood. In other words choice takes place at that point where the truth as the person sees it confronts the illusion produced in him by the power of falsehood. But the majority of a person's actions are undertaken without any clash between truth and falsehood taking place. Many of a person's actions may happen to coincide with what is objectively right because he has been brought up that way and it does not occur to him to do otherwise, and many bad and false decisions may be taken simply because the person does not realize that they are bad. In such cases no valid Behira, or choice, has been made.[2]

Rabbi Dessler's innovation is that much of our behavior lies in the area of positive and negative habituation. His metaphor is a nineteenth-century battlefield. The front is only at one point on the field at any one time. The area behind the lines of each side is not in play. These areas are like those parts of ourselves that have been conditioned to behave and think a certain way through education, our environment, or by our previous decisions. Regarding certain issues, our habituation creates more sensitivity, and in others, less awareness.

For example I was habituated by my parents and public-service advertising campaigns in the 1970s not to throw litter out of the window of my car. I just never do it, and I don't need to think about it. I have internalized a particular sensitivity to the environment from my upbringing. I was also habituated as a white person growing up in an affluent, mostly white town to not see or consider as important the economic struggles of the majority black and Latino communities in the surrounding towns. The issues affecting these communities just did not penetrate my awareness on a daily basis. This type of habituation is sometimes called "white privilege."

The location of each person's choice point in any situation is set by these factors. Only at the edge of our habituation do we have a live option to consciously choose. According to Rabbi Dessler, while the point location is mostly beyond our control, nothing interferes with our ability to choose reality and truth as we know it in any situation.[3] This idea of free will is closer to the determinists that are currently popular, given all we are learning about the brain and how much of our behavior is actually hardwired. We don't have an equally free choice over everything. In the white-privilege example above, I may not be at a point of choosing to be relaxed socially with people from that neighborhood, but it could be a live choice for me to read and learn more about their lives.

Rabbi Dessler teaches that our choice point is always moving.[4] When we make a positive choice, more of reality and truth in a particular area are now clear to us, and our next choice point will be in a more refined place. If we make a choice toward self-deception, our point moves in a direction of dulled awareness and less of the truth is clear to us. If we equate God with the ultimate reality that lies behind everything, as we move closer and closer to a clearer perception of reality in all areas of our life, we get closer to knowing God. With each choice against negative habits we bring more of our divine image into the world.[5] In this way the choice point is an invaluable tool for personal and spiritual growth. Being clear about our choice points helps us understand our growing edge. Where we struggle to choose is where we need to grow. The more we get used to seeing our choice points, the more we really know ourselves and can take charge of how we want to grow.

How does the choice point apply to the various people in the story above? Wanda was chosen to speak because of her courage and leadership in organizing her fellow single parents. However, as a recently homeless African American mother who was raised poor and suffered a lot in her life at the hands of men and welfare bureaucracies, she was also strongly habituated to acting timid and respectful in the face of authority. At the moment she was supposed to stand up and speak, this habituation toward timidity was just too strong to be overcome by the reality of the support she actually had to challenge authority. Unfortunately her choice to stay quiet reinforced her sense of powerlessness.

For me, as one of the organizers, it was beyond my choice point to boldly take over the conference. I was just too scared and inexperienced in asserting myself in that way. It was not a live choice. The reality as I knew it was to stay connected to our team through eye contact rather than just sit still and look away. I did decide that day that a life goal of mine was to be able to act as boldly as Gail, but it would take me a lot more growth to get there.

As an African American woman from the South, Gail was also educated early in life to be timid in the face of white authority figures. Unlike Wanda, she'd received encouraging messages about her intelligence from parents and teachers and succeeded in going to college and law school. As a lesbian she needed to accustom herself to not conforming to authority. For Gail the choice point was on a different level than for Wanda or me because she was already habituated to defying authority. Would it work better strategically to retreat and regroup or take over the conference? Her clear sense of reality was that the director and audience would have been receptive to this kind of challenge, and she was correct. This choice made Gail an even more powerful advocate as she increased her confidence in her own sense of reality.

The director's choice point was between needing to save face in front of her colleagues versus listening to the demands of the protestors. While I'm sure she felt some pull to shut down Gail and prove her toughness to her colleagues, she apparently had enough self-confidence to see clearly that the demands were just. She realized that accepting the demand for negotiation would be the quickest way to move on with the conference.

---

### PRACTICE: *Tracking Your Choice Points*

You know you are in a choice point when you need to struggle to decide what to do. The choice can often be between two or more positive options, like a job choice, or something less significant, like which activity to pursue on a particular evening. The key to the practice is being aware that you are actually in a choice point. With awareness we can assess why we are being pulled in different directions and which side of the choice better reflects reality and truth as we know it.

The practice is to notice your choice points on a daily basis. At the end of the day, or the beginning of the next morning, set aside a few minutes to review the day. What choice caused you deliberation and struggle? For the practice just choose one, even though you might remember several choices. Ask yourself these questions:

What did I need to choose between?

What factors or values pulled me to each side of the choice?

Which side seems closer to reality and truth, and which side seems closer to self-deception?

The first question should be clear once you identify the choice. The second question will take reflection. What antecedent factors may be pulling you in either direction? These can include past experiences, messages from family or society, your values or the values of your community. It is worth spending a few minutes thinking through the issues that lie underneath your pull to either choice.

The third question is especially difficult, but essential. We want to get better and better at noticing the subtle ways we deceive ourselves and strengthening our perception of reality and awareness of our inner sense of truth. You can use a journal and write out your reflections or just set aside time to think. Some people use the hitbodedut process described in chapter 1 to review their choice points.

Repeat this practice daily for two weeks. Notice if you see any patterns to your choice points. For example, do you tend to struggle over choices that involve relationships or how people think about you or how you use speech? Choice points will reveal your growing edge, because it is through difficult choices that we emerge from self-deception into greater awareness of reality.

---

## THE CHOICE POINT AND SOCIAL CHANGE

The choice point is also a powerful tool for organizations and societies to grow into more holistic and healthy collectives with a heightened awareness of reality. Let's take the issue of immigrant migrant workers we discussed in chapter 2.

The placement of the choice point is the society's attitude toward these vulnerable immigrants. How aware and compassionate or how insensitive and indifferent to suffering is the society at large toward this population? There can be many reasons for the level of awareness or insensitivity, including the immigrant experience of the current citizens, the nature of how the education system and leaders speak about low-income immigrants, and past history and prejudices regarding the countries of origins of these migrant workers. If there is much insensitivity, it is not a live choice for such a society to pass compassionate legislation protecting these workers.

In the territory of negative habituation is a stubborn lack of awareness of the suffering of this population, as well as denial of responsibility and blaming the victim. In the area of positive habituation are labor laws passed long ago that give basic workplace protections and regulate wages and the right to organize, as well as social security. These are all good things for workers, but they generally operate under the level of awareness because they are such a fixed part of society.

The challenge for the migrant workers is to get the society to build on its positive habituation in the area of workers' rights and move in the direction of even more awareness of the reality of these workers' lives and contribution to food chain. If we think of the challenge on a vertical axis, the area of positive habituation is on the bottom and the goal is to grow upward, pushing self-deception and illusion out of the way and bringing even more territory under the domain of awareness.

Choice points move a little at a time, so change makers need to strategize about what the next level of dignity would be for this particular society. It might not be passing legislation but could look like major companies supporting a program to raise incomes of farmworkers, like the CIW's Fair Food Program described in chapter 2. Such campaigns raise awareness by creating a choice point for consumers regarding their food purchases. Will they urge their supermarket or fast food chain to help farmworkers or will they ignore the workers' plight?

These choices move the dial on the society's choice point. It is well known in legislative advocacy that it takes many tries to pass a certain bill.[6] The first time around, the legislators and society at large are at such a level of insensitivity about a given issue that the vote on the bill only functions to start raising awareness. As the awareness of a particular issue grows, the choice point moves toward greater sensitivity toward the reality of the issue. Once awareness of the reality grows, the society is at the choice point to actually pass legislation. It is the job of change makers to understand and move a society's choice points so that the society reflects a greater awareness of the reality of its members.

Marriage equality is a remarkable example of this dynamic. In the early 1990s, the best the Bill Clinton administration could do for gay rights was get the military to agree to its "don't ask, don't tell" policy. Marriage equality was roundly dismissed by everyone across the mainstream political spectrum, reflected by the passage of the Defense of Marriage Act (DOMA) in 1996. Despite gay marriage becoming legal in Massachusetts in 2004, President Barack Obama professed his opposition to it becoming the law of the land when elected in 2008. However, four years later Obama included a call for same-sex marriage in his second inaugural speech, and by 2015 the US Supreme Court ruled parts of DOMA unconstitutional. In 1993 it was not a live choice in the United States to adopt marriage equality. There was just not enough awareness of the reality of gay people's lives among the general population. Twenty years of cultural and political activism (including movies like *Philadelphia,* television series with gay characters, and more and more people coming out of the closet) shifted the choice point. By 2015 it became a live choice for those in the center of power to make marriage equality the law of the land.

Change agents can facilitate growth through choice points at the level of the individual, the organization, and the larger society. At the individual level, activists can use choice points both for their own growth and to challenge others to make essential changes in their lives. The action at San Francisco State University showed me that I wanted to grow regarding my ability to take bold leadership at moments of tension. Over the next decades, I took note of leaders who acted with this kind of courage and challenged myself at different points to move out of my comfort zone and be more vocal. While the process was not always conscious, through persistent attention to nudge against my pull toward timidity, my choice point did indeed move over the years.

One striking demonstration of this took place at a gas station on the Merritt Parkway in Connecticut. I was on my way home late one night and stopped in the gas station to get a snack. As I walked into the store, I quickly realized a conflict was escalating. The man of

Middle Eastern descent behind the counter called out to an African American man at the door, "You people are all like that!" The man at the door responded, "What did you say? What did you say!" I made a quick decision to put myself between the clerk and the customer at the door. Looking the clerk right in the eye, I said calmly and firmly, "Stop talking. Stop talking." The clerk's body seemed to relax. I kept standing there looking at him. I then looked back and saw that the customer had gone to his car and left. The clerk thanked me. I bought what I needed and left.

What happened here? My fear of sticking my neck out was outweighed by a strong intuitive sense that I had the skill and ability to make a difference. I just knew what to do. I don't know why, but I also had a clear sense that there was no danger of physical harm. Contrast this to that young organizer shuddering on the side of the conference hall waiting for someone to take charge. I don't think these types of changes happened automatically with age. After years of deciding to challenge myself to act boldly, my choice point shifted to where it really was a live option for me to jump in and de-escalate a racial conflict.

## METHODS FOR MAKING INDIVIDUAL, ORGANIZATIONAL, AND SOCIETAL CHOICES

As change makers we can challenge other individuals to make good choices as well. Ziesl Maayan uses her platform as a nurse to advocate for deep changes in the health-care system, endorsing a move away from being so focused on medication and quick fixes and encouraging more sustainable lifestyle changes that are at the root of so much illness. Maayan's advocacy takes place through the medical education system and also with individual patients. She explains, "The current model is 'Match the pill to the ill.' It does not address the larger context, and this is not a way to approach health. We need to create balance with the way we treat the world and it treats us."[7] One problem with the "Match the pill to the ill" approach is that it bypasses the necessity for people to make different, healthy choices about their lives. Certainly in some cases medication is absolutely necessary for healing. In many cases medication is given when less expensive diet and environmental changes would be just as, or more, effective. Making these types of lifestyle choices is difficult, and this is where the health-care professional can make a big difference.

Maayan describes a middle-aged male patient with high blood pressure and a persistent asthmatic wheeze. He had been taking antiasthma medication for over a year with no change. He had a perception of himself as an athlete. After some probing she found out that his home had mold, his diet was unhealthy, and he actually did very little exercise. He played some hockey on the weekends and played a little with his children. He was actually losing muscle mass and was overweight.

Maayan confronted him about his self-perception as an athlete and challenged him to really start exercising. In addition she worked with him to create a new diet and encouraged him to deal with the mold. While he had years of bad health decisions pulling him to ignore her advice, the pain of the asthma provided him with enough awareness of his choice point to try to make changes. He cleaned the house, changed his diet, and actually started exercising regularly. Each of these was its own choice point that moved him in the direction of healthy living.

After six months he was off blood-pressure medication, and his asthma was gone. This was someone who was living in self-deception about his physical condition and was completely unaware of the impact of environment and diet. Maayan's truth telling and his wife's support helped create a choice point for him, and her advocacy encouraged him to make the healthy choice.

Organizations and campaigns often confront choice points in choosing a particular strategy. The location of this choice point—for example, how much a group feels compelled to give in to political pressure versus standing on principle—will be informed by preexisting factors, such as the political environment, its past decisions, and the fortitude of its volunteers. At any point on this spectrum, the organization or campaign will be able to choose. The challenge, just like with an individual, is to choose toward reality versus self-deception in the situation in which it finds itself.

The Real Food Challenge (RFC) organizes college students to shift campus food services to support just and sustainable farms, fisheries, and food companies. One of the major food-service companies they worked with spread the word not to work with RFC because they suspected the organization was a front for a labor union. Losing these stakeholders on all these campuses would have significantly harmed RFC's efforts. While RFC did not have a formal working agreement with the union, they did support each other and felt aligned in their efforts to create ethical workplaces. The choice point was to obscure the relationship with the union so as not to anger the food-services company or to openly acknowledge the relationship and challenge the company.

David Schwartz, a founder of RFC, explains,

> We decided to come out and fight it clearly. The issue is not who we are aligned with. The issue is that this company is shutting the door in students' faces. We fought the issue on the grounds of student empowerment, and they rescinded the memo. This was a moment when we could have dropped the ties with this company. We had lots of fear—what might happen if we kicked the hornets' nest and angered this food-service organization? Instead, we stood up and fought and sent hundreds of e-mails and calls to their headquarters. One of their competitors reached out to us. It became clear after this that they wanted to have a positive relationship with us.

Fear is often a factor on the self-deception side of a choice point. With the organization's future at stake, it seemed like it could make sense to be careful and avoid alienating the food giant. Instead RFC looked to its core mission of student empowerment and, at the same time, realized their students indeed had significant power in this situation. Schwartz explains,

Fear made us believe that they had all the power—to shut down collaboration, to shut out student participation, to not follow through on commitments, and to make us look bad. But I think when we dug deep, we also were able to recognize our own power—not symbolic, but actual—[in] that this attack actually looked really bad for *them*, and our student base, when mobilized, was totally capable of challenging and changing this company.[8]

By reminding themselves of their core principles and accurately assessing their power, RFC was able to choose a strategy that reflected reality versus fear. Projecting this reality by choosing to articulate its core mission and power won the attention of other food-service companies, which ultimately pushed the adversary back toward RFC. Like an individual who becomes more personally powerful by choosing toward reality, organizations can also win allies and supporters by choosing consistently to express their core values and significance instead of hiding behind decisions that seem safe.

---

PRACTICE: *Organizational Growth through Choice*

This practice requires two or three people from your organization or group who have a big enough perspective on the organization and the choice in question. Decide on a choice to consider and answer the same three questions as above, although this time the subject is your organization:

1. What choice is the organization struggling to make?

   For example, should we join a community-wide vigil that will get us political points with the mainstream organizations in town but will anger some of our membership, or should we decline the invitation to join and produce our own statement that is more true to who we are but will anger the main-stream community and make it more difficult to work with them in the future?

2. What factors or values pull your organization to each side of the choice?

   For example, past experiences taking stands against the mainstream groups can habituate members to being on the outside. This makes it harder to make a decision to join the mainstream, even when it might make sense. The organization may have a need to strengthen its membership, and taking a bold stand based on core values could energize the base even if this makes it harder to work with the mainstream.

3. Which side seems closer to reality and which side seems closer to self-deception?

   You will be thinking about this as an organization. Which choice is closer to reality for who we are and how we want to grow?

---

Societies also have choice points that help them grow toward greater awareness and sensitivity to the dignity of all their members and toward the other. On a societal level, the change makers' role is often to shake fellow citizens out of a sleepiness and insensitivity to suffering that for the most part is hidden from view or willfully ignored. Rabbi Shmuly Yanklowitz, founder of Uri L'Tzedek (an Orthodox social-justice organization), explains, "There is something mystical about enabling others to begin to see and hear invisible and unheard people. I want them to notice that their neighbor or their domestic worker or even someone who they see as their enemy is created in the divine image, which they didn't see before."⁹ By bringing the reality of the suffering of a particular group into awareness, the change maker creates a choice point where one did not exist before.

The type of nonviolent direct action used during the civil-rights movement in the United States during the 1950s and 1960s is a clear example of this type of activism. Reverend Martin Luther King Jr. explains that the goal of nonviolent direct action is to

> create such a crisis and foster such a tension that a community which has constantly refused to negotiate is forced to confront the issue. It seeks to dramatize the issue that it can no longer be ignored . . . There is a type of constructive, nonviolent tension which is necessary for growth. Just as Socrates felt that it was necessary to create a tension in the mind so that individuals could rise from the bondage of myths and half-truths to the unfettered realm of creative analysis and objective appraisal, we must see the need for nonviolent gadflies to create the kind of tension in society that will help men rise from the dark depths of prejudice and racism to the majestic heights of understanding and brotherhood.¹⁰

King's reference to Socrates and half-truths recalls Rabbi Dessler's description of the choice point as a battle between truth and falsehood. Direct action, such as protests and boycotts, forces a community to face where they have been ignoring the truth of the reality of many fellow citizens. Once they see this truth, they have a choice they did not see before. These choice points have the potential to move a society toward more understanding.

Meir Lakein (whose organizing work dealing with teen suicides was mentioned above) argues that creative tension is an essential part of challenging the status quo. Communities choose to preserve a status quo in which some of their members suffer because it feels familiar and safe and people with power somehow benefit from the status quo. Change makers create such tension that the reality of suffering approaches the benefits of maintaining the status quo in the minds of those with power. This tension also makes the status quo feel less comfortable. Lakein explains that this approach is based on

a belief that in public life things are set in a certain way that privileges the status quo and without tension there will not be any leverage to change things. In the United States things are so set that without tension we cannot move people . . . [The tension] forces them to confront us face-to-face and come up with a deal.[11]

These deals, like universal health care in Massachusetts or longer hours for afterschool programs in the inner city, represent a movement of these communities toward greater awareness of the reality of life of those on the margins. The choice point of these communities is now at a more refined and aware level, but the pull to less sensitivity is always there, and new choices need to be made constantly. Change makers keep the realities of people hidden on margins in full sight, to give their communities the best shot possible at choosing toward maximum dignity for the greatest number of citizens.

PRACTICE: *Changing Society One Choice at a Time*

This exercise is best done with two or three other people working on a campaign to move society on a particular issue. Answer the following three questions:

1. What choice point do you want to bring into awareness in your community or society?

For example, your group cares about animal welfare and wants to raise awareness about factory farming. It will be unrealistic to ask the community to stop eating meat altogether. There is some awareness about the benefits of organic vegetables from years of word-of-mouth advertising about community-supported agriculture (CSAs) and local health-food stores. A live choice for your community could be to introduce sustainably farmed meat into their diets at least once each week.

2. What factors or values pull the community to each side of the choice?

For example, lack of awareness about the health, environmental, and animal-welfare aspects of factory farming and habituation to eating inexpensive factory-farmed meat several times each week pull toward ignoring the reality of this issue. Health and religious commitments to animal welfare pull toward choosing to reduce consumption and introduce grass-fed, free-range meat.

3. What tension could you create to raise awareness of the, until now, hidden reality?

---

## SUMMARY

Oppressive conditions and the internal messages of our yetzer conspire to confuse us about our ability to choose. In reaction to an attack by a political opponent, you may feel like you have no choice but to respond. The wisdom of the choice point is that we always have choice about something in a situation. This ability to choose is our endowment as human beings, and it can never be taken away. As individuals, organizations, or campaigns, finding the choice points is the first step in growth. Social oppressions, like racism and sexism, are held in place because people do not believe they have any choice.

Our job as change makers is to demonstrate that choosing toward liberation and reality is always a possibility. Finding good points and increasing awareness through choice reveals the hidden light and connections obscured by oppression. These practices give direction to the motivation and passionate drives discussed in the earlier chapters. The next part of the book, "Walking the Path," offers a practical framework for translating these inner forces into a potent daily practice.

# PART THREE

# Walking the Path

The spiritual resources for working toward sustainable social change emerge from deep within our inner lives. Dig down into your motivations for making change, and you will likely come across a desire to bring some type of connection, goodness, and dignity to the world. Connection, goodness, and dignity are revelations of the hidden light that unites all creation and becomes more visible as we make positive social change. We mobilize this desire by skillfully manipulating our yetzer, the energy source that turns desire into action. Seeking good points in ourselves and others keeps our focus on revealing light and not getting entangled in our own or others' feelings of victimhood and despair. Choice points are those markers in time that hint to us that there is concealed light to be revealed. Attentiveness to these choice points in our personal lives and activism can guide us to where to focus our efforts. Taken together, desire, the yetzer, good points, and choice points provide the spiritual orientation and trail markers for heading on a path of making lasting social change while nurturing our own growth. These inner forces and points for action play out in our daily behavior through our middot, or soul traits.

Many great spiritual systems, especially Mussar, employ the use of middot (singular, *middah*) as a way of organizing spiritual growth.[1] Middot are often translated as "character traits" or "soul traits." They are the qualities of spirit that make up our personalities. From a mystical perspective, they are the interface between our higher soul and how we behave in the world. A middah is literally a "measure" or "quantity" of something. According to Maimonides, our personalities are made up of how much (or the "measure of") anger, patience, trust, or humility we have.[2] In more contemporary language, a middah is measured by how we respond to stimuli. If a colleague screwing up for the third time doesn't rattle us, our middah of patience may be strong.

The middot function along a continuum or axis. For example, at one end of the order/chaos axis is rigid, almost compulsive attention to organization, while at the other is chaotic disorganization. Neither of the extremes is good. Maimonides, among others, instructs us to live at the golden mean—the midpoint on the axis between rigidity and chaos.[3] This midpoint would be effective, flexible organization. Rabbi Salanter taught that we need to develop each middah and its opposite so that we can flexibly call on whatever middah is needed in any moment.[4] A moment may in fact call for rigid order and another for chaos. While we should strive to live most of our life at the golden mean, it is important to be flexible and develop all our soul traits.

One of my favorite metaphors to explain middot comes from the Mussar teacher and organizational leadership consultant Rabbi David Lapin.[5] Rabbi Lapin explains that an airplane has instruments and controls. If you want to see how high you are or how fast you are going, you check the instruments. As humans we also have instruments. Our instruments that give us feedback about how we are doing are our emotional and physical states, the quality of our relationships with others, and the quality of our spiritual lives. If our relationship with our parents is going badly or we are fighting with our spouse or children, this is information for us that something needs to change. If a pilot sees that he or she is flying too low, he or she will not bang on the altimeter to get the plane to go up. Neither does it makes sense for us to fix a relationship by banging on the other person. Just as the pilot needs to use the controls to change altitude, the first thing we need to do to fix our relationships is examine how we may be acting out of integrity with our values.

Our middot are the controls we can use to live in integrity. Only after taking responsibility for own our middot would we address the other's behavior.

If desire and the yetzer are orienting forces within us and the choice point and good point are signposts along the way, the middot are a complex of inner systems that are organized to respond to the world around us in a particular way. Ultimately it is through the middot that we present ourselves to the world on a daily basis. As change makers, how we manage our middot can make all the difference in our relationships and the success of our campaigns. The starting place is in us. This is the work of *tikkun middot*—the transformation of the middot. Of course, the external world and the systems we live within have a significant impact on these middot.

In the choice-point chapter (chapter 4), we saw how the influences from our families and the larger society are the conditions that set up the quality of our inner lives. This is one reason it is so important to change external conditions to support the best possible functioning of our inner lives. At the same time, we can do the spiritual work of understanding how the middot function in our own lives and what we can do to change them. The next four chapters explore key middot in the life of a change maker. We will describe the middah according to Jewish sources, examine how the middah functions in real life, and offer exercises you can do to manage and develop your own middot in the context of making sustainable social change.

## 5

# PRACTICE

I got my first taste of the effectiveness of Mussar practice after I spread negative rumors about a leader I deeply respected. This communal leader ran a business that had just failed. I had inside information that financial mismanagement had something to do with the failure. Several men at my synagogue were informally discussing the business one day after prayer services. These were men I didn't know well, as I was new in the community, and I wanted to make an impression. They were discussing the political issues and I chimed in, implying that it was the leader's mismanagement that led to the problems. Immediately I felt terrible. I didn't have first-hand knowledge of what happened, but I did have a juicy piece of gossip that could get me social capital. In exchange for that capital, I damaged this man's good reputation.

Gossip, or *lashon hara*/wrongful speech, is nearly impossible to repair. I could tell each of these men that I actually didn't know what I was talking about and could apologize to the communal leader, but the faint impression of this information would still remain. For sure, I needed to talk to each of these men and maybe even apologize, but there was another element here that also disturbed me. Why did I make the choice to gossip? Apparently my desire for social capital was stronger than my commitment to speak with integrity. I needed to do something about that. This was early in my Mussar practice and I turned to a thirteenth-century book called

*Gates of Repentance* by Rabbi Yonah of Gerondi. The author compiled verses from the Hebrew Bible and rabbinic literature related to hundreds of commandments and their violations as a guide toward right behavior. I looked up lashon hara/wrongful speech and found a verse from Proverbs (18:21): "Death and life are in the power of the tongue." I took on a classic Mussar practice of repeating a verse for a set period of time, in this case three weeks. I found a private place in my home and repeated the verse, sometimes singing it, for a few minutes each day. I let each word wash over my awareness, noticing the feelings and thoughts that arose. Sometimes the practice brought me to tears because of the deep feelings of respect I had for this leader; other times I felt a strong determination to grow and change as a person. Anger, regret, and hope were all part of the process. After three weeks of practice I could tell that I had strengthened my commitment to right speech, but the only way to really determine the change would be in the arena of my daily life. Many years later, I still notice how much easier it is for me not to share juicy gossip, despite the tempting short-term gain.

A commitment to practice is what enabled me to change. Mussar is a practice-based discipline. While Mussar and Hasidic wisdom offers us brilliant gems about the human condition, much of these insights we intuitively know already. Three hundred years ago, Rabbi Moshe Chaim Luzzatto, in his Mussar classic, *The Path of the Just,* wrote, "I have written this work not to teach [people] what they do not know, but to remind them of what they already know."[1] The challenge is remembering and integrating this knowledge into our behavior. This is why practice is so essential.

The next four chapters, comprising part three, include a wide variety of practices, all drawn from the Mussar and Hasidic traditions. They are all oriented toward breaking down the barrier between the mind and the heart and, in the words of the Mussar master Rabbi Eliyahu Lopian, "making the heart feel what the intellect understands."[2] The structure for the practices is adapted from the work of Alan Morinis and Shirah Bell of the Mussar Institute. These practices can be done with a group, with a partner, or individually. In the Mussar tradition, the group's main function is to support the growth of the individual. The group can be incredibly helpful for providing inspiration, accountability, and companionship. A partner can provide perspective and point out blind spots. However, the group and a partner are not substitutes for personal practice. As in any system of growth, success depends on your personal dedication and commitment to actually doing the practices. The following are brief descriptions of each practice. You will find other resources and a sample group facilitation guide in Appendix A.

## A LEARNING MINDSET

A learning mindset is the first step in Mussar practice. Rabbi Wolbe calls this Hitlamdut, the reflexive Hebrew term for being a learner.[3] He warns that Mussar, as well as any type of self-improvement, can lead one to become arrogant about one's own efforts and judgmental of others who are not working on themselves. I would add from experience that we can also become self-critical as we look at our own traits. The key is to consider everything practice. We are not becoming more patient, we are practicing patience. We are not becoming more trusting, we are practicing trust. A learning mindset removes pressure for the outcome to look any particular way. This subtle mental shift opens emotional space for vulnerability and real learning. It also helps bring humility to our practice. As you try out each trait, keep in mind that you are only practicing humility, patience, dignity, and trust.[4]

## TORAH LEARNING

One of the things that separates Mussar practice from secular approaches to growth is its grounding in traditional Jewish ideas about the soul traits. In thinking about how we want to behave, we draw on this wisdom regarding human behavior, relationships, and spirituality. The first step is understanding a Jewish perspective on a particular trait. These perspectives often become aspirations and directions for our growth. We do not need to necessarily agree with everything we read in Jewish literature about the middot, but these ideas are the starting point for our inquiry.

## FOCUS PHRASE

The focus phrase is one or two sentences that direct the mind of the practitioner toward awareness of the trait. For example, a focus phrase for working on *lashon tov*/thoughtful speech could be, "Death and life are in the power of the tongue."[5] Focus phrases are repeated for a minute or two every morning that one is working on a particular middah. Write the focus phrase on an index card and put it somewhere you will see it at least once each day—like taped to your car dashboard or on your computer. Focus phrases from traditional sources have a particular power, but the phrases can come from any source. Some of the best focus phrases are made up by the practitioner.

## KABBALAH

A *kabbalah* (plural, *kabbalot*) is a small act you take on to facilitate growth in a particular soul trait. For example, if you are working on generosity, a classic kabbalah is to give a small amount of money as many times as possible during the day to build the generosity muscle. A kabbalah needs to be small, measurable, and easily achievable.

It has two purposes—to create a positive habit through regular repetition, and to bring unconscious resistance regarding a certain middah into conscious awareness. The word *kabbalah* comes from the Hebrew root for "accept/receive"; one "accepts" a kabbalah upon oneself.

## CHESHBON HANEFESH/SOUL ACCOUNTING

*Cheshbon hanefesh* literally means "soul accounting." It is a core Mussar practice dating back thousands of years. The practice is called "soul accounting" because we closely track the growth of our soul just as an accountant tracks financial details. Here are two different ways of making a soul accounting:

## Journaling

Rabbi Menachem Mendel Leffin, in his book *Cheshbon Hanefesh* (1810), proposes keeping a record of one's success and failures with a particular middah in a chart form. Each success or failure gets a check mark in the chart and after a period of time one can see a record of practice. Alan Morinis, in his *Climbing Jacob's Ladder* (2002), proposes writing a narrative journal for each day of practice with a middah. I personally find Morinis's type of journaling more effective and rewarding. As described in chapter 2, the first stage of Mussar practice is building awareness and greater sensitivity to our inner worlds and to the world around us. Regular journaling is a time-tested method for building this sensitivity. The yetzer harah makes us forget those small, but significant moments of growth that happen all the time.

The value in journaling is that you can return months later and review your experience with the soul traits. This is particularly valuable before the Jewish High Holidays, a time to review the year as part of Teshuva/Return. Personally, I have found my journal to be one of the most powerful mirrors I have on my life. That said, some people find journaling more difficult and so it is useful to have alternative modes of soul accounting.

## Rabbi Nachman of Breslov's Hitbodedut

As described in chapter 1, *hitbodedut* literally means "solitude." It can also refer to meditation. The Hasidic master Rabbi Nachman's hitbodedut is a particular practice of speaking out one's thoughts to God in a spontaneous way in one's native language. Rabbi Nachman advised his followers to practice it daily as a form of soul accounting. Hitbodedut can be done for any amount of time. It is important to find a place and time during which you have privacy and will not be interrupted. Rabbi Nachman extolled the virtues of doing hitbodedut in nature, but any private place works. Hitbodedut is a powerful practice for developing one's relationship with God. It can also be an alternative soul accounting practice for those who find journaling very difficult.

## SPIRITUAL CHECK-IN

Also known as a *sichat chaverim*, this Breslov Hasidic practice is a discussion between friends in which each person talks about her spiritual life and practice. The purpose of these conversations is to inspire and provide perspective for each other. It is important that partners split time evenly in these meetings, with one person at a time being the focus of the conversation. See Appendix B for guidelines.

## VISUALIZATION

Visualization is a classic Mussar technique for reaching beyond our conscious mind to make an impression in our subconscious awareness (*koach hatzi'ur, hitbonenut*). We create a strong visual image in our mind of the trait and stay focused on this image until we feel emotional arousal. It is through emotion that the thought or behavior gets imprinted on our soul. A classic visualization is of the last moments of the Yom Kippur service as the day gets dark and the fast is almost over. This is a time of great yearning which can be recalled and imprinted on us through visualization. You can choose any moments of deep meaning as an inspiration for visualization. Of course, our contemporary society uses visualization, imagery, and emotional arousal for commercial purposes. We can use these same techniques for spiritual growth.

## CONTEMPLATION

While visualization focuses on concrete imagery, contemplation engages our minds in abstract thought. We focus all of our attention on one idea until that idea becomes seared into our minds. Contemplation can help us understand the different aspects of an idea much better than more casual thought. While emotional arousal can happen during contemplation, the goal is to gain a deeper and more complex understanding of the idea.

## GUIDED MEDITATION

This can be a useful tool for exploring your relationship with a middah in a group setting. The meditation opens the mind and heart to how the middah is at work in your life. It can have elements of visualization and contemplation but is usually not as intense. Guided meditation helps the mind explore an idea or middah and make it more real. Guided meditations are good for group practice.

## SUMMARY

The growth and change described in this book are predicated on practice. Without practice, these interesting ideas will provide little more than fodder for discussion. I encourage you to start small. Any of the above practices will help your growth and you do not need to do all of them to be effective. Start with one practice and then slowly build more into your routine. While it is possible to do these practices on your own, you will be more effective if you do them with a partner and, even better, with a group. I know from experience that I journal, say focus phrases, and do my kabbalot more regularly when I know I have a group or partner to report to in the next week. We humans are social creatures and thrive in relationship. Just as no significant social change happens without relationships, so our practice partners can be essential to strengthening our resolve to make personal change.

# 6

# RESPONDING TO THE CALL

## Anavah/*Humility*

In 1909, Clara Lemlich changed labor history in the United States with her bold call for a general garment-workers' strike. Known as the "Uprising of the 20,000," Lemlich roused her coworkers, who were mostly young, Jewish, and female, by pushing her way to the stage at a rally at New York's Cooper Union and demanding that women stand up for better and safer work conditions. The male leaders of the union were shocked. So was the rest of the country when thousands of women in cities across the United States walked out on their factory jobs.

While this is the most well-known event in Lemlich's biography, her commitment to justice for working people never waned. Known as one of the *farbrente Yidishe meydlech* (fiery Jewish girls), Lemlich helped establish the International Ladies' Garment Workers' Union, was instrumental in the 1917 kosher meat boycott in New York City, and worked for women's suffrage during and after World War I. She organized housewives in the 1920s and 1930s by pioneering the use of consumer boycotts. Investigated by Senator Joseph McCarthy and the House Un-American Activities Committee in the 1950s, Lemlich never stopped organizing. As a resident in a nursing home in California, in her later years, she organized the orderlies to fight for better work conditions.

Why begin a chapter on humility with Clara Lemlich? Lemlich is an iconic and inspirational firebrand of an organizer. She clearly had courage, boldness, and righteous indignation, but what does this have to do with humility? The Hebrew word for "humility" is *anavah*, and its root is *ayin.nun.heh*. This root means "humility" and "lowliness," but these letters are also the same root for "speaking" and "responding." When I respond to the demands of the moment in service and without arrogance or an inflated sense of my own importance, I act with humility. Anavah/humility involves finding the proper relationship between the self and the world around you. One who is appropriately humble neither gets lost in the whole nor sees oneself as the whole. "Who am I?" "What am I being called to do?" "What part of my own concerns do I need to put aside?" These are anavah questions.

Like all soul traits, or middot, anavah/humility exists along a continuum or axis. On the one side is arrogance, and on the other is low self-esteem. Appropriate humility means knowing how much of myself to insert into any particular situation depending on the need of the moment. It is a very dynamic soul trait. To paraphrase the words of Alan Morinis, anavah is knowing the appropriate space to take up in any situation. We start with anavah/humility because it is the middah that most directly speaks to how we understand ourselves in relation to the world around us.

Clara Lemlich boldly stepped up when kosher butchers exploited their working-class clientele or factory owners put lives in danger with unsafe work conditions. Often frustrated by middle-class reformers, she strategically backed away from certain battles even though her inclination was to always fight. When she became a parent, she left paid work and the sometimes dangerous work of organizing in the garment industry and began organizing working-class housewives to fight for lower prices and better education and housing. Lemlich was never bound by one particular arena or strategy for her social-justice efforts. Humility is knowing what is needed from you in the moment and responding accordingly, whether this means boldly stepping up or refraining from responding even when this means setting aside your personal inclinations and prior plans.

## HINEINI/HERE I AM

Think of a time you were with a group of people and someone, maybe a friend of yours, made a racist or sexist comment. A few people may have laughed out loud while the rest of you chuckled uncomfortably or squirmed in your seats. For a moment there was an awkward silence until someone, to everyone's relief, brought up a different subject. What did you feel in that moment after the offensive comment? Angry, shocked, wishing you could disappear, all of the above? Did you have a sense that you should say something? How often do you act on this sense?

This is a hineini moment. *Hineini* is an ancient Hebrew phrase that means "here I am" and has a tone of resolve and service. Our biblical ancestors responded to God's call to service by saying "Hineini." Most of us (at least, I) don't have the privilege of hearing God's call directly. Our task is more often to respond to silence. In moments like the one above, can you hear the still, small inner voice call to you from out of the silence, saying, "This is your time to act" or "This is your time to hold back and try something different"? Some of us jump in reactively to any oppressive comments, while others are numb to any sense of agency in these moments.

Hineini is a thoughtful, decisive response to the call of the moment, often heard from within silence. In the example above, Hineini could mean saying publicly that you found the comment offensive or privately discussing the issue with the speaker or making a light comment expressing disapproval. It all depends on the moment and what you have to bring to it. According to an ancient biblical commentary, when our ancestors responded "Hineini," they were acting with anavah.[1] The actions of two powerful women, one contemporary and the other biblical, will help explain the relationship between hineini and humility.

Gail, the lawyer and organizer described in chapter 4, modeled saying "Hineini" when she bounded up the aisle and took the microphone at the social-services conference. Her hineini moment came when it looked like our action was about to fall apart. The women assigned to stand up and state their demands to the director of social services got scared and stayed seated. As the lead organizer, Gail probably heard the call from the silence more clearly than anyone else in the room. She was able to put aside any fear, anger, doubt, and embarrassment and step forward to challenge the humiliating fraud policy. Hineini means making these kinds of sacrifices and facing this discomfort for the sake of service.

## REFLECTION

When is a time you felt called to advocate for something you cared about deeply?

Were you able to respond to the call?

What factors enabled you to respond or inhibited you from responding?

Turn back the clock to another oppressive situation a little over three thousand years ago. An ancient Jewish story tells us about the time that, in response to the pharaoh's decree that all Jewish baby boys be killed, the leaders of the Israelite community debated the merits of having any children.[2] In a move to defy their Egyptian taskmasters, Amram, the recognized leader, decided he would not have any more children as long as the hated decree was in place. His peers soon followed, divorced their wives, and the Jewish community stopped producing children. Amram's young daughter Miriam, in a remarkable act of self-confidence, argued that this type of righteous defiance would only hurt the community more. "Pharaoh just wants to get rid of the boys. You are getting rid of the boys and girls!"[3] Her impassioned plea that the community keep valuing life, even at the risk of death, swayed the elders. Couples reunited and childbearing resumed. Miriam's younger brother Moses was one of the children born in the years after her bold stand.

What can we learn from these remarkable women about how hineini (saying, "Here I am") is a form of anavah? In both cases these women acutely felt a void. For Gail, the assigned speakers could not fulfill their roles, leaving a vacuum. For Miriam, the leaders were consumed with anger, fear, and defiance, blinding them to the long-term consequences of their policy. They both had to overcome societal messages that they were insignificant—Gail as a black lesbian and Miriam as a female and young person. They both had a clear sense of what was needed to fill the void and that they had something to offer. They also both felt enough of a call to go outside of their comfort zone and actually make the step forward into the void. Anavah involves having an accurate sense of one's self and an accurate sense of what the other or the community needs in the moment. Hineini is what anavah sounds like in these moments.

## THE WISDOM TO NOT RESPOND

Expressing humility can also mean not responding. The only time the word *anavah* appears in the Torah is during a family dispute between Aaron, Miriam, and Moses. The older siblings, Miriam and Aaron, seem jealous of their younger brother's access to God. Like happens in most family disputes, once they let out their frustration, they also bring in other issues. They criticize Moses's relationship with his wife and then complain that they should be just as close with God as their younger brother. We seem to be witnessing a petty family dispute among the leaders of the Jewish people. Why would the Torah want to expose this type of behavior among its leaders? A striking feature of the Hebrew Bible is the honesty with which it portrays its protagonists. The leaders are real people, warts and all. They deceive, lack faith, commit adultery, and express jealousy, as well as act with moral greatness, courage, and spiritual imagination.

In this scene the Torah demonstrates the greatness of Moses's character. As we know from our own experience, nothing boils the blood more than an insensitive remark or act from a parent or sibling. There are so many years of baggage behind these types of comments. For the past year and a half Moses led the people to freedom while his older sister and brother played supporting roles. Ever since he reluctantly takes the helm of leadership, Moses is the focus of the people's criticism and suffers numerous verbal attacks. Now he is criticized by the people closest to him, his older brother and sister. How does he respond? Moses is silent.

How should we understand this silence? Was this the cold silence of someone insulted and withdrawing in anger? At this point the Torah tells us that Moses is the most humble person on earth. What is the silence of humility? Can the silence of humility grow from anger? Does it grow from thinking so little of oneself that it is not worth responding? Rashi, an eleventh-century Torah commentator, hints that this is not the case. He writes that humility implies bearing suffering with patience.[4] Moses is able to experience the emotional discomfort of insult without moving into reaction. This lack of reactivity gives him the emotional space to understand the pain of his detractors and see their insults in context. The silence of humility is a stillness born of deep understanding and empathy, even for one's detractors.

A broad perspective is another aspect of this stillness. Rashi also interprets Moses's humility to be something called *sheeflut*. *Sheeflut* is a hard word to translate into English. It literally means "lowliness," as in *hashfala*, a "low-lying geographic area." While lowliness can sometimes imply low self-regard, I think it means something different in this context. Lowliness implies having an appreciation for the grandeur and vastness of the universe. If I think too much of myself, my grandiose self-image can literally block me from seeing others and the world around me. I don't think too much of myself not because of low self-esteem, but in relation to how clearly

I see the vast universe and my place in it. In fact, low self-esteem is a perversion of humility.

Imagine that you are one of seven billion human beings on a planet that is one of billions of planets in the universe. You are a small part of this vast whole. And you are a significant part of it. Looking at it his way, no one individual stands out too much, like a mountain. We are all low, or close to the ground. Lowliness implies having a broad enough perspective to know one's role in relationship to others around you.

Moses understood clearly his relationship with God as leader of the Jewish people. He knew he was playing a role that was assigned to him and that he was not essentially more special than anyone else. Moses's humble silence was a silence of perspective and confidence that enabled him to not respond while maintaining an open heart toward his critics. Indeed, it is Moses who comes to his sister's aid and prays for her healing when she suffers an illness as a result of her criticism. Rather than giving up or responding reactively to the insults, this silence of humility enabled Moses to assert his leadership and bring healing to his community.

The bold action of hineini is only one aspect of humility. Choosing to not respond, giving space, working with those who insult or believe differently from us—this is the other side. As we see from Moses's example, not responding reactively to provocation is a sign of being able to see the big picture. The following example illustrates how important this underappreciated aspect of humility is to wise social-justice action.

Ruth Messinger was the longtime CEO of the American Jewish World Service (AJWS), a major global human rights and development organization. Before heading AJWS, Messinger served as Manhattan borough president and was a candidate for New York City mayor. Messinger is well-known for her left-leaning politics and boldness in asserting progressive values. She was borough president in the 1980s when real-estate mogul Donald Trump wanted to build a massive luxury housing complex on the Upper West Side of Manhattan. As a liberal West Side elected official, Messinger was expected to strongly oppose this development because it would not be affordable housing and because of Trump's historic antipathy to the left. In a move that surprised her traditional allies, Messinger did not oppose the development but negotiated with Trump. In her own words:

> I thought to myself, "Wait a minute—this is a lot of housing!" It had a lot of money behind it, and it was going to pass the city council for approval anyway. So the question was, what do we negotiate for? There were potentially one thousand units of low-income housing in that area we could get in exchange for our approval, which Trump needed.[5]

Rather than make an ideological stand against the Trump development, the real-estate community, and the powers that be in the city, Messinger negotiated and won one thousand new units of low-income housing for the neighborhood that would not have been developed had she simply opposed Trump.

Messinger's understanding of this experience reflects the quieter side of anavah, one that cedes space and doesn't demand that we necessarily boldly stand up against power:

> So there is this issue of "Do I want to go and stand alone, and what does it take to stand alone?" What I learned fairly quickly in politics was that standing alone is easier than trying to convince other people to stand with you. Standing alone is a self-righteous position . . . There is a place for people who stand alone, but what I've learned is that if we are going to advocate for social change, that is not what you are supposed to do. You are supposed to work together.[6]

This is anavah in a political context. Self-righteously standing alone would be taking too much space. To develop significant low-income housing, Messinger realized she needed to not assert her politics in their most pure form, but give space to developers and their political allies and negotiate.

Messinger relates this type of humility to leadership in general. The prophet is classically the person who speaks truth to power, demanding a certain ideological purity. While prophets certainly play an important role, according to Messinger, this is not leadership:

> Most people say that the most important qualities of a leader are charisma and vision. Actually, the single most important quality is followers. People can do a lot of things, but if other people are not listening, you may be lots of things, but you are not a leader. In a graduation speech to Reform rabbis at Hebrew Union College, I told them that I thought I was going to say that the world needs a lot more prophets for justice. Then I realized that the history of the biblical prophets is that they were reviled in their own time; they mostly derided people and did not get anything done, so forget that. The world doesn't need more prophets; it needs leaders.[7]

Messinger certainly understands the need for the prophetic voice. She herself was a prophetic voice on behalf of Sudanese threatened with genocide in Darfur in 2006. However, her long political experience has taught her that self-righteously standing alone is not an effective method of social-change work. The side of humility that gives space to others and withholds self-righteous response is another important key to making change happen.

---

### REFLECTION

When has holding back, not responding, or giving space been a powerful act to move a situation forward in your life?

What difference in the quality of nonresponse do you notice between giving up and strategically holding back or ceding space to achieve change?

---

## HUMILITY TRAPS

No middah is all good or all bad. Our minds play a trick on us by thinking in binary terms. If something is good, it is all good and its opposite is bad. For example, in a dry area like California, one might think that rain is always good. However, if it doesn't come in the right season, or if there is too much, it can cause mudslides and harm agriculture more than it helps. The right amount of rain at the right time is what is needed. Soul traits are similar. As mentioned earlier, soul traits function on a continuum. Healthy humility is somewhere in between low self-esteem and arrogance. In general we want to function in this middle area. Extreme manifestations of a middah, like arrogance or low self-esteem, may be needed in rare circumstances, but for the most part extremes will do more harm than good.

We mentioned earlier that hineini is an expression of humility because the person who says, "Here I am," lets go of ego to be of service. Once we start letting go of ego, we are in a spiritually rich, but potentially psychologically dangerous territory for several reasons. If we are not very grounded in our own sense of self, letting go of self can backfire. Sometimes we take on giving to others because we are trying to fill a sense of emptiness within. Someone with this profile is vulnerable to not knowing when to stop giving.

There is no end to need in this world. If I don't have a strong sense of self and good boundaries, hineini may end up feeling like being on a never-ending assembly line of fulfilling the needs of others. This can lead to a backlash in which we resent the people or the cause we were trying to serve. On the other hand, if you have an overly developed sense of your ability, you may deceive yourself, thinking that you can solve the whole problem.

Did you ever jump enthusiastically into a cause or effort to help people and only later realize that you didn't set yourself up well and drop the project? A woman who does a lot of work with homeless people once asked me if hineini ever has an end. Ever since she first saw the need of the homeless in her city and said "Hineini—I want to help," she has felt like she can't stop.

Like all the soul traits, humility needs to be balanced. An equally important aspect of humility is knowing that you are a finite, limited human being and do not have to and cannot meet every need. The well-known statement of the second-century rabbi Tarfon in Pirkei Avot (2:16) captures this aspect of humility: "It is not up to you to complete the task. At the same time, you are not free to desist from it."

Stosh Cotler, the CEO of Bend the Arc, one of North America's major Jewish social-justice organizations, relates this ancient teaching to humility. She describes proper humility as a sustainability practice:

> If we look from a macro perspective we have a long, long road ahead, and, as the quote says, we are not free to desist. But we can't have the illusion that we are going to finish it. Who are we to think that we are so great that we alone are the revolution.[8]

Overestimating our own importance and ability to make change can quickly lead to burnout. As Cotler reminds us, practicing balanced humility can keep us in the struggle for social change for the long term.

In a related way, an overzealous exclamation of hineini can lead one to misjudge the complexity of social issues and the long-term commitment needed to tackle them. This is especially true for people coming from the business world, who are accustomed to making quick decisions and seeing results, or politicians, who need quick successes. Again, Cotler reminds us of the importance of humility. Bend the Arc supports grassroots community organizing in low-income communities around the country. Anyone trying to help these communities must have humility. She explains, "I don't have the life experience of those in the communities we are working with who have been the most impacted by economic and racial injustice. I am not going to come up with the solutions. It takes really listening to figure out how to work."[9] Whether it is fixing public education, tackling climate change, or reforming the prison and immigration systems, listening well to the people most affected and deriving multifaceted solutions that fit each community will most likely prove a better strategy than creating a top-down, large-scale effort that seeks to make change quickly. The zealousness that comes with saying "Hineini" and wanting to make change should never override the slow, methodical work of listening to people affected by injustice.

## REFLECTION

Think of a time you said yes to a project and could not follow through. Did unexpected external factors impede your ability to follow through, or did you not have the internal resources to complete the effort? Looking back at the hineini moment, is there anything you can identify or change that might have allowed it to get to completion?

Has saying "Hineini" and jumping into a project ever led you to move too fast and not listen well to the people most affected by injustice? What was the result?

Hineini can also lead to physical and emotional violence. Saying "Hineini" to God or to an ideological cause can be one of the most spiritually uplifting acts available to us. I meld my very self with the divine will or with a purpose larger than myself. This type of spiritual or political devotion is safe as long as one keeps in mind a perspective that balances it with interpersonal commitments, such as treating other people with dignity. When one's devotion to fulfilling a spiritual or ideological call blinds one to interpersonal commitments, hineini can result in suicide bombings or less dramatic ways of nullifying the other who stands in the way of fulfilling your service. Saying "Hineini" is most positively impactful when you are firmly grounded in your interpersonal commitments, have a healthy sense of self, and hand over that self in the service of something greater.

---

**REFLECTION**

In what ways has your commitment to justice, success, or any other commitment made you less sensitive to the needs of others?

Have you experienced this insensitivity from others?

---

False humility, or lowliness without perspective, is another of the humility traps. Almost one thousand years ago, Rabbi Bahya ibn Pequda captured the danger of false humility in his introduction to the very first Mussar book in Jewish history, *The Duties of the Heart*. While Rabbi Bahya was a great Torah scholar and rabbinic judge in Spain, his accomplishments did not prevent him from questioning his own significance:

> When I planned to execute my decision to write this book, I saw that one like me is unworthy of writing a book such as

this. I surmised that my ability would not suffice to analyze all the necessary aspects, owing to the difficulty which I perceived and to my wisdom being insufficient and my mind being too weak to grasp all of the issues, and that I am not fluent in the Arabic language in which I wrote it. I feared that I would toil at something that would evidence my inability, and that it would be a presumptuous undertaking, so that I considered changing my mind and abandoning my previous decision.

But when I designed to remove this laborious burden from myself and desist from composing the work, I reconsidered and became suspicious of myself for having chosen to rest . . . and I know that many minds have been lost out of apprehension, and many losses have been caused by fear.[10]

His concern about exposing his "inability" strikes me as so contemporary in its insecurity and desire for approval. Of course Rabbi Bahya overcame his fear and wrote a book that is still read throughout the world.

---

### REFLECTION

In what ways have you noticed low self-esteem or insecurity get in the way of what needs to be done at any particular moment, in the personal and public realms?

---

We need to know our significance. This is the first step in any spiritual growth and in social-change work.[11] Feeling bad about oneself makes one vulnerable to manipulation and despair. Growing spiritually and creating justice often involves fighting for what is right. It is very difficult to sustain this fight if you feel bad about yourself. You will just be too vulnerable to giving up when the inevitable setbacks and attacks come your way. It can be tricky to tease out low self-esteem from healthy humility because they can present the same way. If one doesn't respond to insult, this could be due to having a broad perspective and understanding one's power and significance. Or it could be the result of believing that one doesn't deserve to be treated any better. The latter is not the humility we are trying to cultivate. A healthy, balanced humility involves having a sense of responsibility and knowing others are there doing their part as well. You are part of something bigger that needs you but is not all about you.

## FLEXIBILITY

Acting with appropriate humility requires discernment. One needs to know just what one has to offer and what the situation in reality is calling for, to know how much of oneself to insert at any moment. This takes a fine attunement to an ever-changing reality. Rabbi Ari Hart provides us with a great example of how saying "Hineini" can mean showing up in very different ways depending on what is needed. Rabbi Hart is one of the founders of Uri L'Tzedek, the Orthodox social-justice movement.

In 2011, Uri L'Tzedek joined with Focus on the Food Chain to demand that Flaum Appetizing pay close to $500,000 in unpaid wages to its mostly immigrant workers whom the company fired when they complained about being underpaid. Flaum, located in Brooklyn, was the distributor of Israeli food giant Tenuva's products in the United States as well as a producer of popular brands of hummus. In 2011, Flaum lost a National Labor Relations Board suit filed by the workers in addition to numerous appeals and continuously delayed paying what they owed. That was when organizers approached Uri L'Tzedek for help, and Rabbi Hart got involved.

Early in the campaign, it was important for Hart to be in the streets, demonstrating alongside the workers. A kippah-wearing Jew demonstrating sent an important message to the Latino immigrant workers that Jews were also on their side. Equally important it sent a message to the owner of Flaum and his community that this wasn't simply an issue of anti-Semitic non-Jews attacking Jews. Hart and Uri L'Tzedek volunteers convinced kosher supermarkets to stop carrying Flaum products until the labor issues were resolved. They won rabbis to the cause, organized students on college campuses, and promoted the boycott for over six months.

Hart describes how he needed to step up despite discomfort during this phase of the campaign: "There was a lot of weight—the weight of the injustice to the workers, but also the weight of the anger directed at us from my own community. I knew this would come, and it took a lot of *emunah*/faithfulness in the process to stay involved."[12] The Flaum owner and his supporters in New York's Orthodox community portrayed Hart and Uri L'Tzedek as traitors and partners to unfair attacks on the company.

After months of trying without success to talk with the company's owner, Hart got through to him. The two men spoke for close to an hour. According to Hart,

This call was a breakthrough because he saw that I wanted to listen to him. I wasn't going to just attack him. I spent most of the time on this call listening to how he felt he was right and that we were bad and would pay for it in heaven.[13]

Eventually the pressure of the boycott, bad press, and financial realities led the owner to reach out to Hart to mediate a resolution. This put Hart in a new and unfamiliar role. He was not a direct party to the conflict or a court-appointed mediator. Yet the reality called on him to say "Hineini" to this new role. Hart spent hours on the phone with the workers' representative and the owner, attempting to hammer out a resolution. While protesting and fighting were the dominant modalities Hart needed to employ in his former role, now listening became supremely important. During one conversation Hart found that it was not that

> the owner was not paying because he was just being a jerk. Rather, I found out that he couldn't afford to pay the half-million-dollar settlement all at once. He just didn't have the money. His unscrupulous lawyers advised him to keep them on retainer at something like ten thousand dollars per month to keep dragging out the case. Once I saw that, I proposed to the owner that perhaps the workers would accept a settlement that was paid out over time. He realized that I was seeing him and his situation and agreed.[14]

Hart's ability to listen to the adversary with empathy and not respond defensively was a key to success and a beautiful example of the quieter side of humility.

Moving between roles in a high-pressure situation takes artful maneuvering and keen emotional intelligence, all the more so when one is acting without clear sanction. If the court had appointed Hart a mediator, both parties would have been clear about what to expect from him. In this situation there was no clear sanction. Hart had simply stepped into a role that reality presented to him. According to Hart, "I almost blew it during the negotiation when I proposed something that was perceived by the workers as favorable to Flaum's. They almost walked away."[15] However, the social capital Hart built over the months in the streets protesting enabled the workers to give him and the process another chance.

The parties successfully negotiated a payment schedule, and the boycott was called off. According to Hart,

> The key was always to represent clearly what I was doing at each point. If I am fighting, I am fighting. If I am bringing together and convening, that is what I am doing. Everyone needs to know about these roles. I needed to be clear both

within myself and with the outside world about what role I was playing at any particular moment.[16]

Hart's ability to transition from a protest stance to a mediation and listening stance was a key part of the success and a skillful example of how humility can make us stretch in ways we never thought possible.

Alan Morinis, the founder of the Mussar Institute, frames humility as "limiting oneself to an appropriate space while leaving room for others."[17] He arrives at this definition by examining two Talmudic passages regarding humility. The first is a story of failed rabbinic leadership in which Rabbi Zechariah, one of the leading rabbis of the first century, was faced with a decision between risking having Jerusalem destroyed by the Roman army and making minor exceptions to Jewish law. He chose destruction, out of fear that people might misinterpret the law. The second is a short passage that labels a person as "humble" who makes a set place to sit in the synagogue. Morinis explains, "Sitting in a predictable place, you make room for others to occupy their own spaces, too. Rabbi Zechariah . . . gave up too much of his 'space,' considering that the space a person occupies can be physical, emotional, verbal, or even metaphorical."[18] Rabbi Zechariah was a leader who failed to live up to the bold leadership his people needed at that moment in Jewish history.

Humility is knowing the proper amount of space to take up in any situation and not rigidly holding on to one's predilection to take up a lot or a little space. We all know people who take up lots of space and always seem to have something to say. Others are quiet and need to be encouraged to speak up. There is nothing intrinsically better about either way of being. The question is, can we be flexible enough to go against our inclinations about taking up space when needed?

In social-change work, sometimes I may need to give space to others, and at times I may need to take up more space. When setting up the peer-counseling class in Bethlehem described in chapter 1, I needed to give space to the younger and less experienced Palestinian counselors to lead the course. Humility meant me taking a behind-the-scenes coaching role. When leading a community-organizing initiative in my synagogue, I needed to take space and advocate for getting on the board of directors and speaking in front of the congregation to introduce our campaign. This may not look like humility, but the situation dictated that I needed to take up that space, even if it felt uncomfortable. Similarly, Rabbi Hart needed to switch gears from protesting and advocating a boycott to giving space and listening deeply to Flaum's owner as he moved into a mediator role. Practice with the middot trains us to develop this flexibility.

---

## REFLECTION

Is your inclination to take up space or cede space to others? How do you know?

What does it feel like for you to act against your natural inclination?

In what ways does your commitment to social or institutional change push you up against your natural inclination for taking up or ceding space?

---

## SUMMARY

Seeing reality clearly is a key aspect of being able to call on just the type of humility needed in each situation, because reality will dictate how I need to show up. Rabbi Yisrael Salanter said that we need to develop every soul trait and its opposite because at different times we will need to call on different traits.[19] One of the early Mussar masters uses the metaphor of a wheel and spokes to describe this ability to finely attune oneself to the needs of the moment.[20] The spokes are the different middot or, in our context, the different ways of expressing humility. If one of the spokes protrudes outside the rim of the wheel, the vehicle cannot move effectively. The needs of the moment, symbolized by the front of the wheel contacting the road, dictate exactly which soul trait in what measure is needed to keep the wheel moving well.

In Rabbi Hart's situation above, reality called for listening, and he needed to set aside his protesting. In my situation, reality first called for me to step up and introduce a counseling method to a group of Palestinians, and then it called on me to step back and support indigenous leadership.

When we ignore reality and express a disconnected inclination toward a certain middah or its opposite, we will neither grow nor make an impact on society. It is the muscles developed from the practice of the soul traits combined with the flexibility demanded by an aware engagement with reality that lead to deep and lasting growth and effective living and leading.

---

## PRACTICE: *Anavah/Humility*

### Jewish Wisdom about Humility
*Everyday Holiness*, Alan Morinis, chapter 7
*Mussar for Moderns*, R. Elyakim Krumbein, chapters 4–5 at http://etzion.org.il/vbm/english/mussar.
For Hebrew language sources and additional material, see www.kirva.org.

### Focus Phrases
Choose a phrase to repeat out loud for a minute or two each morning. You can adapt the phrases to your own language. Write the phrase on an index card and put it somewhere you will see it each morning. Some people tape the card to their car dashboard or computer.

*"Hineini"*

*"The world was created for me"* and *"I am dust and ashes"*

*"No more than my space, no less than my place"*[21]

*"And lo, the Lord passed by. There was a great and mighty wind, splitting mountains and shattering rocks by the power of the Lord; but the Lord was not in the wind. After the wind—an earthquake; but the Lord was not in the earthquake. After the earthquake—fire; but the Lord was not in the fire. And after the fire—a still, small voice."*[22]

## Guided Meditation

This is best done with a group or at least a partner. Have one person read the meditation while the others follow the instructions read by the leader.

Find a comfortable place to sit or lie down.

Feel the weight of your body against the chair or ground.

Rest your hands on your lap or at your sides.

Gently let your eyelids close.

Take three deep breaths, inhaling through your nose and exhaling through your mouth.

Think of a time you really felt called to give of yourself.

This can be from childhood, or at work, community activities or in your family, political or spiritual life.

Remember the moment of the call.

Where were you?

If there was no specific moment but the call developed over time, what do you remember from that period of life?

What were the words of the call? If there were no words, what did it sound like?

How did it feel in your body?

In what ways did you or did you not say, "Hineini/Here I am," in response to the call?

What did you need to put aside in your life or in your personality to respond to the call?

How did your life change as a result of your response?

Allow time for quiet journaling or reflection about what came up during the meditation.

## Visualization

This exercise can be done individually or with a group. If done in a group, choose one person to read the description once through.

Call up an image of a wheel with spokes.

This can be a bicycle wheel or a wooden wagon wheel or whatever wheel you can picture.

The important thing is that it has visible spokes that attach to the center and reach the outer edge of the wheel.

Imagine the wheel traveling along a dirt path.

Zoom in on how the rubber or wood travels over the dirt path, bouncing slightly and crushing granules of dirt underneath.

Put the image in slow motion and pay attention to the exact point that the front edge of the wheel comes around and makes contact with the ground.

The granular nature of the dirt path is the contour of reality as it contacts your life, represented by the wheel.

Imagine the wheel turning, some spokes not reaching the rim and others extending beyond the rim and some just reaching the rim.

As each point of the wheel comes in contact with the dirt path, the spoke at that point extends to reach the rim or retracts to the edge of the rim, so the wheel continues to turn.

The spokes are your traits, some in small measure, others large, and each grows or limits depending on the needs of reality.

What would it mean for you to have this level of flexibility with your soul traits and with taking and giving space as needed? What would you need to decide, change, or give up?

## Contemplation

This exercise can be done individually or with a group. If done in a group, choose one person to read the description once through.

Think of your strongest, most defining trait.

This could be kindness, discipline, courage, loyalty, faith, patience, or any one of the many soul traits.

Think about how you use this trait to help a social-change effort or some community initiative.

Think about the need to use the opposite trait in the same social-change or community effort.

How much would you need to contract yourself to give up your strong trait in this moment?

## Kabbalot

Choose one. The kabbalot are designed to do individually. If you are using this book with a group, give people a few minutes to choose a kabbalah and close the session with people sharing which kabbalah they are going to practice until the next meeting.

Choose one time each day to notice how much space you are taking. This can be at a meeting, at home, with friends, and so on. Are you taking too much space, too little space, or just the right amount? Try out different settings for the kabbalah to get a sense of how your anavah/humility is influenced by different circumstances.

Choose a meeting or time of day that you will take up more or less space than is comfortable to you. This could mean that you will be the first to speak in a meeting or that you will not speak until everyone else has a turn. Your kabbalah could be being sillier and louder than usual with a group of people each day.

Commit to saying "Hineini" and stepping up at least once each day.

## Soul Accounting/Cheshbon Hanefesh

Set aside five to ten minutes at some point in the day to either journal or do the hitbodedut practice answering these questions.

What is one thing you noticed about anavah/humility today? What is this teaching you?

What is a choice point you experienced today that challenged your sense of how much space to take or your ability to say "Hineini"?

What is a good point about yourself or someone else regarding anavah/humility?

How is your level of anavah/humility aligned with what you think God or the universe is asking of you right now?

How is your level of anavah/humility expressing your deep ratzon/desire?

How does the space you, or others, take influence the effectiveness of your change efforts?

## Spiritual Check-in

1. Trade turns listening to each other for two minutes talking about a good point from the day and anything else the speaker wants to get off his or her chest.

2. Journal quietly for five minutes about the soul accounting questions.

3. For ten minutes, take turns listening to each other talk about the experience with the focus phrase, kabbalot, and soul accounting.

4. Then discuss any insights or challenges with anavah/humility that came up during the week.

5. End with a commitment for practice for the next week.

# 7

## CREATIVE DISCOMFORT

## Savlanut / *Patience*

The #BlackLivesMatter movement got its start in the summer of 2013 after George Zimmerman, a neighborhood-watch activist, was acquitted of murdering unarmed teen Trayvon Martin. For Alicia Garza, Patrisse Cullors, and Opal Tometi, and many other African Americans, this acquittal galvanized into action years of pent-up frustration and rage about police brutality toward blacks. The three women created the hashtag and, gaining visibility after additional high-profile black deaths at the hands of police in 2014 in Ferguson, Missouri, and in New York City, mobilized a nationwide movement against police brutality toward African Americans. The movement energized a nationwide debate about the treatment of blacks not just by police, but in the prison and education systems as well.

As the #BlackLivesMatter movement gained momentum, tension arose between the radical founders and younger activists and the more established activists, clergy, and politicians who had been working on these issues for decades. The tensions centered on goals and tactics. While the established activists tended toward reform and working within the system, the younger and more radical folks wanted systemic economic and political change and shunned connections with career politicians and nonprofits. They also expressed resentment at the movement's rage being watered down by the reformists and its power co-opted by establishment organizations, like Al Sharpton's National Action Network. While the established groups organized major marches on Washington to influence Congress, the smaller, radical groups worked to empower people in the neighborhoods by reclaiming streets and creating "cop-free zones."

Core to these conflicts was how to mobilize the anger produced by mistreatment and injustice. The reformers tended to channel the anger into policy changes while the radical groups gave expression to the anger by giving people more immediate and visceral experiences of power, such as reclaiming streets or videotaping police on duty. While reformers risked damping the rage that originally motivated action, the radicals flirted with this rage exploding into hate and physical violence. Indeed, the movement was accused of promoting violence against police. Photographs circulated on the Internet of protesters wearing T-shirts lauding convicted cop killers. How #BlackLivesMatter managed this rage would indeed determine its effectiveness as a social movement.

We know from a long history of social movements—for example, the black civil-rights movement in the mid-1960s and the radical wing of the environmental movement in the 1970s and 1980s—that when righteous indignation morphs into violence and hate, these movements lose both the moral high ground and a significant measure of public support.[1] It is a very fine balancing act maintaining the anger needed to act for change without that anger exploding into verbal or physical violence or dissipating into complacency and comfort. This is called "cold anger." In a document called "The Tent of the Presence," black pastors in the Industrial Areas Foundation[2] describe such anger:

> Anger and grief are rooted in our most passionate memories and dreams—a father whose spirit has been broken by demeaning work or no work; a brother or sister lost to violence or alcohol or drugs; a church burned down by an arsonist; a college career sabotaged by a substandard high school; a neighborhood of shops and families and affections and

relationships ripped apart because banks wouldn't lend to it, because insurance companies wouldn't insure it, because city officials wouldn't service it, because youth wouldn't respect us, because teachers wouldn't teach in it. Anger sits precariously between two dangerous extremes. One extreme is hatred, the breeding ground of violence. The other extreme is passivity and apathy, the breeding ground of despair and living death. Anger that is focused and deep and rooted in grief is a key element in the organizing of black churches.[3]

Anger that is rooted in grief, grief for lost family members, lives stunted by racism, opportunities denied: the Jewish experience has its own reasons for grief—lives lost to suicide bombers on Israeli city streets, children traumatized by nights in bomb shelters in Sderot and Kiryat Shmoneh, anti-Semitic attacks at Jewish community centers around the world, and of, course, the Holocaust, which is fewer than seventy years in the past. How do we cultivate anger to grow from grief without exploding into rage? Maimonides's words address this same concern:

One should not be of an angry disposition and be easily angered, nor should one be like a dead person who does not feel, but one should be in the middle—one should not get angry except over a big matter about which it is fitting to get angry, so that the person will not act similarly again.[4]

The middle path is anger born of significant grief with the purpose of setting things right. It is not just about satisfying the need for emotional release, but is generative and purposeful. How do we cultivate such cold anger?

This is the work of *savlanut*, often known as "patience," but more accurately translated as "bearing." To root our anger in grief, we need to be able to bear this grief, to sit with it and not push it away too quickly. The root of explosive anger is the inability to bear emotional discomfort. Grief is extremely uncomfortable. It is much more emotionally satisfying in the short term to let the anger explode out rather than sit with feeling so bad. Have you ever exploded in anger at a coworker, supervisor, parent, or lover? You know that sweet, satisfying feeling at having "gotten it all off your chest."

I lived in Israel during the violent Second Intifada. I remember the news reports of angry mobs of Israeli Jews pouring onto the streets and vandalizing Arab cars following suicide bombings. I completely understood this reaction and could feel the desire to destroy well up in me. The downside is that these outbursts almost never resolve anything; they often make things worse and leave us ultimately feeling bad about ourselves. On the other hand, some people turn this anger in on themselves, which manifests as depression and, in the worst cases, suicide. Whether the anger is turned outward or inward, the inability to bear grief leads to destructive outcomes. The key to bearing grief or any difficult emotion is connection—connection to others, to ourselves, and to God. Cultivating these connections is the work of savlanut.

We can learn some things about how to balance this tension between hot and cold anger from the life of Moses. As mentioned in the last chapter, the eleventh-century commentator Rashi calls him a "savlan"[5] when he bears his siblings' insults, but his life does not embody savlanut, or bearing. Rather, a defining characteristic of his life is his struggle finding the midpoint that motivates positive change between hot, explosive anger and apathy. When we first meet the adult Moses, he is coming out of the Egyptian royal palace, where he was raised as a prince. We can imagine how complex his identity is having been raised as an Egyptian royal while knowing he was born a Jew.

He leaves the palace to see what is happening to his people of origin. He is shocked at the brutality with which his adopted people treat the Israelites. With no authorities looking on to suppress his rage, he kills an oppressor and buries his body. Flash-forward some sixty years to when Moses ascends Mount Sinai to receive the tablets of the law from God. He spends forty days in an epiphany with God and then descends the mountain to find the Israelites dancing around the Golden Calf. He smashes the holy tablets, grinds the stone into dust, and forces the offenders to drink the deadly mixture.[6] Moses's hot anger bursts forth again later in the desert when dealing with a water shortage. God instructs Moses to speak to a chosen rock and that rock will give forth water. Instead Moses calls the Israelites "rebels" and strikes the rock twice to get it to give water.[7]

At other times Moses is a model of profound bearing. Twice he saves the Israelites by boldly standing up to God and arguing on their behalf with great compassion when he could easily have given up in frustration. After the Golden Calf and the debacle with the spies who convinced the Israelites not to enter the Land of Israel, God was ready to hit the reset button, wipe out the Israelites, and start over with Moses.[8] Both times Moses argued persuasively that the right thing to do was show compassion in the face of rebellion. Yes, there were consequences in both instances—the main perpetrators died, God's direct presence was removed from the camp, and the Israelites needed to wander in the desert for another thirty-eight years—but these consequences were balanced with love and compassion. The Israelites were given the Tabernacle to create a space for God in their midst, and God created clouds that would accompany the Israelites on their wanderings through the desert. In both instances the people were given an opportunity to do teshuva, to return to themselves and their source. What greater act of compassion is there? The power of cold anger is that it can create something new out of the ruins of racism, rebellion, and violence.

The clearest example of the creativity that comes from cold anger is in Moses's encounter with God in the aftermath of the Golden Calf incident. Here God appears beyond frustrated and proposes to eliminate these rebellious people and start over with Moses,[9] saying, "Leave me alone so my wrath can burn at them."[10] This is the divine equivalent of that moment just before exploding when I can taste how good it will feel to unleash my anger at my partner, my children, my students, or whoever violated my will. Notice that God says, "Leave me alone." This is key to understanding hot and cold anger.

We can only rage when we feel isolated. When my son gets very upset, he wants to be alone in his room to rage. Think about the last time you exploded in anger. Were you feeling connected or disconnected from the person who was the focus of your anger (and this can mean yourself as well)? I experience this type of rage when I feel that the other person does not understand me and judges me for something I am not. Not being understood is an experience of disconnection. God knew it would be impossible to rage at the Israelites if God was in communion with the people through Moses, their leader. In a dramatic exchange, God says to Moses, "Leave me alone so my wrath can burn at them."[11] Moses refuses to let God be alone and says, "Remember your covenant with Abraham, Isaac and Jacob."[12]

Moses reminds God of the intimate connection between God and the Israelites. Then a powerful thing happens. Instead of raging, God's anger cools and something new is created—teshuva. Before this moment there were only two possibilities: obedience or destruction. Connection at the moment of anger opened the possibility for something new, something born of love, which was the opportunity for repair and reconciliation. It wasn't that God was no longer angry or had forgiven the people. No, God was still angry and may have felt grief for the trust and level of relationship God thought had existed. The difference now is that God was reconnected to the people. This tension of anger and connection breaks open the heart and lets cold anger flow with creative force. While explosive anger is destructive and apathy produces nothing, cold anger is life-giving and generative. This is what is at stake with savlanut.

### REFLECTION

When is the last time you expressed hot anger and what led to this outburst?

What are some models of effective and ineffective uses of anger and patience you have experienced in trying to make social change?

How do you "reduce the temperature" when you feel triggered and angry?

---

## SAVLANUT IN ACTION

The following activists demonstrate the creative power of combining motivating anger with bearing. Stephanie Pell is a human rights lawyer with years of experience helping vulnerable immigrants and children navigate the complex and often rigid bureaucracies of family and immigration courts. She describes herself as easily triggered and angered by people who seem to mistreat or speak badly of others. This makes her vulnerable to shutting down and not engaging with these types of people.

One summer during law school, Pell worked in the Legal Aid Juvenile Rights Division advocating for children whom the state deemed at risk of neglect and could be removed from their homes. Often she would get angry and judgmental toward the parents for their neglectful and abusive behavior. She quickly found that her righteous anger was getting in the way of actually helping the young people in her care. She describes how that later changed:

> I was able to drop down into a more compassionate place and try to imagine the kind of life these parents have. This made it easier for me to connect to the children because they love their parents so much and do not want to leave home. When I could stop demonizing the parents as evil, I was able to connect with the children because they loved their parents.[13]

Pell's ability to temper her anger with compassion gained her the trust of her young, vulnerable clients and enabled her to be a more effective advocate because of this trust. It also enabled her to think more clearly about whether it made sense for the child to stay or be removed from the home.

Pell's use of compassion echoes Rabbi Nachman's advice about managing anger. He writes, "You must break the force of your anger with love. If you feel yourself becoming angry, make sure you do nothing cruel because of your anger. You must make a special effort to have compassion for the very person you are angry with. Sweeten your anger with compassion."[14] Note that he is not instructing us not to feel anger. It is appropriate to feel anger when confronted by injustice. He tells us to "break the force of the anger" by sweetening that bitter emotion with compassion.

Pell's instinct was to hit back at these parents with the force of the law as punishment for how they mistreated their young people. This may have been just another cruel gesture in response to cruelty. Righteous anger needs sweetening, which creates a balanced response. This balance is the cold anger that leads to creative solutions. Once she was well connected to her charges, Pell could better negotiate a resolution that met the real needs of these young people.

Michael Oshman, the environmental activist and social entrepreneur, similarly uses compassion to advance his message of environmental stewardship. As described in chapter 1, Oshman was shocked as a nineteen-year-old to see photos from outer space that showed an actual hole in the ozone layer. The reality of the destructive human impact on the environment motivated him to convince restaurants to stop using Styrofoam and other harmful materials. While he was deeply concerned about environmental damage, he was, "committed to not being an angry activist."[15] In his personal life, he would bring a reusable bowl with him to meals where the hosts had disposable plates. He was often the first person these people had ever met who held out the possibility of such behavior.

Oshman claims,

I am deeply committed to not doing environmental damage, and I don't want to cut you down emotionally or shame you for behaving in ways that are normal in our society. Rather I demonstrate that we are on the same side. I believe that . . . everything in the environment, including us, uses things efficiently. We forgot how to do this for a while, but we will get back there. It might take fifteen or fifty years, and we will get there.[16]

This belief in the ability of humans to ultimately do right by the environment gives Oshman a compassion for people. He sees people as much as the solution as they are the problem. His consistent prodding and hand holding, helping business do the right thing, grows out of an ability to connect with compassion with the very people who cause the environmental damage he is so concerned about and wants to change. It is this combination of passion and compassion that makes his work so effective.

## THE LONG VIEW

Savlanut, or bearing with discomfort, is key for bringing a long-term perspective to social-change efforts. Certainly much social-change activism needs to respond to immediate needs. For example, black church burnings need to be met with the prosecution of perpetrators, street vigils against racism, fund-raising, and advocacy to remove racist symbols from public places. At the same time, lasting social change often takes years if not decades. How do we engage in fixing the world while holding a perspective that our efforts could take generations? Indeed, this long-term perspective is one embraced by many activists after years of participation in social-change efforts.

The Israeli-Palestinian conflict is one of the world's most vexing national disputes. Rabbi Shaul Judelman, cofounder of the coexistence organization Roots, along with a Palestinian partner, has no illusions about the complexity of creating change in the Holy Land. Recalling the words of his teacher, the peace activist Rabbi Menachem Froman, Judelman explains, "For the Israeli-Palestinian conflict generations is a reasonable framework."[17] Inspired by Froman's perspective, Roots builds relationships between Israeli settlers in the West Bank and local Palestinians in a way that is not meant to address an immediate, acute need, but to create long-term "climate change," as Judelman calls it, with the goal of creating conditions for a more peaceful and just future.

Judelman, a veteran of the World Trade Organization Seattle protests in 1999 and a longtime environmental activist, critiques much Western activism as too fast paced. He relates that Froman always argued that process is the key in this conflict. While there certainly are injustices and violence that need to be addressed in the present, an indigenous approach to peacemaking would go slowly and focus on relationships. What is needed is a shift in the culture of the relationship formed between Judaism and Islam over the past century. According to Judelman, Rabbi Froman insisted that "if we only think in two- and four-year terms we are missing the other frequencies that go on in these conflicts. These are long-term, generations-long processes."[18]

David Schwartz, the food-justice activist introduced in chapter 4, echoes these sentiments about the need for a long-term perspective. In his work organizing college students to shift campus food services to support just and sustainable farms, fisheries, and food companies, he comments that the day-to-day battles with big business and campus politics can be hard and depressing. The more one knows about the system, the more one realizes how broken the world is. "Despair can lead to really bad social policy. Despair tempts me to join a radical punk anarchist collective," quips Schwartz. "This is not social change the way we imagine it."[19]

For Schwartz, changing the time scale is key. He explains,

If I am on the time scale of the media cycle, it is all bad news. But if we look at longer sweeps of history, especially historical moments where progress was made, we can breathe easier and dream bigger. If we take a generational perspective— like, what is a forty-year plan to change the food system?—I am very motivated by the possible.[20]

Schwartz notes how helpful Jewish tradition is for cultivating this long-term perspective. He says,

> I feel sad for lots of activists who do not have a cultural tradition to call on for that kind of strength. The Jewish tradition is thousands of years old and allows for the kinds of rituals that mark time and help us appreciate time in a different way . . . Knowing that people have been discussing these issues for thousands of years helps [one to] not feel overwhelmed by the fierce urgency of now.[21]

Schwartz's experience testifies to the value of a long-term perspective for creating good strategy and for sustaining activists themselves.

Rabbi Jill Jacobs, the executive director of T'ruah: The Rabbinic Call for Human Rights, claims that a long-term perspective is a key to her ability to sustain activism. Jacobs is one of the foremost North American Jewish social-justice activists leading campaigns for worker justice, ending human trafficking, and fighting for the human rights of Bedouins and other vulnerable minorities in Israel. She is the author of numerous books and articles about Judaism and justice. She explains, "When I was younger, I had a sense that we needed to fix everything now. If we could just stay up all night seven days a week, we could fix everything. Now I know it is a marathon, and an election is every four years." However, she cautions, "It is not nothing—people die in the meantime. People died in Iraq because of a bad Supreme Court decision, but things can always change in the other direction."[22]

Judelman, Schwartz, and Jacobs, activists in different realms and in different parts of the world, all share the same insight: a long-term perspective is essential to sustained social change engagement. The fierce urgency of now is real and demands a response, but it can also be an illusion. The skilled change maker knows when to respond and when to adopt a long-term perspective on an issue.

Cultivating savlanut, the ability to bear discomfort, is key to developing this skilled discernment. Hot anger wants immediate release. When I am vulnerable to being triggered and feeling righteous indignation about some perceived injustice, I am in reactivity mode. I am not necessarily thinking clearly about how to right the injustice. I just want to avenge the injustice. This type of reactive response is closely related to the yetzer harah, the drive for immediate gratification, and is the opposite of the long-term perspective described by our change makers above.

As described in chapter 2, the yetzer is not necessarily negative, it is just a drive for immediate gratification. This drive certainly serves its purpose in fighting injustice, but it is not a reliable tool for long-term change. Reactivity is simply too unstable to serve as a base for a successful change strategy. The Talmud highlights the problems with reactivity when it tells us, "If one tears his garments in anger, or breaks his vessels in anger, or scatters his money in anger, he should be in your eyes as one who serves idols. For such is the craft of the Yetzer Harah. Today he tells a person, 'Do this,' and tomorrow he tells him, 'Go and serve idols,' and he goes!"[23]

The passage describes a person filled with hot anger. He tears his clothes, breaks dishes or furniture, and impulsively spends money. He is out of control. Whatever the perceived injustice or violation of his will, he cannot create space in himself to sit with how bad the injustice or violation feels. Rather, he immediately reacts with anger. The hot-anger reaction provides temporary relief for the uncomfortable feelings. This is the yetzer in its classic role finding immediate relief. What is the relationship with idol worship? In the mind of the Talmud, idol worship is one of the most mistaken things a person can do. Once a person loses control and just reacts to get immediate gratification, reacting to other impulses becomes easier. Discipline weakens. If the idol worship seems to meet some immediate need, the person will worship the idol even though doing so violates his belief system.

How does this relate to social change? My desire to feel effective and make a difference against oppression can be a form of idol worship. I am worshiping the idol of my own abilities and importance. A long-term perspective on any social issue by necessity diminishes my individual significance because so many people need to be involved over the course of generations. I need to bear the discomfort of the injustice, be it racism or economic oppression, and not go toward despair and close my heart nor go toward thinking I can solve the problem immediately through some action. I need to think strategically in partnership with lots of other minds because complex social issues need thoughtful solutions worked out over many years.

Idol worship is also confusing a part for the whole. If I am unable to bear discomfort, I will grab on to any partial solution that eases discomfort even though I know a real solution is more complicated. For activists moved by current suffering, it is a constant effort to stay aware of this suffering and know that a long-term perspective is needed to make sustainable change. Reverend Martin Luther King Jr. gave expression to this tension at the end of his powerful "Letter from Birmingham Jail":

> If I have said anything in this letter that is an overstatement of the truth and is indicative of an unreasonable impatience, I beg you to forgive me. If I have said anything in this letter that is an understatement of the truth and is indicative of my having a patience that makes me patient with anything less than brotherhood, I beg God to forgive me.[24]

Mastering this tension is the practice of savlanut.

## STAYING CONNECTED

Remembering our connection at the moment strong feelings emerge is key to developing our ability to bear discomfort, as Moses demonstrated in the episode with God described above. This connection can be with ourselves, with others, or even with God. I had a visceral experience of this during my first year of teaching high school.

A group of four boys sat in the back of my ninth-grade class. They were standing and playing with something on the wall before class started. I looked over at them as I stood to begin my class session and asked them to sit down. Two of the boys sat. I asked again and did not get a response. I looked out over the class-room full of students and asked again, this time in a louder voice, for them to sit down. One more boy sat. Kevin remained standing occupied with the object on the wall.

I could feel my blood rising and my heart pounding. The students sat in tension waiting to see what I would do. Kevin and I were in a classic adult-adolescent showdown of the kind more experienced teachers and youth workers skillfully avoid. The thoughts racing through my mind sounded like, "How could Kevin defy my will like this and not sit down when I ask? This is outrageous!" I was filled with righteous indignation. "I am the teacher, and he is the student, so he must listen to me. I am completely justified in letting loose and screaming at him right now." This was how my logic went.

I could almost taste how sweet it would be to pour out my wrath on this fourteen-year-old rebel. Just as I was about to "pull the trigger," I remembered my savlanut practice and a source I was meditating on that week:

> There is not a moment in which a human being is not sustained from the flow of divine abundance. There is not a wrongdoing that a person does, in which, at that same moment, the divine abundance isn't sustaining him . . . While the human is committing this wrongdoing with this very power from God, God suffers the insult . . . This is why Micah the prophet calls to God, 'Who is like you, God?' You are a God of kindness, doing good. You have the power to take vengeance, but you are patient and wait for people to return in teshuva. Behold, this is a trait that people need to acquire—patience, to be able to withstand insult and still not withhold your goodness from the other.[25]

I repeated a paraphrase of this last line in my head several times as I stood looking at Kevin: "I will not withhold my goodness from you; I will not withhold my goodness from you." I could feel my heartbeat slow down and my muscles unclench. I could take a deep breath now that my blood was not pounding so hard. I felt love for Kevin. I said in a calm but firm voice, "Kevin, you need to sit down, so we can start class." Kevin looked at me and sat down. Kevin and I went on to develop a good and respectful relationship over the rest of his time in high school, a relationship that would have been difficult to achieve had I actually raged at him in public.

It is possible that the practice suggested by the "Date Palm of Devorah" text needs to be filtered through a prism of power relationships. Perhaps this technique of not withholding goodness works when the insulted party has more or equal power to the defiant party, like a teacher and student. What if the person experiencing insult has less power? Is it still appropriate for that person to cultivate patience? Whereas insult by the less powerful party can be experienced as defiance, insult by the more powerful party can be experienced as injustice. In the face of injustice, does it still make sense to cultivate connection? I actually think it does.

Roots cofounder Ali Abu Awwad is a courageous Palestinian nonviolent activist who models patient resistance. Born into a politically active family, he was jailed with his mother during the First Palestinian Intifada in the late 1980s. In jail he studied nonviolence and engaged in a seventeen-day hunger strike. He became a Palestinian Authority security official during the Oslo process in the nineties and was shot in the leg by a Jew during the Second Intifada. While recuperating he learned that his brother had been killed after unintentionally stumbling into an altercation between the Israel army and stone-throwing Palestinian youth. He went through a cathartic grieving process with the Bereaved Parents Circle, a group of Palestinians and Jewish Israelis all of whom lost a family member to war. His Roots partner Judelman recalls Ali saying, "It was the first time I saw an Israeli cry. I couldn't believe that [they] really had tears." At a public presentation, he finally reached a point where "I wanted to give up being a victim." Knowing that neither Jews nor Palestinians will leave the land where they live, he said he asked himself, "Do I want to be right or do I want to succeed?" "The hate and anger keeps eating at you so you look for a solution," he said, and he came to believe that "there can be no harmony until we [Palestinians and Jews] see the humanity of the other side."[26]

Abu Awwad understands the corrosive effect of hate. "Seeing the humanity of the other side" is a way of forging basic human connection, which helps transform hate into something more generative. Abu Awwad spends a good amount of time with the Jews of the West Bank, acknowledging their suffering but also challenging them to revise their own exclusive narrative about the Holy Land. In this way he continues to give his goodness to those who defy him by being citizens of a country whose military controls his people in parts of the West Bank. At the same time, he is building a Palestinian nonviolent resistance movement and, with Rabbi Judelman, a new model of coexistence in the heart of the Israeli-Palestinian conflict. Abu Awwad's ability to stay connected, to "see the humanity of the other," while feeling grief, is a model of savlanut, which nurtures the cold anger that can make real change.

### SUMMARY

Anger is a useful emotion that can motivate action to create social change. To be effective, this anger needs to be purposeful and nonreactive. Savlanut/patience is the trait for developing this type of cold anger. Savlanut calls on us to feel anger, but modify it by drawing on compassion and maintaining a human connection with the instigators of our anger. Maintaining this connection will channel the energy of the anger into something prosocial and generative. The creativity that grows from confronting injustice with appropriate savlanut can produce sustainable solutions that make a lasting difference.

PRACTICE: *Savlanut/Patience*

## Jewish Wisdom about Savlanut

For Hebrew language sources and additional material, see
www.kirva.org.

*Everyday Holiness*, Alan Morinis, chapter 8

*Gateway to Happiness*, Rabbi Zelig Pliskin, chapter 11

*Advice*, Rabbi Nachman of Breslov, translated by Rabbi Avraham
Greenbaum, pp. 128–30, Breslov Research Institute

## Focus Phrases

Choose a phrase to repeat out loud for a minute or two each morning. You can adapt the phrases to your own language. Write the
phrase on an index card and put it somewhere you will see it each
morning. Some people tape the card to their car dashboard or computer.

> *"Sweeten anger with compassion"—Rabbi Nachman of Breslov,
> Advice*[27]

> *"No matter how insulted I feel, I will not withhold my goodness
> from you"—R. Moshe Cordavero, "The Date Palm of Devorah"*

> *"I will bear the burden with you"—Pirkei Avot, 6*

## Guided Meditation

This is best done with a group or at least a partner. Have one person
read the meditation while the others follow the instructions read by
the leader.

Find a comfortable place to sit or lie down.

Feel the weight of your body against the chair or ground.

Rest your hands on your lap or at your sides.

Gently let your eyelids close.

Take three deep breaths, inhaling through your nose and exhaling through your mouth.

Bring into your mind a person whose behavior triggers in you an anger response.

Let yourself notice his or her facial expression and body language.

Imagine this person doing the type of activity that triggers you.

Feel your reaction in your chest, stomach, or anywhere else that gets tense.

Keep inhaling and exhaling as you notice the quality of these feelings.

What do the feelings look like? Where do you notice them in your body?

Let your body react to these feelings—this can include yawning or shaking.

Now say in your mind, "I will not withhold my goodness from you; I will not withhold my goodness from you."

Let yourself feel the reaction in your chest and elsewhere from being triggered and again think, "I will not withhold my goodness from you."

Note that goodness does not mean doing whatever this person wants.

Imagine opening your heart to this person.

Feel your heart open and imagine goodness and love flowing from your heart to this person.

Keep inhaling and exhaling slowly through the nose as you imagine your goodness flowing to this person.

Bring your attention back to your heart, chest, or anywhere there was tension.

What is the quality of this tension now?

Take three more big inhales and exhales.

Slowly open your eyes.

Allow time for quiet journaling or reflection about the meditation.

## Visualization

This exercise can be done individually or with a group. If done in a group, choose one person to read the description once through.

Choose an image of something that angers you and motivates you to work for social change.

This can include a childhood neighborhood that lacked a supermarket, a child with disabilities being mistreated, a friend or relative hurt by violence.

Visualize the image with all of its details.

Let your mind fill in details and keep your attention on the image.

Notice your feelings as you see the image.

If your mind wanders, keep bringing your attention gently back to the image.

What would it mean to you to sweeten this image with compassion?

Keep the image in your field of vision and bring compassion to the image.

How might bringing compassion to your anger open creative ways of channeling this anger?

## Contemplation

This exercise can be done individually or with a group. If done in a group, choose one person to read the description once through.

Choose a social change effort you care about.

What would success look like in this effort? For example, reversing climate change, ending racism, or resolving the Arab-Israeli conflict.

Contemplate the idea that this effort will ultimately succeed.

It may take decades or centuries, but it will succeed.

For the duration of the contemplation, keep bringing your attention back to this idea that over time you will succeed.

## Kabbalot

The kabbalot are designed to do individually. If you are using this book with a group, give people a few minutes to choose a kabbalah and close the session with people sharing which kabbalah they are going to practice until the next meeting.

Choose a person who bothers you and decide to stay connected by feeling or expressing love in his or her direction at least once each day.

Apply a long-range perspective to a project or social-change effort in a planning or strategy conversation.

## Soul Accounting/Cheshbon Hanafesh

Set aside five to ten minutes at some point in the day to either journal or do the hitbodedut practice answering these questions.

What is one thing you noticed about savlanut/patience or anger today? What did this teach you?

What is a choice point you experienced today on the continuum of anger and patience?

What is a good point about how you or someone expressed savlanut/patience today?

In what ways did you notice anger and patience being used effectively or ineffectively in a social-change effort?

How is your savlanut/patience aligned or not with your understanding at this moment of God's will for you or what the universe is calling for from you right now?

How is your level of savlanut/patience expressing or working against your own deep desire/will?

## Spiritual Check-in

1. Take turns listening to each other for two minutes talking about a good point from the day and anything else the speaker wants to get off his or her chest.

2. Journal quietly for five minutes about the cheshbon hanefesh/soul accounting questions.

3. Take turns listening to each other for ten minutes talk about the experience with the focus phrase, kabbalot, soul accounting, meditation, visualization, and contemplation.

4. Then discuss any insights or challenges with savlanut/ patience and anger that came up during the week.

5. End with a commitment for practice for the next week.

# 8

# CREATED IN THE DIVINE IMAGE

## Kavod/*Dignity and Honor*

Marlene Juarez worked as a nanny for a family near Boston, taking care of four children ranging in age from 6 months to 6 years old; she organized play dates, cooked, did laundry and cleaned a large house. Both parents worked full time and in some weeks asked Juarez to work as many as 60 or 70 hours. Juarez had recently emigrated from Honduras, and was afraid to complain. She couldn't afford to lose her job. But, once, she requested a few hours off to deal with a personal matter—and in response, her employers docked her pay.

"If you're reducing my pay when I ask to work less hours," she said, "shouldn't you increase my pay when you ask me to work more hours?"

"They said no," Juarez recalled. "They said I had no right to overtime."[1]

This is a fairly common story, with 67 percent of domestic workers receiving no extra pay for overtime labor, according to a report by the National Domestic Workers Alliance (NDWA). These employees are among the most exploited and invisible in the US workforce. These are the people, mostly women, who take care of elderly parents and young children, clean homes, and make it possible for their employers to go to work each day. They are systematically excluded from protection as one of two groups (farm workers being the other) who were left out of the landmark 1938 Fair Labor and Standards Act, which set federal wage and hours guidelines.[2] According to a study on domestic labor,

> Domestic workers' vulnerability to exploitation and abuse is deeply rooted in historical, social, and economic trends. Domestic work is largely women's work. It carries the long legacy of the devaluation of women's labor in the household. Domestic work in the US also carries the legacy of slavery with its divisions of labor along lines of both race and gender. The women who perform domestic work today are, in substantial measure, immigrant workers, many of whom are undocumented, and women of racial and ethnic minorities. These workers enter the labor force bearing multiple disadvantages.[3]

Efforts are under way to end this exploitation. Over the past decade, seven states (including California, New York, and Massachusetts) passed versions of a "Domestic Workers' Bill of Rights," giving nannies, housecleaners, and home-care workers the right to a minimum wage, overtime, written contracts, vacation, and other benefits long guaranteed to most people in the US workforce. The NDWA serves as a national clearinghouse and organizer of these efforts. The main motivation for this organizing comes down to dignity. As the NDWA explains on its website,

> Domestic workers care for the things we value the most: our families and our homes. They care for our children, provide essential support for seniors and people with disabilities to

live with dignity at home, and perform the home care that makes all other work possible. They are skilled and caring professionals, but for many years, they have labored in the shadows, and their work has not been valued. These workers deserve respect, dignity and basic labor protections.[4]

It is ironic that the workers who care for the people we value most are among the most devalued in our society in terms of wages, protections, and status. As mentioned above, the value society assigns to these workers is closely aligned with how our society values women, people of color, and immigrants in general. A visceral sense that all people deserve to be treated with dignity and value motivates much social-change activism, including these efforts to raise the status of domestic labor. How we assign value is the central feature of *kavod*, the trait of honor, dignity, and respect.

## KAVOD IS CENTRAL TO OUR HUMANITY

The word *kavod* comes from the Hebrew root *kaf.vet.daled* (K.V.D.), meaning "heavy," "weighty," or "significant." When we give someone kavod, we are saying, "You are significant and deserving of recognition and good treatment." If kavod implies weight or gravitas, the opposite is *kal*, or "light." We disrespect someone by treating them lightly, as if they are not significant—and kal is the foundation of the word *klala*, or "curse." It is a curse to treat people as if they are not significant by not giving them attention, or underpaying or mistreating them.

Notice how Marlene Juarez was treated in the example above. Her employers clearly felt they could treat her "lightly," ignoring her request for overtime pay. As an immigrant woman working in the home, her employers could ignore her significance and take advantage of her vulnerable economic situation.

Rabbi Wolbe explains that everything in this world has value.[5] We express how much we value things by assigning them a monetary value. Human beings are different in that we can't put a monetary value on a person. We express how significant we think someone is by the kavod we give them. Kavod, or dignity and respect, is how we express value.

## REFLECTION

Think of a time you were treated lightly. What did it feel like?

When have you been considered significant? What let you know that others could see your significance?

When have you treated someone else lightly? Why did you do this?

When I deny someone kavod, or my organization or society creates conditions where people are denied kavod, I ignore something essential about human beings. One of the first things we learn about human beings in the Creation story in Genesis is that we are made "in the Divine image."[6] According to Rabbi Yitz Greenberg, being made in the divine image endows all humans with three essential dignities: all humans are infinitely valuable, equal, and unique.[7]

Infinitely valuable means that people have value beyond their usefulness to me or to society. Their value is essential and not instrumental in any way. This is a good thing to remember in capitalist societies that only value people for what they can produce. Equal means that, in an essential way, no one is more or less valuable than anyone else. Unique means that each particular person has something to offer the world that no one else ever did or ever will. As far away as we are from actually treating all people with the dignity they deserve, Genesis sets a goal to which we can aspire.

This radical statement about the value of a human is the reason why religious people and organizations, for all their problems and regressive tendencies, are often at the forefront promoting the dignity of the individual against state-sponsored efforts to deny this dignity. Advocacy against the death penalty, liberation theology in Central America, the sanctuary movement, the civil rights movement, and the Polish solidarity movement against the Soviet Union are three clear examples where Christian and Jewish religious groups were, and continue to be, instrumental. There is a deeply humanist impulse in a religious consciousness that understands all people to be created in the divine image.

Awareness of this reality about human dignity is, according to some, the central principle of Judaism. Close to two thousand years ago, the sages Ben Azzai and Rabbi Akiva debated over which was more important: humanity created in the divine image or the golden rule ("Love your neighbor as yourself").[8] In the same discussion, Rabbi Tanchuma points out that the golden rule is vulnerable to how a person feels about himself or herself and how he or she has been treated in the past. If a person feels mistreated and internalizes that mistreatment, he or she may want to bring others down and mistreat them as well. In such a situation, remembering that all people are created in the divine image could encourage the respectful treatment of others even when one feels bad about oneself. In this way being created in the divine image is a more durable and universal principle. In fact, the human being is the closest thing there is in this world to the image of God.[9] One way to make God's presence more palpable in this world of hiddenness is to treat other humans with the respect they deserve as infinitely valuable, equal, and unique beings. This also means influencing our organizations, companies, and societies to end the mistreatment and devaluing of fellow humans created in the divine image.

Why would people be mistreated if we are all infinitely valuable? The many social theories that deal with this issue come down to one main thing: dehumanization. Social scientists, anthropologists, and now brain scientists teach us that, as social animals, we instinctively notice difference. While our first reaction to noticing difference may be simple interest, in many cases we are taught to see difference as dangerous and threatening. Oppressive regimes have always understood this and manipulated their people to see those who threatened their dominance as "other" or less human in some way. Pharoah of the Exodus story did this as did the Nazis, who perfected the dehumanization of Jews and other "undesirables," like people with disabilities and homosexuals.

One way an oppressive regime dehumanizes is by denying certain classes of people the kavod they deserve as humans. In the case of the Nazis, they first denied Jews basic rights as citizens, including the right to own businesses, study and work in universities, and participate in the public life of the society. On top of this, Nazi propaganda portrayed Jews as less than human and animal-like in their mannerisms and customs. In the mind of a generation of Germans, Jews were so "other" and less than completely human that they did not deserve the kavod/dignity due to "real humans." As the Third Reich progressed, Jews were denied more and more kavod to the point that Jewish life itself became so insignificant that the Nazis implemented the mass extermination of Jews because it was more cost-efficient to kill Jews than to keep them alive. In the late nineteenth century, the Mussar master Rabbi Simcha Ziesl Ziv claimed that a human being cannot live without kavod, so essential is it to our understanding of ourselves as people.[10] The Nazis understood this and perfected denying whole classes of people dignity. A cursory look at the policies and propaganda used in the African slave trade and the genocide against the native peoples of North America, as well as any number of oppressive campaigns, reveals the use of similar and sometimes as extreme methods of dehumanization to both justify and reinforce the denial of kavod.

The goal of most, if not all, social-change efforts is to restore human dignity. A cursory look at the websites of human rights organizations reveals that most name "human dignity" as a key goal. The NDWA claims that it is "winning improved working conditions while building a powerful movement rooted in the human rights and *dignity* of domestic workers, immigrants, women, and their families."[11] Rabbi Jill Jacobs, of T'ruah, claims her motivation to be "improving the conditions people live in."[12] Rabbi Shmuly Yanklowitz, a leader in the prison-reform movement, describes his motivation, which we quoted in chapter 4, in terms of revealing the divine image:

> I think there is something mystical about enabling others to begin to see and hear invisible and unheard people. I want them to notice that their neighbor, their domestic worker, or even someone who they see as their enemy is created in the divine image which they didn't see before. Opening hearts around that human dignity aspect is essential to my activism.[13]

Pope Francis in his encyclical on the environment and statements about the negative impacts of global capitalism bases his arguments in the imperative of human dignity.[14] Reverend Martin Luther King, Jr., in his early writings from the 1950s, based his arguments for the necessity of a movement for black civil rights on the need for black Americans to regain a sense of inner dignity lost from years of unequal treatment.[15] Indeed, the primary goal of the massive efforts for social change around the globe is to create conditions in which all people are treated with the dignity they deserve simply for being human.

---

### REFLECTION

Choose a person from a racial, ethnic, religious, class, gender, or sexual orientation group that is different from yours. In what ways do you think about and/or treat this person with anything less than full respect?

Why do you think you do this?

How does your company or organization treat people with dignity?

How does it not treat people with dignity?

---

## SEEKING HONOR

Giving kavod is essential to people's well-being, but seeking kavod is destructive to both the seeker and the larger community. Close to two thousand years ago, rabbis noticed that "jealousy, desire and [seeking] kavod drive a person from the world."[16] Rabbi Joshua Lesser, of Bet Haverim in Atlanta, describes how this desire for recognition weakened the Occupy Atlanta movement in the fall of 2011. The Occupy movements spread across the country that fall inspired by the Occupy Wall Street protests in which people set up tent encampments in the center of New York's financial district. The goals of the protests, which popularized the slogan "We are the 99 percent," were to draw attention to the devastating impact of increasing economic inequality and to agitate for change in the US economic system. At their heart, the protests were deeply committed to pure democracy and consensus leadership.

Even still, Lesser points out that certain people, usually white men, would always be the one's speaking onstage. An unnamed competition existed for who would get recognition as leaders of the movement. Lesser reflects,

What I've noticed and personally wrestled with is how to honor the prophetic voice, which is about restraint and the message, and not get caught up in needing to be the vehicle. There is a certain amount of status in the social-justice world to be the spokesperson. There is a tension between who does the work and who gets to speak.[17]

Movements and campaigns are never the product of one person, but given the way the media works, it is often important for one or two people to be the public face of the movement. Who will be this public face and get recognition for the efforts of many awakens deep desires for kavod. Once unleashed, kavod-seeking can divert attention from ending poverty or racism to managing bruising ego battles over who gets to speak in front of the press. No organization or movement is immune from the jealousy and internal competition that churns in the wake of kavod-seeking.

What does it mean that jealousy, lust, and honor-seeking "drive one from the world"? Jealousy, lust, and honor-seeking all involve reducing others to instrumental objects. When I feel jealous of a colleague's accomplishments and status, I am not really seeing that person. I am only seeing my lack and what I want. Lust is a drive to satisfy one's own sexual desires through intimate contact with another person. That other person's needs are secondary or irrelevant. When I seek kavod, I do not care what anyone else around me needs or wants. All I notice is my own desperate need for recognition, attention, and praise. Others are either obstacles to getting this recognition and need to be removed or instruments to be manipulated to help me get kavod.

These three traits drive one from the world because they disconnect us from the humanity of the other. They are also insatiable. There is a famous rabbinic saying that no one dies with even half of their desires filled. If we love external recognition, we may get temporary relief by receiving lots of praise, but the desire will come back stronger once the spotlights dim and the crowds go away. Trying to fulfill these desires drives one farther and farther away from real connection to others and to oneself and in this way drives one from the world.[18]

The desire for external recognition runs very deep for most people. I know personally that nothing gets me off balance as much as the sense that I am not receiving the recognition I feel I deserve. This can come from not being mentioned by name for my contribution at a public event to something as small as not being acknowledged with a smile from someone at a social gathering. It is often shocking to me how vulnerable my self-esteem can be in these moments. Most of us did not get anywhere near the attention we needed as very young children, and, as we described in chapter 2, this leaves us with an outsized feeling that we need recognition.

This distorted need gets exaggerated by the way praise is used to manipulate young people. Certain types of praise can negatively influence self-esteem in young people.[19] If a child is repeatedly praised for a certain innate characteristic, that child may unconsciously decide not to take risks for fear of losing the praise. The classic examples are intelligence and physical beauty. If a child is told repeatedly that he is so smart, he may get a self-esteem boost about his intelligence, but he also may limit the intellectual risks he takes because he is afraid of not "being smart." In addition, his sense of being smart is tied to others telling him so, and thus he may be inclined to only do things that will get others to tell him he is smart.

My wife and I half jokingly say we are addicted to praise. We both were early readers and did very well in school. At an early age, we came to understand that if we did what our teachers wanted, we would get lots of praise and feel really good. We obliged and were perfect students all the way through graduate school. However, as adults both of us struggle with dreaming big, taking risks, and doing things that will upset others. So much of our self-esteem is invested in what others think of us. The impact of this external-oriented self-esteem is not just personal. As mentioned above, the drive for attention can wreak havoc among change agents within organizations and in coalitions. On an individual level, someone who depends on external recognition can be easily manipulated and challenged to stand up in the face of injustice, especially if doing so is unpopular.

Rabbi Abraham Isaac HaKohen Kook writes,

The more one lacks a sense of inner-wholeness or completion, the more nature will seek to gain such wholeness and completion on an outer level. It is only in a state of low-level spirituality that there will be aroused in a person a desire to glorify himself before others, both with the virtues he possesses and with others he does not possess. It is therefore important for a person to enhance his sense of inner wholeness and completion, and his self-assessment in relation to others shall always be in the proper measure.[20]

Rabbi Kook points to an inner lack as the stimulant for kavod-seeking. The more we sense something missing inside, the more we will look to fill ourselves with attention and praise from the outside. The key is developing an inner-directed source of self-esteem and dignity. Our social-change efforts can actually provide many opportunities for developing this inner kavod.

---

### REFLECTION

In what ways do you notice people vying for recognition in social-change efforts? In other areas of your life?

How does this competition for recognition impact your organization, family, or change efforts?

In what ways do you love external recognition?

Name a time that you sought out this recognition? What happened?

---

## INNER KAVOD

James Kofi Anan was sold into slavery by his family at age six. James is from the impoverished town of Sankor, Winneba, in coastal Ghana, which I visited on an American Jewish World Service rabbinic delegation in 2012. The fishing industry in Ghana depends on child slave labor, and many poor families sell their children to small-time fishermen in the hope that their children will gain a skill while making some money for the family. These children live a brutal existence filled with long workdays, punishing labor untangling fishing nets and diving into cold water, and getting little rest and almost no time for play.

James knew that this was wrong. He knew he shouldn't have been sold and was determined to escape. After several failed attempts and painful beatings, he eventually did escape at thirteen and made it back to his hometown. Upon his return, his father rejected him, and he was forced to live on the streets. Miraculously James fed himself on mangos and coconuts from the trees. He used his skills as a fisherman to earn money and put himself through high school and college. All the while he knew he deserved to succeed.

Eventually he got a job with Barclays Bank, rose to be a manager, and decided he wanted to give back. He returned to Sankor, determined to save every child from slavery. He started one child at a time, and after ten years he now runs a major educational, social-service, and advocacy organization called Challenging Heights, dedicated to ending child slavery in Ghana and around the world.

The most powerful part of this story for me is the fact that James always knew that what was happening to him was wrong. He never believed he deserved to be a slave or to receive the mistreatment heaped on him by his master or his community. This clarity about his inner-kavod gave James the strength he needed to keep fighting for all those years.

James's story highlights that cultivating an inner sense of one's worth is much more valuable than receiving kavod from external sources. We will explore Jewish sources that expand on this idea and show how giving kavod and cultivating inner kavod can function as a reinforcing cycle of virtue. In addition to giving kavod to others, navigating attacks and adversity is another proven method for developing the kind of rock-solid self-worth that enables one to be like James and bring concrete change to the world.

## INNER VERSUS EXTERNAL KAVOD

The second-century rabbinic sage Ben Zoma asks, "Who is honorable? The one who gives honor to others."[21] Rabbi Shalom Noach Berezofsky, the Rabbi of Slonim, explains this passage as follows:

> When the Mishnah asks, "Who is dignified?" it does not mean, "Who is made dignified by other people," as is the common understanding. What value is there in being dependent on other people giving you dignity? Rather, "Who is dignified? One who gives dignity to all people" is teaching that the gaze of one person to another is like glancing in the mirror—if his face is dirty he will see in the mirror a dirty face. So it is the same when a person looks at the other—the amount that he is pure and refined internally, so he will look more generously upon the other and see good attributes. On the other hand, if he is infected with bad attributes and behaviors, so he will see bad attributes in everyone else. Therefore, the truly dignified person is the one who treats all people with dignity, who appreciates all people. This behavior is the true sign that he is dignified himself.[22]

Rabbi Berezofsky asks, "What value is there in being dependent on other people giving you dignity?" If the source of our dignity is located outside ourselves, it is not durable. In this sense, being dignified does not mean others heap accolades on you. Rather, it refers to a deep awareness of one's intrinsic dignity that is projected outward by treating others with dignity. It sometimes seems that we get inner kavod by receiving kavod. This is the lure of fame. If I can get top billing and lots of applause and recognition, I will finally feel good about myself. This is false! That good feeling lasts for a few moments, maybe a few days at best. If inner kavod is dependent on external recognition, it will only last until this external recognition ends. A teacher of mine says that even if six billion people applauded us, we would focus on the one person not applauding. When our kavod is dependent on external recognition, it is insatiable and unreliable.

Shunning external kavod was also a central feature of Novardok Mussar. Novardok was one of the big three Mussar schools and focused on developing an unshakable sense of trust and inner moral compass. Rabbi Yitz Greenberg credits his ability to create organizations and tirelessly promote pluralism and interfaith dialogue while sustaining withering criticism from his own Orthodox Jewish community to his Novardok education. Rabbi Greenberg describes his Novardok training:

> We had a va'ad [Mussar group]. We kept a spiritual diary of the week that tracked where you failed. Then the group would tear you apart and tell you where they thought you were off. On the one hand, you get this tremendous critique in the va'ad and reshape your behavior patterns. On the other it only matters what God thinks of you. If you are intimidated or moved by their criticism or moved by their praise, it is a problem for you. It is only about you and God. I think that really helped me stick to my guns and not give in or be over-swayed by Orthodox or other conventional consensus.[23]

While I doubt whether these old-school techniques of harsh peer critique, tearing down, and focus on failure would work with today's Mussar students, the emphasis on inner-directedness is undoubtedly valuable for the task of social change. Impervious to public opinion, but with a well-toned moral compass and connection to God, Greenberg has advocated boldly for human dignity for many decades.

The same dynamic works in organizations and campaigns. Social-justice victories usually involve getting a powerful person or entity to change a policy or direct more resources for a prosocial purpose. Activists can hang their self-esteem on the recognition they get from politicians, CEOs, or others with power. This is a dangerous practice. David Schwartz explains,

I heard this from [veteran community organizer and Harvard professor] Marshal Ganz: "Never look up for power; only look around you." If we only see validation and success because some other entity or decision maker gave us something, then we are just perpetuating the same idea—that all power flows from the elite, the wealthy. Rather, we need to believe and act on the idea that we have the power and we always have. If we win, it's not because someone gave us something; *we* got that win. And continuing to love and build the community and power that got us there is our task.[24]

Just as individuals need to cultivate an inner sense of dignity, so do social-change organizations become "dignified" by acknowledging the intrinsic value and power they have as a result of their members. To be sure, they need to influence decision makers, but their dignity comes from within. Developing inner dignity rather than relying on external accolades gives us as individuals and our organizations a durable foundation from which to pursue social change.

## DEVELOPING INNER KAVOD

Jewish wisdom gives us two main ways to develop an inner sense of dignity: treating others with dignity and managing adversity and attacks. As we saw above, treating others with dignity reveals our own inner dignity. There is a feedback loop here. When I treat others with dignity, I become more aware of my own dignity, which enables me to treat people even better. The converse is also true. When I judge others negatively, ripping them to shreds in my mind, I can't be feeling good about myself. When I catch myself being so judgmental, I know it is a sign I am lacking in my inner dignity.

Rabbi Nachman's good-points teaching from chapter 3 models this dynamic of giving kavod and developing inner kavod. He starts by instructing the reader to search for and find the good in others.[25] He exhorts us to find the good in ourselves only *after* finding good in others. Rabbi Nachman starts where we are. It is hard to see ourselves clearly. But I can see you. I can see that you are good. Now, if it is true that you are good and valuable and significant just for being human, then it is only reasonable that I am too, given that I am also human. Treating others with dignity and finding the good points is one technique for developing inner kavod.

Rabbi Nachman has another technique that I have found very powerful but more difficult. We develop a sense of our own significance through dealing with adversity. I don't just mean that we learn about our skills and talents when we are put to the test. This also happens, but the inner kavod that can develop in adversity is just that, an inner sense of strength not necessarily related to any action. Rabbi Nachman writes about the experience of purposefully not responding to insult and verbal attacks.[26] How could this be a way to develop inner kavod? It sounds more like a way to feel bad about oneself. I finally understood this teaching when a close colleague of mine suffered stinging attacks for her role in a communal controversy.

Nancy Kaufman is a lifelong advocate for women's rights, the empowerment of marginalized people, and intergroup relations. The head of the National Council of Jewish Women, Kaufman was the executive director of the Jewish Community Relations Council of Greater Boston for over twenty years, from 1990 to 2010. Community relations councils (CRCs) are the organized Jewish community's representatives to government and other religious and ethnic groups, as well as advocates for Israel to the general population. Under Kaufman's leadership the Boston JCRC mobilized the Boston Jewish community to engage at a deeper level in social-justice activism, building strong connections with Black, Latino, Christian, and Muslim leadership throughout the city. Between 2004 and 2008, a divisive controversy erupted between certain parts of the Jewish community and the Muslim community, which was building a major mosque and cultural center in the Roxbury neighborhood of Boston. Certain members of the Jewish community joined with others to accuse the Islamic Society of Boston (ISB), the mosque's developers, of connections with radical Islam and of paying less than market value for the land. They supported an abutter to the proposed mosque, who filed a lawsuit against the city to stop the mosque from being built on land given to the ISB by the city of Boston. In response the ISB filed a defamation lawsuit against their accusers. The controversy divided the Jewish community between those who were suspicious of the people behind the mosque project and wanted to stop it and those who welcomed, whether cautiously or openly, this new development in the local Muslim community. Kaufman describes being under significant pressure to make public statements denouncing the lawsuit filed by the ISB against its opponents. Indeed, in November 2005 Kaufman's JCRC publicly supported the right of these opponents to question aspects of the deal between the city of Boston and the ISB to build the mosque.

This controversy put Kaufman in a difficult position. As a leader of citywide interfaith social-justice efforts, she had close relationships with some leaders of the ISB. Through the Greater Boston Interfaith Organization, they stood on the same side of a number of public policy battles, including the fight for universal health care in Massachusetts. At the same time, she represented the organized Jewish community, which included some of the opponents of the mosque project. Kaufman's instinct was to capitalize on years of organizing and relationship building between the Jewish and Muslim communities and directly ask her Muslim colleagues to clarify the accusations concerning anti-Semitism and possible connections of certain ISB board members with radical Islam. She also wanted to urge both sides to drop the lawsuits, so dialogue could take place. However, she met significant resistance from some in her own community for suggesting that a dialogue with people from the ISB should take place. As an organizer and bridge builder, she found herself in a crisis of personal integrity because she was being asked to sign combative public statements she didn't believe in. Kaufman explains,

> What was most disturbing was there wasn't a willingness to talk to the opposing party and, in fact, any dialogue was denounced. Why? And what were we so afraid of that we couldn't even have a conversation. The minute I would

attempt to talk to anyone "from the other side" I would get slammed and asked, "Why did you talk to that person?"[27]

During this time Kaufman was the object of attacks in the local Jewish newspaper by some who strongly opposed the mosque. In the end, Kaufman tried several creative ways to organize a dialogue, including getting the Harvard Kennedy School and Divinity School to host a one-day gathering of interfaith leaders to discuss the situation. She also organized a series of seminars with prominent experts to discuss the nature of the charges and whether the ISB was a real threat to personal security.

While she did not publicly organize as powerfully as she might have under different circumstances, she did maintain her behind-the-scenes advocacy to get the parties to drop the lawsuits. Eventually both lawsuits were dropped, and the ISB went on to build the mosque. According to Kaufman, her reluctance to take a strong stand against the mosque led to loss of trust in her and her organization by some members of the community. Kaufman sees this as an unfortunate outcome but describes the whole incident as "one of my greatest leadership challenges. I think I came out with my personal integrity intact. I fought the battle; I fought the war; I lost them both, but I lost with my integrity intact."[28]

Eventually Kaufman moved on to the national stage, becoming the CEO of the National Council of Jewish Women. She describes feeling a certain inner quiet and confidence that she didn't have during her time at JCRC. She attributes some of this to her experience coming through the battles over the mosque. She absorbed stinging ad hominem attacks in person and in the local press, and she found herself still standing with her integrity intact. She did not respond with anger or with threats of her own. Even though she needed to hold back at times when she simply wanted to speak out, she feels her sense of purpose deepened through the whole experience. This visceral sense of integrity is a core ingredient of inner kavod. Kaufman strengthened hers through the way she dealt with these challenges.

Rabbi Nachman teaches that we develop inner kavod, or what he calls "divine kavod," by not responding reactively to attacks.[29] His metaphor is blood pounding in the heart. This blood, or *DaM* in Hebrew, is symbolic of the yetzer, the drive for instant gratification. When we are attacked, our yetzer wants to act out and lash back in defensive anger. This is the DaM/blood boiling. The key move in the moment is to transform this DaM/blood into *DoM*/Stillness, which is a play on words in the Hebrew.

The spiritual result of cultivating inner quiet and stillness in response to provocation is that God endows you with an inner spaciousness. The hard work it takes to transform the yetzer for anger into stillness is a way of honoring God. This withdrawal of the ego makes more space for God. With this mastery the practitioner senses more spaciousness and inner dignity.[30] This inner, divine dignity is not something anyone can take away with accusations and insults. Born out of a graceful nonreactive response to attacks, the sense of well-being and inner dignity grows stronger with each successful encounter with transforming the yetzer from DaM/blood to DoM/stillness.

Kaufman endured many attacks during the battle over the mosque. Each accusatory op-ed in the local Jewish paper and each call for her resignation would increase the DaM/blood, or desire to attack back. Each time she needed to do the hard work of getting perspective, exercising patience, and modulating her response. In the words of Rabbi Nachman, she needed to sacrifice her yetzer harah each time she was attacked. Her main tool was to remember that she represented something bigger than herself and she had a responsibility to her organization. This is how she constricted her own ego and made space for God's kavod. Over time her nonreactive responses and quiet building of support from allies in the community helped her cultivate the stillness that enabled her to listen to her inner voice. Listening to this voice in the stillness enabled Kaufman to emerge with her integrity and inner dignity not only intact, but stronger than ever.

This practice of meeting opposition with stillness and quiet helped Rabbi Nachman's followers successfully navigate violent and enduring attacks from fellow Hasidic groups in the mid-1830s.[31] In one dramatic incident, Rabbi Natan Sternhartz, the leader of the Breslov Hasidim, was being led to jail by the police on false charges while being pelted with insults from the opposing Hasidim. The young Breslovers were outraged at seeing their leader so degraded. They wanted to attack back. Rabbi Sternhartz saw this and signaled to them, like a quarterback calling plays, "Lesson six, lesson six." The young Breslovers knew this meant "Respond to insults with stillness" and cultivate divine inner dignity, and they were able to overcome their anger. After several years the opposition to the Breslovers died down and the opposing groups disappeared into history. Meanwhile, 180 years later, Breslov Hasidism is thriving around the world.

---

### REFLECTION

Did you ever suffer attacks for your change efforts? If so, think of one particular incident.

What did it feel like? Describe the different feelings and thoughts you had at the time.

How did you respond, and what would you do differently?

How did your response affect your sense of your own dignity?

---

### SUMMARY

Giving kavod is essential to human life; seeking kavod is destructive to the individual and the community while developing inner kavod is the foundation of sustainable social change. Inner kavod is probably the most important and durable element of this trait for making change. Survivors of oppression—from victims of domestic violence to genocide—experience the erosion of self-esteem.[32] Victims internalize the mistreatment and think of themselves as slaves, ugly or worthless. In many cases the victim will then turn around and visit this same mistreatment on his or her own people.

Returning to the example of James Kofi Anan, this is one of the reasons so many former child slaves become slave owners themselves once they have their own fishing boats. Once inner kavod is lost, it is nearly impossible for an individual or people to fight against the oppression. James's story is inspiring in that it offers a picture of what one person can do who has a sense of inner kavod and will not believe the lies about himself. James responded to humiliation with inner conviction and a fierce determination to succeed. One success built on another until James's self-esteem could not be shaken. At a certain point, James dedicated his life to treating all people with dignity by working to end child slavery in his home country and around the world. James's life testifies to the ability to break the cycle of mistreatment and make significant change while growing one's own dignity. In this way kavod is both a means to the end and the end goal itself. If the end goal is a world where everyone is treated with dignity, the main way to get there is by developing our own inner dignity to such an extent that no one will put up with anything less than complete respect for everyone.

PRACTICE: *Kavod/Dignity*

## Jewish Wisdom about Kavod
*Everyday Holiness,* Alan Morinis, chapter 13
"The Moral Principles," Rabbi Abraham Isaac HaKohen Kook, translated by Rabbi Ben Zion Bokser

For Hebrew language sources and additional material, see
www.kirva.org.

## Focus Phrases

Choose a phrase to repeat out loud for a minute or two each morning.
You can adapt the phrases to your own language. Write the phrase
on an index card and put it somewhere you will see it each morning.
Some people tape the card to their car dashboard or computer.

> *[Ben Zoma said]: Who is honorable? One who honors all others.*
> *Pirkei Avot 4:1*

> *He (Ben Azzai) used to say: "Do not be scornful of any person and*
> *do not be disdainful of anything, for you have no person without*
> *his hour and no thing without its place." Pirkei Avot 4:3*

> *"It is only in a state of low-level spirituality that there will be*
> *aroused in a person a desire to glorify himself before others, both*
> *with the virtues he possesses and with others he does not pos-*
> *sess."—Rabbi Abraham Isaac HaKohen Kook*

## Guided Meditation

This is best done with a group or at least a partner. Have one person
read the meditation while the others follow the instructions read by
the leader.

Find a comfortable place to sit or lie down.

Feel the weight of your body against the chair or ground.

Rest your hands on your lap or at your sides.

Gently let your eyelids close.

Take three deep breaths, inhaling through your nose and exhaling
through your mouth.

Imagine yourself or someone else as made in the divine image.

What is the worth of the person (yourself or other) whom you are imagining?

How much is your car, your home, your bicycle, or anything you own worth?

The person (yourself or other) is more valuable than these things.

Add up all the value of everything in the world and we are worth more than that.

What would it take for you to really believe that?

What does it mean to be unique?

Imagine one ball, and then two, then twenty, one hundred, five hundred. As far as you can see, balls. All different from each other in some way.

All unique.

This is humanity—we are all different from each other in some essential way.

What does it mean to be equal?

Two plus two equals four.

Two pounds of coffee beans and two pounds of quarters—they are not the same but have equal weight.

Our souls are unique but have equal weight as divine.

What would it take for you to really believe that we have infinite value, are equal and unique?

Allow time for questions, journaling, or reflection about the meditation.

## Visualization 1

This exercise can be done individually or with a group. If done in a group, choose one person to read the description once through.

Recall a time you were criticized or insulted, especially if it happened in public.

Imagine your heart in that moment pounding hard with adrenaline.

Blood pumps quickly into your left ventricle, and your heart expands and contracts.

Expands and contracts quickly.

Sit with this image until you can see the blood raging in your heart.

Take a deep breath.

Now imagine the blood slowing down to a steady pace.

The walls of the ventricle return to pumping in a regular, moderate rhythm.

In and out smoothly and gently.

The blood is now a slow, lazy river.

In comparison to the raging torrent moments before, the heart seems still in its gentle, but steady beat.

Out of this stillness, a sense of spaciousness grows in your chest.

This spaciousness allows breath and air to circulate through your chest and cool down your heart.

Imagine this spaciousness filled with clarity about your divine inheritance as an image of God.

## Visualization 2

Eating quickly while walking through the market is the Talmud's image of not having self-respect. What is your image of self-respect, of knowing you are made in the divine image? What are you wearing? How are you walking and carrying yourself? What are you talking about? What do you look like?

## Contemplation 1

This exercise can be done individually or with a group. If done in a group, choose one person to read the description once through.

Contemplate the idea that social-change activism is about making the divine image in each person more manifest in the world. What would it mean for social-change efforts if this were really the goal?

## Contemplation 2

Contemplate the possibility that you never again need to seek praise or recognition. What would you feel? What impact would this have on your life?

## Kabbalot

The kabbalot are designed to do individually. If you are using this book with a group, give people a few minutes to choose a kabbalah and close the session with people sharing which kabbalah they are going to practice until the next meeting.

Choose someone in your family, organization, or community and deliberately do something to honor him or her. Choose a different person each day. Vary between people who have more power than you (e.g., your boss or a superior at work) and people who have less power than you (your children or someone you supervise).

Practice turning DaM/blood to DoM/stillness. Each day when confronted with an insult, attack, or some perceived slight to your honor, be still and quiet for at least one minute before responding.

Notice each day at least once how you seek praise.

Once each day notice yourself doing something good or doing something well.

Once each day notice someone else doing something good or doing something well.

Choose one thirty-minute period during the day, and during that time do whatever you can to honor anyone who comes your way.

Do one thing each day that demonstrates kavod for yourself.

## Soul Accounting/Cheshbon Hanefesh

Set aside five to ten minutes at some point in the day to either journal or do the hitbodedut practice answering these questions.

What is one thing you noticed about kavod/dignity and honor today? What is this teaching you?

What good points did you notice in yourself or others?

What choice points did you notice in honoring others?

In what ways do you seek praise and recognition?

In what ways do you and the people you work with to make change model or not model the dignity you are trying to bring to others?

How is your kavod aligned or not with your understanding at this moment of God's will for you or what the universe is calling for from you right now?

How is your level of kavod expressing or working against your own deep desire/will?

## Spiritual Check-in

1. Take turns listening to each other for two minutes talking about a good point from the day and anything else the speaker wants to get off his or her chest.

2. Journal quietly for five minutes about the soul accounting questions.

3. Take turns listening to each other for ten minutes talk about the experience with the focus phrase, kabbalot, soul accounting, meditation, visualization, and contemplation.

4. Then discuss any insights or challenges with kavod that came up during the week.

5. End with a commitment for practice for the next week.

# 9

## BALANCING TRUST WITH EFFORT

### Bitachon / *Trust*

Dov Halpern worked for over a year cultivating a family foundation to fund a new computer lab. His organization, Helping Hand, was transitioning from a sole focus on hunger relief to also offering employment assistance to people working their way out of poverty. This computer lab would give low-income job seekers a place to improve their skills, create resumes, and search for employment. The family foundation pledged the $85,000 needed to renovate the room and purchase fifteen computers.

On the day construction began, Helping Hand's development director called with bad news. The matriarch of the family foundation decided she wanted to do something else with the $85,000, and they would not be fulfilling their pledge. The development director felt hurt and furious with the foundation and dreaded telling her boss, Dov, this news. This loss of funding could jeopardize the entire project, which was one of the organization's major strategic initiatives that year. Dov's immediate reaction surprised her. He said, "That family foundation must not have had the merit of funding this room, and the money will come from somewhere else."[1]

The development director was shocked at Dov's calm in the face of losing this money. However, within two weeks one of Helping

Hand's wealthy donors passed away and left $80,000 in her will to the organization. That $80,000 built the new computer lab.

Most of us, including myself, would not respond with Dov's calm when he got the bad news. A more typical reaction might look like the anger and grief expressed by the development director. However, Dov's reaction is an excellent example of *bitachon*, the middah of trust. Trust does not mean believing that everything will work out the way you want. Sometimes things don't work out how you want. Trust means acknowledging you are not always in control, knowing you can rely on other people or God to help you work things out, and believing that there is purpose and meaning in life's challenges. Trust seems like a counterintuitive trait for change makers and particularly activists who, by definition, take matters into their own hands. We will see that balancing initiative with reliance on something outside yourself is key for sustainable social change.

## EFFORT AND TRUST

The balance of effort with trust is a major theme in the Bible. Take, for example, the Jewish people's exodus from Egypt.[2] Why didn't God just burden the Egyptians with plagues and free the Israelites? Curiously, God asks Moses to take the lead in approaching the pharaoh and demanding the Israelite's freedom.[3] Only after the pharaoh rejects these requests does God intervene with the plagues. Why does God need Moses for the Israelite liberation?

God and Moses's relationship models a core spiritual reality referred to by many teachers as *hishtadlut* and bitachon.[4] *Hishtadlut,* from the root Shin. Daled. Lamed., means "effort" and refers to the work we do to achieve our goals. *Bitachon,* from the root Bet. Tet. Chet., means "trust" or "security" and refers to relying on others, God, or something beyond our control. Hishtadlut and bitachon exist in a dynamic tension. A life of one without the other would be frustrating or absurd while in balance they produce a life filled with striving and meaning.[5]

If you are reading this book, you are probably well practiced at hishtadlut. Hishtadlut involves planning, strategizing, organizing, advocacy, lobbying, fund-raising, and service. In the premodern Jewish communities of Europe, the *shtadlan* was the court Jew who had the cash, clout, and connections to intervene with the bishops and kings to protect his people. In the story above, the staff and volunteers of Helping Hand put in lots of effort creating a strategic plan, deciding to add employment assistance, cultivating donors, and hiring contractors. The computer room would never have been built without all that effort. For people concerned with social justice, hishtadlut is so fundamental to what we do that there doesn't seem like there is anything else. This is where bitachon comes in.

In our modern, secular society, bitachon is a strange and uncomfortable concept. It calls for giving up control and having faith in something outside of ourselves. In our ego-driven, can-do culture, bitachon can seem like a cop-out. Bitachon is an inner quality; it is quiet, subtle, and hard to measure. It is the confidence that comes with knowing you can rely on something that is not completely in your control. In Dov's case he relied on the worthiness of their cause, his knowledge that there was more money out there, and the fact that there were greater forces at work, including God, in the decisions people make about how to spend their money.

There are compelling reasons why bitachon is so challenging. For moderns, whose belief in an all-powerful, all-knowing, and loving deity has been severely weakened by over two centuries of rationalist, scientific thinking and the horrific violence and suffering of two world wars, to simply rely on God to take care of you rings hollow. How can I trust a God who allowed Auschwitz to happen? There is no stronger challenge to the idea that we can rely on God than that. As a result of this very reasonable rejection of relying on God or anything outside of ourselves, many moderns, and particularly Jews, act as if there is nothing outside our own effort. This belief belies that reality that it is indeed possible to strike a graceful balance between human effort and trust. The biblical story of the manna from heaven gives us a glimpse at the deeper issues involved in balancing effort with trust and the costs of not doing so.

## BITACHON AND MAKING A LIVING: THE MANNA TEST

Just days after the Israelites crossed the Reed Sea on their way out of Egyptian slavery, accompanied by ample divine pyrotechnics, God gives them a test to see if they have internalized the faith they professed at the sea. God provides manna bread but only allows the people to take exactly what they need and not save any for the next day. If they do save it, it rots.[6]

Why did God choose food as the object of this test? Food is symbolic of our livelihood. Providing for our own material well-being and that of our family has been one of the core sources of anxiety throughout human history. Will we have enough to eat? The feeling of scarcity awakened by this question is closely connected to the yetzer harah. As we described in chapter 2, an overly developed feeling of scarcity can lead to greed, violence, and the worst aspects of human behavior.

The manna test was carefully crafted. God could have just given every household the amount of manna it needed to fulfill its daily nutritional requirements. Rather, they had to work for their food by collecting the manna from the field. This requirement echoes God's curse to Adam in the Garden of Eden after eating the forbidden fruit that from now on he would need to work the land to get its produce.[7] Part of being human is that we need to work for our food.

But this comes with another challenge. We feel pride in our labor and our ability to make things and support ourselves. The Torah warns us not to say, "My own power and the might of my own hand have won this wealth for me."[8] The Torah is calling on us to do something quite counterintuitive and perhaps paradoxical. We need to use our capability to earn a livelihood (symbolized by collecting the manna) and, at the same time, recognize that it was not just our own capabilities that earned us this livelihood (symbol-

ized by the need to trust that more food will be there tomorrow).
Thus, we don't get to do whatever we want with it (symbolized by
the need to not hoard the leftover manna).

This is an important statement about our relationship to the
natural resources of the universe. In an ultimate way, we are stew-
ards and not owners in that we are not privileged to do whatever we want with the world's natural resources. There is a way of
being in relationship with these resources that keeps them coming in the future.

Dov Halpern and his staff worked hard to bring in financial
resources to help the poor and grow their organization. At the same
time, he remembered it wasn't their efforts alone that brought the
money. This balanced perspective enabled him to lead with determination and equanimity when the inevitable failures struck his organization. This mistake about ownership and control is the source
of much suffering in our personal and communal lives, including
our current environmental crisis. In the words of Pope Francis, "A
selfish and boundless thirst for power and material prosperity leads
both to the misuse of available natural resources and to the exclusion of the weak and disadvantaged."[9] A bitachon perspective helps
quench this thirst with just the amount of resource that ensures all
of us and the planet can thrive.

We need to train ourselves to exert effort but always know the
end result is out of our hands. This is no simple task. The practice of *tzedakah,* or "charity," common to all faith communities, is
designed to do just that. We earn money through our effort but
need to recognize that a portion of those earnings actually belong
to the needy. We are not in full control even though it seems that we
earned the money. In the 2012 presidential election, Barack Obama
related to this idea when he cautioned business owners and entre-
preneurs against thinking that their success was all of their own
doing. While one particular phrase from the speech, "You didn't
build that," was ridiculed by Republicans, President Obama's senti-
ment aligns well with our perspective. In the book of Deuteronomy,

Moses warns the people against thinking that their future success and prosperity will be solely the work of their own hands.

What is wrong with crediting your hard work, ingenuity, and skill for your success? You did, in fact, build that. President Obama's point was that so many other inputs beyond one's own time, effort, and money go into making a business a success. There is infrastructure that contributes to success—the highways, airports, Internet and phone lines that are all partially funded by taxpayer money. There is the educational system that taught the workers in the business and so on. What President Obama should have said was "You didn't build that by yourself." That is the Torah's warning. You didn't do that by yourself. You are not alone in this world. You are embedded in a greater reality that includes other people and the life of the spirit. When we ignore this reality, we put our life and change efforts at risk.

## EFFORT WITHOUT TRUST

The influence of bitachon on our efforts is subtle but essential. Effort without bitachon can feel desperate and alienate potential allies. It can also lead to quick burnout. As noted in the introduction, I got my start in activism after seeing the impact of date rape after years as a fraternity member turning a blind eye to such abuses. I was filled with anger at male-dominated institutions, the military-industrial complex, and pretty much all of mainstream society. I refused to be complicit anymore and wanted to do something to change the system and end mistreatment of all vulnerable people. I began canvassing for California state senator Tom Hayden's political action group and working for a radical documentary film company.

The dark side of accepting responsibility was that I felt like I could never rest. I didn't deserve to rest. Women were still being mistreated, and the CIA was still undermining governments in Central America. I vividly remember going to a Dodgers game and questioning how could I morally account for wasting four hours at a baseball game when so much injustice raged around the world. Twenty years later I can look back and say I needed to relax a bit.

But there is actually a deeper issue. I was all hishtadlut and no bitachon. It was all about me. I wasn't going to be complicit anymore. I needed to do something. My ego was so invested in making change that I felt desperate. It felt as if my identity and well-being were on the line. I remember feeling quite dark and cynical much of the time. In fact, it is the one time in my life when I was actually fired from a job.

After a little more than a year of this, including deeply alienating my girlfriend, I instinctively moved toward a more serious engagement with spirituality. It was during this period that I experimented with Buddhist chanting and eventually found my way to Jerusalem, where I learned about Torah, God, and Jewish practice. I was still angry, but this spiritual support provided me with a sense that it was not all about me and I could rely on other people and something bigger than myself.

My activism changed. As described in the introduction, I got involved with a homeless shelter dedicated to community organizing and delighted in how we worked together to change public policy. I experienced joy working together with other good people and laughed a lot more. I saw ending oppression as a long-term commitment and later got involved in a lifelong effort to make social justice a defining element of Jewish life in North America. Because hishtadlut and bitachon are a paradox, there is always the danger of slipping into divided thinking, where it is all up to my effort or there is nothing I can do. It is a constant practice to make an effort and then sit back, make and effort and then sit back. Sustainable activism is never static.

How do we know when to rely on bitachon, trusting in ourselves, others, and God, and when to engage in hishtadlut, taking action to accomplish our goals? Rabbi Shlomo Wolbe once asked a student how his Torah learning was going. The student replied, "With God's help I will learn." This irked the rabbi. God gave you a brain and the ability to learn. Real trust in God is using all the tools God gave you. Only after you have exhausted your God-given gifts can you turn to God for additional help.[10] In social change we need to put in lots of effort before stepping back and letting the process unfold.[11] There are no guidelines for all situations that will tell you exactly when to step back.

In Uri L'Tzedek's campaign for the Flaum workers, described in detail in chapter 6, Ari Hart needed to know when it was time to stop applying pressure and let Flaum make the next move. Meir Lakein describes how young organizers often misbalance effort and trust. They are under so much pressure to get cards signed or turn out people for meetings that "it is very, very hard not to treat people as means to your end . . . In the end you are desperate to get something done." Lakein explains that the goal is

> to get beyond that and really see who the other person is and make space for them, even if it will make your life harder, because of the relationship and commitment . . . This can even mean that a rabbi counsels a congregant to go elsewhere because she will be served better by a different community.[12]

This takes a lot of trust and letting go of a specific outcome.

Zeisl Maayan describes the importance of letting go in her work as a nurse. Early in her career, Maayan would call patients in between visits and try to tweak the directions she'd given them. She wanted to hold all the pieces of their care and control the outcome. This gave rise to deep anxiety. Maayan explains, "I am more in touch with that place in myself to let myself let go and know that God is doing that deep holding and not me."[13] Over time Maayan learned how to balance giving attention and care to her patients with knowing the outcome was not in her hands.

Education may be the field where effort and trust are most pronounced. Almost by definition it is nearly impossible to see immediate results in education. The changes and growth we hope will take place in our students and in our schools take years to manifest. Rose Sadler, an urban educator, describes a particularly challenging student and the seeming futility of all her efforts. This student often sat in the back of the classroom not doing any work. Sadler explains,

> Even though it never felt like we as teachers were able to do enough to successfully support this student's learning in the classroom, in the long term we all worked hard to make sure he felt seen and cared for. This student ended up coming back to visit us after graduation more than any other student.[14]

Sadler and her colleagues needed to give this student lots of care and attention and then let go and trust their efforts made a difference.

For change makers, letting go is deeply counterintuitive. We are all about striving and doing. But without a healthy balance of effort and trust, we make ourselves susceptible to burning out, mistreating the very people we want to help, and undermining our best intentions.

---

### REFLECTION

Where are you on the continuum of trust and control?

In what ways do you try to control things too much? What is the impact on yourself and others?

In what ways do you take too much credit for your successes or failures?

Are there any areas of your life where you think you have too much trust and could use taking more initiative?

---

A note for full-time activists and communal workers: The classic Jewish framing of effort and trust concerns making a living. In the traditional Jewish world, there is a certain ideal to work for money as little as possible and devote most of one's time to spiritual pursuits. The idea is to have trust that God will provide the income you need with your minimal efforts. As distant as this practice sounds to the modern ear, many professional activists live in somewhat the same way, but the ideal is social-change activism and not spiritual pursuits. Many of us dedicate our lives to changing the world with minimal compensation. According to Rabbi Daniel Roth, a religion and conflict-resolution expert, "Funders take advantage of social-justice workers and think they do not need real salaries because they are such idealists."[15] As activists and communal workers, we need to ask ourselves hard questions about the sustainability of this work.

REFLECTION

What does it do to you, your family, and the people you are trying to help if you don't have enough income?

Are you able to support your family?

Do you have negative beliefs about money, such as money is "dirty" or "bad"?

How does this impact the sustainability of your activism?

Let's not leave ourselves out of the equation of effort and trust. Too much trust in our ability to survive on low incomes can ultimately undermine our change efforts. Social change of any kind is a long-term investment. What kind of financial situation do you need to stay in this for the long term?

The awareness that we are part of something much larger than ourselves and the ability to lean into this larger whole as a source of support are key for renewal. There are many possible sources for this kind of support. For some this source is God, for some it is other people, and for others it is the goodness of the universe. How we name the larger web in which we locate ourselves is less important than consciously connecting with this source. In a bitachon practice, we are constantly going back to our source, knowing that we are only part of something bigger than ourselves.

The prophet Jeremiah uses water as a metaphor for God as the source of renewal when he says, "Two evils have My people committed: they have forsaken Me, a freshwater spring [*makor mayyim hayyim*], to hew themselves cisterns [*borot*], cracked cisterns that can hold no water."[16] A freshwater spring's water flows out of its source, whereas the water in a cistern is collected from somewhere else. It is separated from its source.

In another passage Jeremiah relates trust to water, saying that the person who trusts in God is like a tree planted by water and "shall not see when the heat comes, but its leaf shall be green; and shall not be anxious in the year of drought, nor shall it cease from yielding fruit."[17] Water is the source of well-being. A tree with its roots by the water is always connected to this source or life and vitality. Bad things may happen, like a drought or heat, but because of this connection to its source of life, the tree keeps creating and producing fruit.

This is how Jeremiah describes a person who has bitachon. Having bitachon doesn't mean bad things won't happen. There will be famine and drought. The person with bitachon will not get confused by suffering but will be able to stay life affirming and generative for self and others.

This is especially important for those change makers confronting the impact of oppression on a daily basis. Experiencing the human suffering resulting from environmental degradation, mass incarceration, domestic violence, or racism on a regular basis can leave us feeling broken. For me, the core belief that functions like Jeremiah's water is that God and the universe are good and benign. As humans we are not doomed to suffer, but rather, we are here to enjoy the beauty and mystery of life. Suffering is part of life, but it does not give it its character. This perspective was particularly helpful living in Jerusalem through the brutal violence of the Second Intifada and when my wife suffered with a debilitating chronic illness for six years. When confronted with these challenges, I returned to this belief and reframed the daily struggles as mysterious gifts and chances to learn. This is when I remembered. More often I forgot and was just as irritable, despairing, and angry as the next person. But when I could remember, this trust was very much like cool water that gave me life when everything seemed like drought.

---

### REFLECTION

What are your sources of renewal in the face of challenges?

What aspects of your change making seem most like "famine and drought"?

How can relying on your source of renewal give you new energy when faced with these times of drought?

---

## CONFIDENCE

Bitachon also means "confidence." When I know I can rely on someone, something, or myself, I am more confident and willing to take risks. I remember first noticing this kind of self-confidence as a young athlete. Between the ages thirteen and fifteen, I spent every summer and hours each day after school mastering soccer moves. I made various travel teams, won all-star awards, and became captain of my high-school team. To this day when I get on a soccer field, I trust that my body will know what to do with the ball, even though I rarely play anymore. I know I can rely on muscle memory in my body even though my mind is not actively controlling the way my feet move, as it was when I was learning these skills.

This is a basic form of bitachon that all of us use every day. If you drive a car you are probably self-confident that your foot will use the brake pedal in the right way to stop short in front of a child who jumps out in the street without needing to think about how to use the break. If you didn't have this level of bitachon, driving would be a terrifying task. It is useful to notice the many ways you are confident in your own mastery of your body and environment that enable you to function well every day.[18]

Confidence in our human relationships and in God alters the perspective we bring to confronting challenges. Rabbi Shlomo Wolbe teaches we can have a perspective of closeness or a perspective of distance.[19] A perspective of closeness enables healthy risk taking and bold action while a perspective of distance leads to fear-driven timidity. With a perspective of closeness, we remember the hidden lines of connection that join us together with others, God, and our deepest selves. This perspective helped the leaders of a Boston interfaith community organization survive a potentially devastating political disagreement.

In 2006 Massachusetts voters needed to decide on two ballot initiatives: universal health care and an amendment to repeal marriage equality.[20] The Greater Boston Interfaith Organization was a major player in the campaign for health-care reform. Rabbi Jonah Pesner of Temple Israel and Reverend Hurmon Hamilton of Roxbury Presbyterian Church were the clergy leaders of this initiative. At the same time, Rabbi Pesner and Reverend Hamilton were on the opposite sides of the marriage-equality debate, with Pesner as the public face of the campaign to defeat the amendment and Hamilton a vocal supporter. Tensions came to a head when liberal supporters of gay marriage and black church supporters of repeal found themselves in opposing rallies on the Boston Common. Feelings ran so deep on this issue that they threatened to break apart the ten-year-old interfaith organization. It was at this point that a perspective of closeness made a difference.

GBIO's lead organizer advised the clergy members to leave the disagreement alone and focus on health care. However, according to Pesner, "If we were really taking relationships seriously, we had to deal with it."[21] The GBIO's model of leadership development, as an Industrial Areas Foundation affiliate, was based on clergy and congregants building relationships through one-to-one meetings.[22] Pesner, Hamilton, and other clergy had been meeting one to one and sharing their personal stories for close to ten years. It was on the strength of these relationships that the clergy felt they could rely and thus directly address their bitter disagreement.

First, Pesner and Hamilton met one to one to discuss their relationship to marriage equality. Pesner spoke about his gay brother, and Hamilton shared his concerns about out-of-wedlock births and the fear of polygamous marriage in the African American community. They widened the circle, and more clergy had similar meetings. Hamilton and other black church leaders attended a house meeting where Temple Israel members spoke about the realities of discrimination in health care, child raising, and visitation rights suffered by gay couples. All the participants were courageous in their honest sharing and empathic listening. Pesner describes the outcome of these meetings:

> None of us was trying to change the other's mind. That would have been a fruitless effort of exchanging positions. Instead, we were seeking deeper relationships. In fact, I believe the way we religious leaders practice community created a turning point in the debate. What had been a poisonous atmosphere of vitriolic attacks and caricature-like

articulations of opposing views became a respectful conversation. Opposing leaders assumed good faith. They stopped debating the issue in the press. At the end of the day, both sides spoke out in defense of the true concerns of the other. And so we became a community created in God's image, not just a coalition.[23]

This is what can happen with a perspective of closeness. There was no question that the houses of worship had opposing positions on this issue. But from a perspective of closeness, the leaders had confidence that the relationships built over the past ten years meant something. They had confidence that the stories they shared with each other over the years opened a place in the heart where some compromise might be possible. With this perspective the leaders engaged each other in difficult, yet openhearted attempts to stay together as an organization despite their differences. The confidence gained from this perspective made all the difference in GBIO staying together despite being on opposite sides of this contentious issue.

---

### REFLECTION

Try applying this perspective of closeness to one of your projects or campaigns. How might you approach things differently from a perspective of closeness?

---

Confidence is so important to social-justice work because it provides an antidote to despair and its companion, desperation. According to Rabbi Eliyahu Dessler, when our motivations are informed by a lack of trust, our impulse to act is filled with "haste and confusion," while when based in healthy bitachon, we act from a place of "calm deliberation, composure and tranquility."[24]

What is it like when someone approaches you with desperation in his or her voice? I am thinking of students of mine who feel desperate about a test or a summer program or college applications. Sometimes I just see the intense emotion and desperation, and it is hard to even hear the actual request. I feel bad for these students, but I don't really want to help them. Of course I will help them because that is my job, but their desperation leads them to sound demanding, impatient, and entitled. This is not how you want to sound when trying to win allies.

People can tell when you feel desperate by the tone of your voice and, in Rabbi Dessler's words, by your approach. When we can access the soft, internal truth that we are deeply connected to others and something much bigger than ourselves, despair melts. Bitachon does not make things easier. It makes them seem less desperate. And this relaxed confidence wins over allies much better than urgency.

---

### REFLECTION

What it is like when a change maker approaches you with urgency and desperation?

In what ways do you approach making change with desperation or discouragement?

How do you think this affects your effectiveness?

What would help you approach whatever change you want to make with more relaxed confidence?

---

Bitachon was such an important middah for Rabbi Yosef Yuzel Horowitz, the founder of the Novardak school of Mussar, that he would give his students drastic challenges so they could grow in this trait. He instructed a student who was afraid of the dark to spend the night in the cemetery saying psalms. He gave a student who was afraid of humiliation the challenge of going into a bakery and asking for nails and into a hardware store asking for bread. The point of both these challenges was to condition the students to have bitachon and realize that nothing harmful would happen to them if they faced their fears. The students of Novardak went on to found over one hundred yeshivas throughout eastern Europe, withstanding tremendous opposition and threats from Russian authorities.

This type of confidence in God and one's own self-mastery is also key for social change. How can we challenge ourselves, our fellow community members, families, and workmates to change if we are timid? Timidity is a tool of the oppressive system. Trust in God, or something greater than ourselves, is an element in building what Rabbi Tzvi Miller calls "bulletproof" self-esteem.[25] With such self-esteem we can say, "Hineini/Here I am," despite the opposition. This is where trust and humility, as described in chapter 6, meet. The sixteenth-century *Shulchan Aruch* ("Code of Jewish Law") opens with an exhortation to cultivate the quality of "holy boldness" to serve the Creator. The author understands that living as a traditional Jew in the sixteenth century meant confronting lots of opposition from Jews and Gentiles alike and would take strong self-esteem and trust in oneself and God. We can apply this same teaching to ourselves as social-change agents. Parents, friends, and powerful figures in our lives will oppose the changes we know need to happen. A bitachon perspective can help us develop the holy chutzpa needed to continually speak out for justice and a better world.

In what kinds of situations do you get the most timid?

When do you have the most confidence?

Where are you on a timidity-confidence continuum, and what is one thing you could do to become more confident?

What would you have to face if you were going to be less timid with your friends, family, or colleagues? With your political opponents?

## SUMMARY

Bitachon requires a mindset shift. We live in a world of ego, of effort, and of materialism. Everything in Western society promotes these values: do more; buy more; it is all about you. Bitachon pulls in a different direction: I am a small part of something bigger; it is not all about me; I depend on others. These values can seem like weakness in our society. As we've seen, the opposite is true. Bitachon and hishtadlut, a source of renewal and confidence, can actually make our social-justice efforts deeper, more effective, and much more sustainable and enjoyable for everyone.

This concludes the "Walking the Way" section and our exploration of key character traits for social change. Of course there are dozens of other traits that could have been included, but these four seem to me to have the broadest impact on our behavior. There are very few people who don't have something to learn about these middot.

The next and final chapter is about Shabbat, the Jewish Sabbath. Shabbat is neither an inner process nor a character trait. Rather, Shabbat offers the change maker an immersive experience of renewal, making possible the long-term use of the rest of the tools in this book for sustainable social change.

# PRACTICE: *Bitachon/Trust*

## Jewish Wisdom about Bitachon/Trust
*Everyday Holiness,* Alan Morinis, chapter 22
For Hebrew language sources and additional material, see
www.kirva.org.

## Focus Phrases
Choose a phrase to repeat out loud for a minute or two each morning. You can adapt the phrases to your own language. Write the
phrase on an index card and put it somewhere you will see it each
morning. Some people tape the card to their car dashboard or
computer.

> *"Blessed is the person who trusts in the Lord, and whose hope
> the Lord is. For he shall be like a tree planted by the waters, and
> that spreads out its roots by the river, and shall not see when
> the heat comes, but its leaf shall be green; and shall not be
> anxious in the year of drought, nor shall it cease from yielding
> fruit." (Jeremiah 17:7–8)*

> *"A perspective of closeness"—adapted from Rabbi Shlomo Wolbe,
> Aley Shur, vol. 2, p. 576.*

## Guided Meditation
This is best done with a group or at least a partner. Have one person
read the meditation while the others follow the instructions read by
the leader.

Find a comfortable place to sit or lie down.

Feel the weight of your body against the chair or ground.

Rest your hands on your lap or at your sides.

Gently let your eyelids close.

Take three deep breaths, inhaling through your nose and exhaling through your mouth.

Think of a project or campaign you are doing or have done in your social change efforts, family, or community.

What was the goal of this project?

What effort did you put in over the course of the project or campaign?

Scan the project to remember all the effort you put in.

How strongly did you believe that your efforts would make all the difference?

Now imagine that the outcome was actually dependent on God's will or greater forces outside of your control.

Try to bring that awareness into your effort.

Hold both at the same time: you put in lots of effort to achieve your goals and decide that the outcome is ultimately dependent on God or forces outside your control.

You trust that you've done what you can.

Keep holding both perspectives at once.

How does holding both effort and trust affect how you engage in this project or campaign?

How does it influence how you relate to others who are involved?

How does it influence how you related to the community or individuals the project is trying to affect?

How does it influence how you feel about your own contribution?

Take a few minutes for journaling or reflections after completing the meditation.

## Visualization

This exercise can be done individually or with a group. If done in a group, choose one person to read the description once through.

Imagine a spring of water in the side of a mountain surrounded by green grass and rocks.

The spring's source comes from deep within the earth, where the water is constantly replenished by melting snow and rain.

The water is cool, clean, and refreshing to drink.

It is impossible for the spring's water source to ever run dry. It is a 100 percent reliable source of life-giving water.

What would it mean for you to have something in your life you can rely on 100 percent?

## Contemplation

This exercise can be done individually or with a group. If done in a group, choose one person to read the description once through.

Contemplate the idea that God is really there and that the moral arc of the universe does bend toward justice. Ultimately the world will be repaired, social justice achieved, war ended, and humanity will be at peace with the earth and larger universe.

How does believing in this outcome influence the way you think about your change efforts?

## Kabbalot

The kabbalot are designed to do individually. If you are using this book with a group, give people a few minutes to choose a kabbalah and close the session with people sharing which kabbalah they are going to practice until the next meeting.

Make one effort in your work or home life each day as if you really believed God or a higher power was in charge and involved in a benevolent way.

Do a renewing activity each day. What is the source of your renewal?

Focus on one request you receive each day. Does it seem to come from despair or relaxed confidence? Try also noticing a request that arises from within yourself.

## Soul Accounting/Cheshbon Hanefesh

Set aside five to ten minutes at some point in the day to either journal or do the hitbodedut practice answering these questions.

What is one thing you noticed about bitachon/trust today? What is this teaching you?

What good point did you notice in yourself or others regarding bitachon in your change efforts?

What choice point did you have regarding effort and trust?

What is your state of renewal or despair regarding social change right now?

How is your bitachon aligned or not with your understanding at this moment of God's will for you or what the universe is calling for from you right now?

How is your level of bitachon expressing or working against your own deep desire/will?

## Spiritual Check-in

1. Take turns listening to each other for two minutes talking about a good point from the day and anything else the speaker wants to get off his or her chest.

2. Journal quietly for five minutes about the cheshbon hanefesh/soul accounting questions.

3. Take turns listening to each other for ten minutes talk about the experience with the focus phrase, kabbalot, soul accounting, meditation, visualization, and contemplation.

4. Then discuss any insights or challenges with bitachon that came up during the week.

5. End with a commitment for practice for the next week.

---

# PART FOUR

# *Rest*

One of the most rewarding moments of a difficult hike is when I remove my heavy backpack after a tough climb and let my body collapse against a tree trunk, rock, or mossy area on the side of the path. The minutes spent at these rest stops are some of the most memorable and gratifying of the hike. Shabbat, the Jewish Sabbath, is just such a rest stop.

This last chapter is a description of Shabbat as a fundamental social-change ritual. Shabbat gives us an experience of the world as it could be if we really succeeded in our strivings. This book is all about striving for personal growth and striving for social change. Paradoxically Shabbat is about nonstriving, acceptance, and deep rest. We are good, just the way we are, and the world is good, just the way it is. Engaging these deeply counterintuitive propositions is essential for the long-term well-being of change makers and their efforts. If we cannot appreciate the good that is, how can we build a world that expands on this goodness? Shabbat offers an appreciation of goodness and renewed motivation to work for change. Just as we began with motivation, so we end with the motivation for lifelong service that can be generated when one is inspired by a taste of the world as it could be.

## 10

# SHABBAT AS A SOCIAL-CHANGE RITUAL

I had my first real taste of Shabbat while driving through the Utah desert on my way to settle in San Francisco as a young adult. I had been to some Friday night services and dinners, and even spent a summer in Jerusalem with a Shabbat-observant community. But I had not yet experienced the life-altering nature of this twenty-five-hour sundown-to-nightfall period. I was on a very lonely stretch of Interstate 80, driving in my Toyota Tercel packed full of all my possessions, when I noticed it was late Friday afternoon. For the first time, I was cognizant of the choice to observe or not observe Shabbat. Should I power through and get to Oakland by tomorrow or stop and have Shabbat? Something in me called out, "Why not?"

This was the late 1980s, before GPS, so I pulled out my US map and found a campground not far away. By the time I arrived at a set of empty campsites nestled in between two large, craggy red-dish brown hills, the sun was close to setting. I quickly set up my dome tent and put together a meal of canned vegetables and fish. I don't recall whether I even had challah or grape juice. As the sky darkened, I said what I knew of the Friday evening prayers, had my meal, and lay down in the tent.

I could already sense something different. The decision to stay for twenty-five hours opened up spiritual possibilities I'm quite sure I would not have noticed had I just stopped for dinner, or the night, with the intention of traveling on. I sensed a spaciousness and yearning that at once felt ancient and barely recognizable. The next day I took full advantage of that spaciousness with long walks, relaxed prayer, meditation, and reading. Time seemed to stop, and many moments in the day had the fullness of forever. I remember noticing a flower whose petals seemed impossibly red. I gazed at these bold petals in meditation; eternity winked. Decades later the spiritual vitality of these moments is with me as if no time has passed.

What made this Shabbat so powerful? I've asked this question many times in the years since, out of curiosity and the very human impulse to recreate and control. I don't think it was merely the solitude or the mystical desert landscape. I believe it was the decision to stop and give space to experience life in a different, less controlling way. This is the essence of Shabbat—a time to stop, give up control, and if lucky, glimpse real wholeness.

## SHABBAT IS ESPECIALLY RECOMMENDED FOR ACTIVISTS

This discovery of Shabbat in the desert came just in time. As a newbie activist in my early twenties, I saw oppression and injustice everywhere. As mentioned in the introduction, I was zealous for my causes, and these causes were many—US imperialism in Central America, violence against women, homelessness, and nuclear power and weapons were a few of the social ills I felt compelled to change. The Talmud teaches, "If you have the ability to influence the people of your city not to do wrong and you do nothing, you are also responsible for the wrongdoing."[1] This is the rabbinic statement on complicity. I did not want to be complicit. If my fraternity fostered an environment where women were demeaned and objectified, I needed to say something. If my city replaced low-income housing with luxury high-rises, I needed to advocate for more housing. If my country covertly undermined democratically elected governments overseas, I needed to join efforts to stop this behavior.

In a democracy complicity seems to have no end. One the one hand, if I can make a difference, I have to act. On the other hand, it is physically impossible to act in every situation in which I am complicit. Thus, I am stuck being complicit in wrongdoing. This realization produced in me a moral crisis that seemed to have no solution. My physical and emotional limitations banged up against my sense of moral urgency to repair the world. What to do?

Shabbat is a Jewish response, providing tools to navigate such moral and ultimately irreconcilable dilemmas. Shabbat comes from the Hebrew root Shin. Bet. Taf., meaning "stop," "cease." Built into the deep structure of creation is a time to stop: "God ceased on the seventh day from all the work that God had done. And God blessed the seventh day and declared it holy."[2]

There is a rhythm to the universe. We act and build and create and repair for six days, and then we stop. Marge Piercy's poem "Wellfleet Shabbat"[3] captures this rhythm in a more profound way than is possible in prose:

*The hawk eye of the sun slowly shuts.*
*The breast of the bay is softly feathered*
*Dove grey. The sky is barred like the sand*
*When the tide trickles out.*

*The great doors of the Sabbath are swinging*
*Open over the ocean, loosing the moon*
*Floating up slow distorted vast, a copper*
*balloon just sailing free.*

*The wind slides over the waves, patting*
*Them with its giant hand, and the sea*
*Stretches its muscles in the deep,*
*purrs and rolls over.*

*The sweet beeswax candles flicker*
*And sigh, standing between the phlox*
 *And the roast chicken. The wine shines*
*Its red lantern of joy.*

*Here on the piney sandspit, the Shekhinah*
*Comes on the short strong wings of the seaside*
*Sparrow raising her song and bringing*
*Down the fresh clean night.*

I love this poem. It gives a sense that nature itself moves to the rhythms of Shabbat. Of course, there is no Shabbat in nature. In fact there are no weeks in nature either. The sun and the moon set the course for days, months, and years, but weeks are imposed on nature. This is the genius of Shabbat. It imposes a rhythm on the unceasing, steady beat of our activity. Until the final perfection of the world, there actually is no end to our work, just like there is no ceasing to the activity of nature. However, on Shabbat we cease as if our work is finished. Modeled on God's ceasing creative activity at the end of the sixth day, we cease our activity, look over what we've done, and we rest.

Shabbat is a radical idea. The ancient Greeks derided the Jews as lazy for taking a whole day off from work. From sundown on Friday to nightfall on Saturday, twenty-five hours in all, traditional observant Jews cease all creative activity that involves the domination and manipulation of nature. In place of traditional work, Shabbat is filled with prosocial and spiritual activities like prayer, family and communal meals, walks in nature, naps, reading, and song. Shabbat is an incredible statement of principle that declares: I am more than my productivity. In such a materialist and technologically connected society as ours, this day is an even bigger statement. A day without money, economic consumption, and being plugged in is about as countercultural as it gets in present-day Western culture. For one day I refuse to define myself by what I do, watch, or buy.

This all sounds wonderful for the regular working person. But what about for social activists and all people working to make the world a better place? We have an urgent mission. There is real human suffering, and the world's climate is changing before our eyes. It seems like our work should be exempt from Shabbat. Jewish law deals with competing priorities all the time. Perhaps social-change activism is so important that it should continue even during Shabbat.

A close look at the reasons for the exemptions and restrictions on Shabbat reveals the exact opposite. *Tikkun olam* ("the repair of the world"), because of its importance, must cease on Shabbat. According to *halacha* (traditional Jewish law), one is exempt from Shabbat to save a life. Thus, many Jewish observant doctors and emergency personnel can work on Shabbat. Similarly, a seriously ill person and their caretakers can violate Shabbat restrictions, such as driving, using electricity, and cooking. While several reasons are given in the Talmud for these exemptions, I find the following verse the most compelling: "You shall keep My laws and My rules, by the pursuit of which *you shall live:* I am the Lord."[4] The rabbis interpret this verse to mean we should live by these rules, such as Shabbat, and not die by them. When Shabbat observance may cost life, it is a mitzvah to not observe Shabbat.[5]

How about social change? Would the organizing, advocacy, relationship building, acts of kindness, and fund-raising that generally make up our activities to improve the world fall under the category of "Live by them and don't die by them"? What if we are working to eradicate child slavery or toxic waste or nuclear weapons? These are life-and-death issues. However, they lack the immediacy needed to fit this category. "Live by them and don't die by them" means that if I keep Shabbat, I or someone else will most likely die or become more ill as a direct result of this Shabbat observance. Of course there are grey areas. However, with most tikkun olam activities, with the exception of health care, war, and immediate search-and-rescue missions, the results are more distant. Conceptually, there is a different category that better captures social-change activism. This is the *mishkan,* the sanctuary/tabernacle in the desert: "And let them make me a sanctuary that I may dwell among them."[6]

The mishkan was an amazing thing. As described in the book of Exodus, it was a portable temple, funded by communal donations, constructed by human hands, and a dwelling place for God's presence.[7] Once constructed, it was the most holy physical place in the universe. Death and imperfection could not enter the sanctuary. It was a place of wholeness, holiness, and peace. The mishkan, and later the Temple in Jerusalem, was a microcosm for the entire world. The Israelites needed to construct the mishkan in such a way that God's presence would dwell in it. Similarly, we need to build our societies in such a way that God's presence will dwell with us. While the mishkan was made of gold, silver, and bronze metals, wood, and leather, donated by rich and poor alike, our societies are built out of the institutions, associations, systems, and policies adopted by the entire community. Activists work to make these societies places where wholeness, holiness, and peace can dwell by creating just policies and social systems. While organizing to eliminate human trafficking does not save a life this hour, it moves society toward justice and is thus related to the holy work of constructing the mishkan.

It is exactly this holy work that the Torah teaches us must cease on Shabbat.[8] The Talmud teaches us that we learn about which activities are prohibited on Shabbat from the creative activities done in the mishkan. The mishkan is our model of creative activity. There is nothing more creative than building a space in which God's presence can dwell. Paradoxically it is this holy work that must cease on Shabbat. An essential part of the process for building a space for God's presence is to stop and notice God's presence. The awareness of wholeness is essential for the task of creating a space for wholeness, but in the creative act, the awareness is elusive—thus, the need to stop and retune ourselves to holiness.

This same dynamic is at work with social change. As we work to build a better society, we need to stop and notice the goodness and perfection that already exists. We need to remember the goodness and perfection in our own unique experiences to remember why we work to make a better, more perfect world for all. Activism so often involves polarization and anger, which, over time, are corrosive to the soul. Without taking time to stop, we can become embittered and cynical about the world. This is the paradox of ceasing the work of tikkun olam in order to fully realize tikkun olam. This paradox holds the answer to the dilemma about complicity and urgency. We need to stop and notice the big picture, the relationships we are trying to create, what creation can be, and the fact that the world is already good, to dive back in and effectively advocate for change. The truth about living righteously lies in holding the paradox of the real and the ideal.

It is true that the world is a mess, rife with exploitation and environmental degradation. It is also true that this world brims with beauty, perfection, and unbelievable human kindness. We need to fully immerse ourselves in this paradox, and Shabbat offers a solution. Dr. Parker J. Palmer, an educational philosopher, challenges us to embrace paradox: "In certain circumstances, truth is found not by splitting the world into either-ors but by embracing it as both-and. In certain circumstances, truth is a paradoxical joining of apparent opposites, and if we want to know that truth, we must learn to embrace those opposites as one."[9]

Rabbi Shaul Judelman, introduced in chapter 7, talks about how important this paradoxical aspect of Shabbat was to him coming off participating in the 1999 World Trade Organization protests in Seattle:

> I came to Israel months after these powerful, but very polarizing protests. If it was against the WTO, police brutality, or environmental work, the Us versus Them was a clear tenet throughout. I was just learning about Judaism and the idea that once a week you stop and get to come to terms with the world the way it is supposed to be. You stop your activity and spiritually have to let go of all the things I am trying to fix. You see that we are all in this together—the suits and the greenies and the turtles, everyone. Activists need to let go. There is a sense that it is all going to hell in a handbasket, and people burn out because the situation is so urgent. The way they present their case is so heavy.[10]

Rabbi Yitz Greenberg echoes the impact Shabbat can have on the activist's tone. He writes that Shabbat "gives the revolutionary a sunniness that comes from joy realized and mellows the puritanical fervor of the radical mission."[11] Holding the paradox between the real and the ideal helps activists not only live better lives, but also be more effective at winning allies by projecting not just anger and urgency, but also the joy that comes from experiencing wholeness.

## SHABBAT, WHOLENESS, AND HOLINESS

The word most associated with Shabbat is *kodesh*/holy. *Kiddush,* from the same Hebrew root Kuf. Dalet. Shin., is the ritual over grape juice or wine that starts Shabbat. *Holiness* is a tough word to define. To adapt Supreme Court justice Potter Stewart's famous formulation, "I know it when I see it," you know holiness when you experience it. Holiness is hard to describe because it animates our interiority more than our five senses. The word *kadosh* and its noun form, *kedusha*/ holiness, literally means "dedicated for a special or divine purpose." Someone or something holy is of God. Since God is One, experiencing holiness brings an awareness of the connection of all things and a broad perspective based on awareness of this ultimate oneness. It's opposite, *chol,* means "mundane" or "common" and reflects a sense of emptiness and disconnection among the parts that make up our lives. Nothing is particularly special. How do we experience holiness? When the angels describe God in Isaiah's prophecy as "Holy, Holy, Holy," the intention is that God is completely other and distinct from everything created in the universe.[12]

From these definitions it seems that holiness is experienced in very special moments when all the conditions are exactly right. Indeed, the most holy physical place in the world was the *kodesh kedoshim*/the Holy of Holies in the ancient Temple in Jerusalem. This was the location of the Ark of the Covenant, which contained the tablets brought down by Moses from Mount Sinai. Only one person, the high priest, was allowed to enter the Holy of Holies on one day of the year, Yom Kippur, at one particular time, during the special sacrificial service. So spiritually dangerous was this task that the high priest would enter the Holy of Holies with a rope tied around his ankle, so he could be pulled out lest something go wrong during the ritual and he die. In our materially oriented world, think of a scientist mixing incredibly potent chemicals that require 100 percent precise proportions or—*boom!* Holiness is potent, real, and very elusive.

If this were the whole story about holiness, Judaism would probably be a monastic religion with only a few highly dedicated and trained adherents. Fortunately there is another, democratizing aspect of holiness found most commonly in the mystical or spiritual schools of thought. Back to the angels: "Holy, Holy, Holy" is just the beginning of their proclamation about God. The sentence ends, "The entire earth is filled with God's glory."[13] The Jewish mystical tradition described it this way: "There is no place devoid of God."[14] Many Jewish spiritual teachers explain that it is possible to grasp God's presence—which is the essence of holiness—within every created thing.[15] Alan Morinis titled his book of Mussar, *Everyday Holiness*, to reflect the sensibility that we can access holiness by working on ourselves in the context of the mundane stuff of everyday life.

So, is holiness something distant and almost inaccessible, or does it exist on the tip of our tongue and with our next decision? Like many things in Judaism, it is both. Judaism's vitality over the millennia comes from this dynamic of distance and closeness. According to the kabbalistic drama of the universe described in the introduction, all creation was in the form of vessels. God's light/holiness shattered those vessels into little shards. Our human task is to identify and release these sparks of light/holiness in the shards through intentional living and thus repair the broken universe. Each time we see the potential in someone and help him or her realize that potential, we raise up sparks. When we make a blessing over food, thus recognizing the miracle of produce and the efforts of all those involved, we raise up sparks. When we align our middot (like those discussed in this book) with our values, we raise up sparks. Holiness may be special and separate, but it is readily accessible with discipline, learning, and effort. Our human task is to make this material world brim with the holiness that attests to its divine creation and reveals the connections that lie just under the surface of perception.

The dynamic between Shabbat and the six weekdays reflects the tension between transcendent and immanent holiness. During the six weekdays, we are so busy that it is hard to notice the constant flow of miracles that is this world. Even with the majestic charge to raise up the sparks, various deadlines, meetings, classes, and errands keep most people firmly grounded in the material aspects of the world, even for those of us in helping or more spiritual professions. Shabbat is like tuning a radio onto a different frequency: the holiness station. When we give ourselves permission to stop, the sparks of light shine brighter and a new, holy dimension of the world comes into focus. Shabbat trains our eyes and souls to sense holiness and connection, orienting us and making it possible to bring this perspective into our activism all week long. When grounded in awareness of these connections, our daily efforts to get one more restaurant to establish ethical labor and environmental practices, or convince three more legislators to sign onto a letter, fit into a greater vision of a world complete.

Social-change work by necessity takes place in small, incremental steps. When in the trenches of a campaign or helping one more person, it is easy to forget how each of these actions and successes is one more pole, curtain, or peg in the mishkan. Shabbat restores a perspective of how these individual acts connect to a greater whole. In addition, a perspective of connection supports us to bring more patience, trust, and creative thought to our work. Two aspects of Shabbat practice help us experience this orientation toward holiness and connection—protecting and celebrating.

There are two versions of the Ten Commandments in the Torah. In the first version in Exodus, we are told, "Remember the Sabbath to keep it holy."[16] In the second version in Deuteronomy, the charge is to "protect the Sabbath Day to keep it holy."[17] What is the difference between protecting and remembering? The Hebrew word for "protect" is *shamor*, which is the same word as "guard." What does a guard do? A guard watches over something to make sure it remains intact and able to function. In a spiritual sense, the guard ensures that the essence of the guarded item remains vital.[18]

The Talmud tells us that Shabbat is a gift from God to the Jewish people out of God's secret treasury. We are given Shabbat as guards. Shabbat has an inherent holiness, and our job is to protect that holiness. How does a guard protect that which is in his or her charge? Of course the task differs if we are talking about a donkey, an iPhone, or a toaster oven. In any case the guard will want to have a place to put the object that is well protected. What is the equivalent of a safe or desk drawer regarding Shabbat? Just as a safe is a bounded, closed-in area, so too do we create boundaries and metaphoric fences around Shabbat.

The Torah has two main categories of mitzvoth—positive and negative, or dos and don'ts. The don'ts are the boundaries. Don't carry objects from inside your house to out in the street; don't light or extinguish a fire; don't write or erase writing; don't plant or harvest crops; and the list goes on. As mentioned above, these don'ts are based on the creative activity used to build and maintain the Tabernacle in the desert. What was done to build that holy sanctuary is not done on Shabbat. By creating rules that limit activity, the sages created a boundary around this twenty-five-hour period to protect its holiness.

I experienced this most powerfully in my early days of observing Shabbat. The year before I began my practice, I worked as a high-school teacher in New York City. As a first-year teacher, I needed to use most of my Sundays for class preparation. Saturday was my one day off. This was my one day to do something fun and rejuvenating. This was my one day to visit friends and places in the city I hadn't yet visited. You get the idea. There was a lot of pressure for this one day to fulfill a lot of needs. I remember one Saturday morning, lying in bed, feeling very stressed out about whether I should go to the zoo or the Metropolitan Museum of Art or for a walk by the river on my day off. Paralyzed by the options, I would often feel disappointed about the choice I made because there were so many other options not chosen. What a relief it was when I started observing Shabbat. "Well, I can't use money, so the zoo is out; I can't travel on the train or bus, so the Met is out. What can I do?" Have a meal with friends, read, rest, go to synagogue, and walk to the free museum in my neighborhood to enjoy art. I felt such relief and freedom at living within the boundaries of Shabbat. The spaciousness I mentioned at the beginning of this chapter filled the day. By limiting the ability of my ego to call all the shots, I gained access to something much deeper than a visit to the zoo. I gained access to the holiness of Shabbat.

Reigning in our ego brings us back to the middot. The trait from our last chapter, bitachon/trust, is a big part of Shabbat observance. In fact, the first Shabbat in the Torah is framed as a test of trust. This test is given together with the manna described in the last chapter. After God promises to make bread fall from the sky, the Torah says,

> But on the sixth day when they count what they have brought in, it shall prove to be double the amount they gather each day . . . Tomorrow is a day of rest, a holy Sabbath of the Lord . . . Then Moses said, "Eat it today, for today is a Sabbath of the Lord; you will not find it today on the plain. Six days you shall gather it; on the seventh day, the Sabbath, there will be none." Yet some of the people went out on the seventh day to gather, but they found nothing. And the Lord said to Moses, "How long will you people refuse to obey My commandments and My teachings? Mark that the Lord has given you the Sabbath; therefore God gives you two days' food on the sixth day. Let everyone remain where he is; let no one leave his place on the seventh day."[19]

Can we stop acquiring and hording? Why do we need so much stuff? Shabbat is a test of trust because it is a day we need to accept that what we have is enough. We make our best efforts six days a week, and on Shabbat we trust that God has provided for all our needs. This trust gets tested in little ways all the time in Shabbat-observant homes. "Oops, I forgot to fill the water urn before Shabbat!" Our guests will be OK without tea or coffee. How one responds to these mini trust tests can be the difference between a tension-filled or tranquil home.

My wife and I were in the process of bidding on a condo on a Friday afternoon. As it got closer and closer to sundown, the brokers kept wanting to negotiate because the owner was going to accept a bid that night. We were competing with another buyer who wouldn't reveal his final bid. Minutes before Shabbat we faxed a bid and told the broker we would be out of touch until Saturday night. We would have no chance to respond to a higher bid from the other buyer. We needed to accept that the fate of this condo was now out of our hands. This was a test of trust. We both accepted that God was in charge at this point, which gave us a deep sense of peace.[20] Protecting Shabbat (*shmirat* Shabbat) with boundaries helps us grow in trust because it forces us to acknowledge that, ultimately, this world is much bigger than any of us. Despite how much we want it, control is elusive.

Ziesl Maayan describes how letting go of control on Shabbat helps her keep doing her life-changing nursing work. Maayan specializes in functional medicine and helps patients adopt healthier lifestyles while working to change the medical system to prioritize the individual patient over profits. She describes how crucial Shabbat is for her work:

> There is no way I could have done school or what I do if there wasn't Shabbat. The more plugged in we are—to have a day where all of that is gone is amazing. But also there is a deep way that when you really let Shabbat in, there is this letting go of deep holding. All week I hold on so tight to all the details of helping my patients. I don't find anything else that touches that deep holding as Shabbat. I don't put my patients out of my mind, but there is a letting go and presence that happens in Shabbat that doesn't happen any other time.[21]

Letting go, while still being fully committed to change over the long term, is the gift of Shabbat.

If Shabbat were just about the boundaries, it would get awfully repressive. There is not much enjoyment in just protecting.

Boundaries are important, but an exclusive emphasis on boundaries can make one feel quite empty. Think of a glass of water. The glass represents the Shabbat restrictions, and the water represents the things we do to express the holiness of the day. These activities are what help us remember, or celebrate, Shabbat.

Remembering Shabbat includes saying blessings over wine or grape juice, eating especially delicious food, and wearing special clothes. Shabbat is not just a day of refraining from activity. It is a day of special activity. The first-century sage Shammai would look for extraspecial cuts of meat at the butcher during the week and save them for Shabbat.[22] Yossi Moker Shabbos, a figure from ancient Jewish lore, paid huge sums of money for the best delicacies on Shabbat. In my family we all have our Shabbat clothes and our special Shabbat meal. For many families this is a roasted chicken. As a vegetarian family with an affinity for the Far East, we love our soba noodle soup and sushi. If holiness means "special" or "different," we respond to holiness by doing something special and different from the rest of the week.

*Oneg* Shabbat, or "delighting in Shabbat," is another way we fill the day. Oneg, which also means "joy," includes singing, eating sweets, chatting with friends, playing games with our children, walking in nature, and taking nice long naps. These are some of the great things in life that we are working so hard to achieve. Once we succeed in creating environmentally sustainable social systems that honor the dignity of all people, our lives would look a lot like oneg Shabbat, including lots of time for song, play, and human connection. By living this ideal once a week, the dream maintains its motivational pull by remaining within our mental grasp.[23]

## PRACTICE 1: *Create a Shabbat/Rest Practice*

This can be as short as one hour, and it doesn't need to be on Friday night and Saturday. Of course, if you practice during the time marked by

Friday sundown to Saturday at nightfall, you will have others to join with in your rest and celebration, and you will be aligning your rest time with that of other Shabbat-observing Jews in your area. The main thing is to choose a beginning and end time and stick with your commitment, at least once. You can choose whether you want to repeat the experiment.

Create a boundary around this time that will help you really take a break from your world-changing and other regular activities. This boundary can include turning off your phone and/or computer or just not checking e-mail. It could include not driving a car. Whatever you choose as your boundary markers, they should remind you that you are not carrying on with regular life for this time period.

What oneg, or delights, do you want to do during your Shabbat? You may want to fill it with silence, reading, play, prayer, communal meals, singing, or walks in nature. Choose activities that really help you rest and that you love. These are activities that remind you of your best self and of how connected you are.

Entering and leaving Shabbat are as important to the practice as the rest itself. Think about your Shabbat in advance, and plan for how you will create your boundary and the elements you want to bring with you into the time. Mark the beginning of Shabbat with a ritual. This can include lighting candles, taking a bath or shower, putting on special clothes. These rituals will help your unconscious make the shift from regular time to Shabbat time. Use a *havdala* ceremony to end Shabbat. *Havdala* means "separation" and traditionally includes verses from Psalms, blessings, wine or grape juice, spices, and candles. You can use the traditional ceremony (found in most prayer books and online) or make up your own havdala, to mark the transition from your Shabbat to back into the world. The important thing is to re-enter with intention. Include in your ceremony naming an intention you have for how you want to be or something you want to do during the coming week.

## PRACTICE 2: *Living the Ideal*

You are working for social change to accomplish something. Perhaps you organize domestic workers, so they can work with dignity, free from harassment. Or you are trying to get government regulations changed to reduce greenhouse gases, or you are working to improve relations between Jews and Muslims or working to end police violence against black men. What is one element of success that you can experience right now? For example, regarding domestic workers, at the core of this campaign is dignity. In an ideal world, all people would work with dignity, including you. What is one way you can treat yourself with dignity? For some people it is exercising or getting enough sleep. For others it is wearing clean, pressed clothes. Do this thing for at least a week, and pay attention to what dignity feels like. This experience of dignity is a taste of the world you are trying to create for everyone.

As an environmental activist, make sure you actually spend time enjoying the natural world through daily hikes or periodic camping trips. If you work to make the world better for young people, make sure you spend fun, unpressured play time with young people to remind you how much you enjoy these relationships. These are all examples of ways you can get a "taste of the world to come" on the way to achieving our social-change goals.

## Summary

Shabbat is called "a taste of the world to come."[24] To the contemporary sensibility, "the world to come" is a strange concept. To come when? Is there another world? The most useful understanding I've come to is that this is a world of pure spirituality. If we live in a world, this world, where the spiritual and material are all mixed together, the world to come is all spiritual. In the world to come, thoughts and emotions communicate automatically without the need for air to vibrate in vocal cords and project sounds. The intuitive sense that all things are connected is a mundane reality, experienced by all. In the world to come, meaning is clear and no longer hidden behind mistaken interpretations of victory and suffering. This all-spiritual world speaks the language of our soul but is beyond our grasp as incarnate creatures. We can taste, glimpse, and hear faint notes from this all-spiritual world. Sharing a good laugh, achieving a long-sought-after victory, comforting or receiving comfort, creating beauty are all activities that can bring us a glimpse of that world.

Shabbat is a day each week when our experience of this world is amplified. Pure spirituality is more accessible than usual. A world of peace and justice is about as close as we can get to creating the world to come here in this world. Once a week we can get just enough of a taste of what real peace and justice feel like to reignite our ratzon/motivation to keep going for another six days. Our charge is to bring this taste of spirituality, or connection, meaning and joy, into the week. Ultimately Jewish tradition holds out hope that each day will be *yom sh'kulo* Shabbat, a day that is "completely Shabbat." May our efforts to change the world be part of bringing this into reality.

# CONCLUSION

In my last months of writing the manuscript for this book, Pope Francis released *Laudato Si': On Care for Our Common Home*, his treatise on the global ecological crisis. In it, he clearly states the connection between the inner life and environmental destruction. Gratitude, sobriety, and humility are among the traits he calls on humanity to develop, not just as individuals, but as communities dedicated to responsible global stewardship. He points to greed and fear of scarcity as causes of the overconsumption driving climate change. This book is a Jewish approach to transforming our inner lives in the process of, and for the sake of, transforming the world. Its premise is that inner and outer change must coexist and be mutually reinforcing.

The challenges we face as a human race, be it climate change or the Israeli-Arab conflict, are too big and complex to be solved quickly. We will need all the resources at our disposal to engage with wisdom, nuance, determination, and fortitude over generations to heal and reverse the dynamics that led to these crises. The good news is that Judaism, and other traditions, have plenty of the resources needed to root social-change activism in the deep waters of ancient wisdom. This book presented a path made up of clarifying deep motivation, channeling unconscious drives, seeking good, making choices, and aligning behavior with values as a way to live a life a service. It is my hope that those who read this book will find their lives and their social-change efforts deepened and made even more effective, so we can fulfill our roles as full partners with the source of all life in the completing of creation.

## ACKNOWLEDGMENTS

This book represents close to thirty years of experiences, learning, conversations, and thinking. I feel deeply grateful for the many people who mentored me and walked this path of Judaism and activism with me. I learned much of what I know about activism, organizing, and anti-oppression work from Jacqueline Debets, Malcolm Garcia, Michael Saxe-Taller, Dr. Sander Connolly, Judy Blochowiak, Nancy K. Kaufman, Joel Nogic, Jaye Alper, Cherie Brown, Marya Axner, and Diane Balser and Meir Lakein. My Christian colleagues, particularly the Reverend Eugene Rivers, Reverend Ray Hammond, and Bishop Krister Stendhal, gave me living models of faith and justice integrated.

While I had a warm Jewish upbringing, my real engagement with the transformative power of Judaism began as a young adult. Rabbi Shira Liebowitz recommended I study at the Pardes Institute. There, Rabbis Meir Schweiger and Aryeh ben David unlocked the awesome power and depth of Torah study. Rabbi Yitz Greenberg's teachings gave me a broad picture of Judaism and my place therein. He later became a personal mentor, particularly in the area of Mussar. I'm privileged to be in the orbit of such a great man. Rabbi Dr. Ariel Burger introduced me to the teachings of Rebbe Nachman of Breslov and was instrumental in practically every Torah endeavor I've undertaken. Rabbis Shaya Karlinsky and Yitzchak Hirshfeld of Yeshivat Darchei Noam helped me to learn Gemara and introduced me to Mussar and Rabbi Shlomo Wolbe. Rabbi Natan Greenberg is my rabbi. From the first time we met I knew I needed to learn Torah with him as my primary spiritual guide. It is his vision of intense avodah (spiritual practice) integrated with openness to the world that motivates me and that I try to express in this book. Rabbi

Dr. Marc Gopin inspires me with his union of ancient wisdom and conflict transformation. Rabbi Erez Gazit gave me a picture of a deep and committed Torah-based spiritual practice.

Dr. Alan Morinis, more than anyone else, is responsible for the growing awareness of Mussar in North America. He is my teacher, colleague, and friend. His influence echoes throughout this book and I am especially thankful to him for recommending me to Shambhala Publications. As a first-time author I am grateful for the good people at Shambhala, particularly my editor Beth Frankl, whose enthusiasm, advice, and hand-holding has been a constant source of invaluable encouragement. Thank you as well to assistant editors Audra Figgins and Gretchen Gordon.

Rabbi Beth Lieberman provided excellent editorial advice in turning a rough manuscript into a successful book proposal. Thank you to readers Rose Sadler, David Schwartz, and Mimi Michner. My friends and peer coaches Dr. Benyamin Lichtenstein, Dr. Marilyn Paul, and Rabbi Natan Margalit kept me moving forward. My good buddy, John Englander, is the best writer I know. I am grateful for his work on the Shabbat chapter and his lifelong companionship. To all the folks who agreed to be interviewed for this book—thank you for your passionate dedication to justice and your inner lives. I am grateful to the Dorot Fellowship in Israel Task Force, particularly Steve Jacobson, for their ongoing support of this project.

This book would not have been possible if I hadn't had years of opportunities to teach Mussar and Chassidic practices. For that, I am thankful to all my students and colleagues. Rabbis Marc Baker and Lisa Goldstein—friends, chevrutas, and extraordinary leaders—gave me the opportunity to teach respectively at Gann Academy and with the Institute for Jewish Spirituality. The Mussar Institute, on whose board I served, has been a wonderful home for learning and teaching.

I am grateful to Kurt Schneider for always pushing me to think and dream big. To my childhood friend Billy Smithline, who was so full of life and whose premature death motivated my spiritual search. My parents, Alan and Liz Jaffe, are unceasingly generous.

The values they taught—community, family, and education—continue to guide my life. Anything I have accomplished is due to them. I love my two boys, Tani and Binyamin, beyond words. They are mensches and keep reminding me to play. I am deeply blessed to spend every day with my soul-mate, Janette Hillis-Jaffe. Her wisdom, beauty, fierceness, compassion, and goodness enrich me and all who know her. I never knew such love was possible.

Finally, I am grateful for a life-long relationship with the Holy One, whose will I try to discern and in whose service I try to live my life. My prayer and hope is that this book creates more space in our hearts and the world for God's presence and the deep connections that come with the awareness of the Source of all Life.

# APPENDIX A: FACILITATOR'S GUIDE

The ideas presented in the book are probably not surprising or new for many readers. They are things you know intuitively or have heard before. The important thing is practice. The goal of this book is to support the change maker and the project of social change with ancient Jewish wisdom for right living. This wisdom will only have an impact if it is internalized, and internalization only comes from practice and repetition. Over 250 years ago, Rabbi Moshe Chaim Luzzatto wrote in the introduction to his classic, *Mesilat Yesharim* (*Path of the Just*), that while his book contained few new ideas, its power lay in the repetition and internalization that make the words come alive. You can do the practices in the book alone, but they will be more effective if you have a partner or, even better, a group with whom to practice. I speak from over a decade of experience with these practices: absent a partner or group that meets regularly, it is almost impossible to stay committed. This appendix is a guide for convening a practice group. Every other week is a good pace for these groups to meet because it gives time to settle into the practices and meet with your partner on the off week. Some groups choose to have one facilitator for the entire duration, and others switch off each session.

## 1. *Contemplative Opening (10–15 minutes)*

Help people make the transition to the contemplative space of the group through the following two activities, in whatever order makes most sense for your group. Depending on time, you can do one or both.

*Opening meditation/reading/song/video (5 minutes):* The purpose of this activity is to help people open the affective part of their being. Different participants can be assigned to bring a short reading, video, and so forth to share with the group.

*Dyad/check-in (5 minutes):* The purpose of the check-in is to direct each person's attention to the present. Each member of the pair gets two minutes of uninterrupted attention before switching.

Good points: The first speaker says something positive about his or her day or week. It can be something as small as enjoying a meal.

Getting attention: The first speaker then gets the full attention of his or her partner for the remainder of the two minutes. He or she can use this attention anyway he or she wants. The speaker can talk about something troubling from the day, sit in silence, think through something on his or her mind. The attention of the listener will help the speaker clear his or her mind and be present for the group. The listener can ask questions as appropriate.

After the set amount of time, the speaker and listener switch roles.

## 2. Va'ad (35–40 minutes)

*Va'ad* is the classic Mussar movement term for a group of people who join together to support each other's growth. The purpose of the va'ad is to provide group attention and accountability for each member regarding the practices of the past period of time.

If this is your first meeting, the process will be different than what is described below. For your first meeting, discuss the ground rules found in appendix B. Then invite each participant to share a moment when they learned something about themselves from their social-change efforts. You can ask any question that connects the inner life and social change. Give people three minutes each to share. After everyone who wants to share has done so, skip to the *Silence* prompt below.

*Review (3–5 minutes):* Allow some time for people to review their journals and think about what they want to say during their time in the va'ad. Remind them of the practices from last session.

*Sharing (3 minutes per person):* Try to keep the va'ad sharing to no more than thirty minutes. If the group consists of more than eight, you may want to break up into groups of three or four to save time.

Note: The time boundary is important during the sharing. Have a timer with a bell that will alert the speaker that time is up. People can finish their thought or sentence, but if they go on considerably longer, the facilitator needs to remind them that their time is up. Maintaining the time boundary is essential to ensuring the safety of the group.

Cross talk is not permitted during the sharing portion of the va'ad. It is OK to say thank you or something equally benign after someone speaks, although warm and accepting body language is just as good. If a member starts to give advice or comment, it is very important to interrupt and remind the group to avoid cross talk during the va'ad so as to maintain safety. You can refer to the guidelines.

*Silence (1 minute):* It is important to provide this quiet time to honor and process what was just shared, before entering a discussion.

*Discussion (10 minutes):* This is for open discussion and the sharing of observations about the practices, ideas, or traits. Ask people to share insights or questions they have about practice. If you separated the group into small groups, bring everyone together for the discussion.

Note: It is not the time for giving or seeking advice. If someone does give advice, direct that person back to sharing about his or her own experience of what was said or about the issue. If someone asks for advice, redirect the question to be about the issue in general and not his or her specific case.

## 3. Break (5 minutes)

## 4. Study (35–40 minutes)

The purpose of study is to explore the Jewish wisdom about the concept, or trait.

*Introduction (3–5 minutes):* Each session can focus on a different chapter, or you can spend more than one session on a chapter. The facilitator should read the chapter in advance and choose which sections to learn together as a group, if you are not going to read through the whole chapter. The facilitator gives a brief overview of the chapter.

*Partner learning (10–15 minutes):* In pairs, have the group learn the selections from the chapter and answer any reflection questions. You may also choose to stay together as a group to read the material. Please note that groups work best when there are a variety of modalities, including full group discussion, dyad work, and individual contemplation.

*Discussion (10 minutes):* Discuss the main points in the readings with a focus on the reflection questions if those were included in your selection.

## 5. Practice: (15 minutes)

*Review the practices (10 minutes):* Each chapter has practices either at the end or interspersed in the chapter. Choose the practices on which you want to focus, and review them with the group. You can use this time to try a practice like those described in chapters 2 and 4.

Solicit questions about the practice and experience from others with the practice as a form of mutual support among the group. For example, ask the group if they have questions about using focus phrases. If someone says he or she is having trouble finding an opportune time to say the phrase, you can ask what others have found helpful in terms of making time to say the phrase. For the middot/trait chapters, review the practice sheet carefully with the group.

*Decide on practices for between group meetings (5 minutes):* In pairs or in silent contemplation, each member decides on a personal practice. For the character traits chapters, these can include a focus phrase, personal kabbalah, or time and place for soul accounting.

*Closing circle (5 minutes):* Each person shares at least one practice that they will try out before the next meeting.

Note: Have spiritual check-in partners set a time to meet before the next group session. They should set this time before they leave this session.

# APPENDIX B: VA'AD/GROUP GUIDELINES

Practice groups work best when participants feel safe enough to share with each other about their personal journeys and practice. To create a container that encourages such sharing, ask that participants agree to the following guidelines (adapted from the Institute for Jewish Spirituality's document "How We Make for Safety").

1. Know that there is genuine freedom in the group. We do not engage in "forced sharing." Every invitation to speak and participate is just that: an invitation. Passing or staying quiet is perfectly acceptable.

2. We do not engage in "fixing . . . saving . . . advising . . . or setting each other straight" (Parker J. Palmer). Each of us is here to refine our ability to listen to the still, small voice inside. Trust that we will all find our own way and refrain from acting on the desire to give advice. Open questions that help the speaker probe deeper into his or her inner life are welcome at designated times.

3. Give your full attention to the person speaking. Do not engage in side conversations. Use "I" statements when speaking. Be aware of how much space you are taking up.

4. Respect difference. Remind yourself that other people are not failed attempts at being you! Cultivate curiosity.

5. Each person in the va'ad commits to both conventional and "double" confidentiality. Conventional confidentiality means that we do not speak to anyone outside the group about what is shared in this group. "Double" confidentiality means that

when a person shares a confidence that we sense makes him or her vulnerable, we do not raise the issue again with that person or anyone else in the group, without the invitation of the person in question.

# APPENDIX C: SPIRITUAL CHECK-IN/ *SICHAT CHAVERIM* GUIDELINES

The check-in has the following purposes:

- To help one another access his or her best thinking about how to develop the middah/practice in question and how to model this behavior for others.

- To hold one another accountable for progress toward self-determined goals.

- To inspire one another by hearing about each other's practice.

Schedule a regular time to meet with your partner. Ideally this meeting will be midway between the group meetings. Please allot no less than one half hour for the check-in.

## Good Points/Letting Go (4 minutes: 2 minutes each way)

- Choose someone to be the talker and someone to be the listener.

- The talker starts by sharing one thing that is new and good since the last time they saw each other. This can be some small positive thing, like a visit from a friend or a good inter-action with a coworker, family member, or friend. It does not necessarily have to pertain to the middah you are studying.

- The talker then shares about any little upsets or distractions that might get in the way of being present for this session. The listener uses active-listening skills to keep the other person talking without interrupting.

- Switch roles, and the other person now gets three minutes to speak.

## Journal (5 minutes)

Take five minutes to write a new journal entry and/or review your journal entries from the past few weeks.

## Presentation (20 minutes: 10 minutes each way)

- Choose someone to present first.

- Start by reviewing the practice goals you set at the last group meeting.

- State at least one thing that is going well (a good point) with your practice.

- The presenter can then talk about any particular aspects of practice that he or she would like help thinking about. This can be something from personal practice or modeling the middah for others. It can also include thoughts and questions about our readings.

## The Listener

The role of the listener is to act as a peer coach. A peer coach can use open, honest questions to elicit the best thinking of the presenter without inserting judgment or advice. The presenter can ask for feedback at the end of his or her turn if he or she wants.

Switch roles and follow the same steps.

# NOTES

## A Note about Jewish Sources

I refer to biblical sources by their more commonly known English names: for example, Genesis, Leviticus, Samuel, Isaiah, and Psalms. Unless otherwise indicated, I use the Jewish Publication Society Hebrew–English Bible for biblical translations: *Tanakh: The Holy Scriptures: The New JPS Translation according to the Traditional Hebrew Text* (Philadelphia: Jewish Publication Society, 1985). I use the original Hebrew titles for less well-known postbiblical sources. These sources are known collectively as the Oral Torah and they range in date from the second Jewish commonwealth (440 B.C.E.–70 C.E.) until today. These include the Mishna, the Talmud, the Midrash, commentaries and legal codes, and question and responses from legal authorities. Originally passed down from teacher to student orally, these teachings were eventually committed to writing. Mishna is a collection of teachings of Jewish legal theory. The Talmud is a massive work of over two thousand pages of extended discussion and debate based on the Mishna. The Babylonian Talmud was the product of Jewish society along the Tigris and Euphrates rivers during 200–600 C.E. The Jerusalem Talmud was the product of similar discussions in Israel during 200–400 C.E. The Midrash are homiletic and legal commentaries and interpretations of verses in the Bible dating from the second commonwealth until today. The legal codes attempt to codify behaviors for right living discussed in the Talmud. The codes date from the eleventh to the sixteenth centuries C.E. The legal responses are a fascinating genre of correspondence between religious adherents and religious authorities about how to interpret the law in different times and circumstances over a period of close to two thousand years through today.

This book draws widely from sources in the Oral Torah, especially the volume of Mishna known as Pirkei Avot, "The Ethics of the Fathers." This is one of the earliest pieces of ethical literature in the Oral Torah. You will also find references to various volumes of Midrash and Talmud, such as Midrash Tanhuma and Talmud tractate Derekh Eretz Zuta about ethical behavior. This is all in addition to the Mussar and Hasidic sources quoted throughout. Unless otherwise indicated the translations are my own. Jewish literature has an endless, oceanic quality to it. This short note should give the reader a basic sense of the breadth of this sea. May the sources you learn in this book give a sense of its awesome depth.

## Introduction

1. See Leviticus 19 and many sections of Deuteronomy, including chapters 8–11.
2. Mishna Avot; Tractate Derekh Eretz Zuta. Several collections in the oral tradition are sources of wisdom about ethical behavior. The most well-known include a volume of the Mishna, Pirkei Avot, and Derekh Eretz Zuta, a volume of Talmud dedicated to interpersonal relations.

## Part One: The Compass

### Chapter 1. Motivations for Change: What Do You Yearn For?

1. Rabbi Shlomo Wolbe, *Aley Shur* (Jerusalem: Beit HaMussar, 1986), 2:257–58.
2. Rabbi Shlomo Wolbe, *Essays on the Days of Desire* (Jerusalem: publisher unknown, 2005), 3–5.
3. This inclination is called the *yetzer harah* in traditional literature and is the subject of chapter 2.
4. Leviticus 19:1.
5. Rabbi Nathan of Breslov, *Advice (Lekutei Etzot)*, Avraham Greenbaum, trans., (Jerusalem: Breslov Research Institute, 1983), 245. For a Hebrew version, see Rabbi Natan of Breslov, "Ratzon v'Kisufim 1," in *Lekutei Etzot* (Jerusalem: Odesser Foundation, n.d.), 626. Rabbi Nachman writes that ratzon is the reality, or being, of the soul. I thank Rabbi Ariel Burger for making me aware of this source.
6. I heard this idea from Rabbi Michael Rosen of Yakar Jerusalem in September 2000.

7. This dynamic affects women in a particular way. One aspect of women's oppression is that many girls and women are taught that their complete worth lies in taking care of others. This message can make it difficult to know what one really wants separate from the needs and desires of others.

8. Rabbi Shmuel Shapira was one of the great Breslov Hasidim in Jerusalem in the second half of the twentieth century. Every day he immersed in the *mikva*, or communal ritual bath, as was customary among Hasidim. As he got older and had a difficult time moving, he had a helper named Yitzhak pick him up and accompany him to the mikva in the morning. Finally Rabbi Shmuel became too ill to go to the mikva even with Yitzhak's help. The first morning he couldn't go to mikva, he called out, "Yitzhak, is that you?" His wife came into the bedroom and reminded Rabbi Shmuel that Yitzhak wasn't coming any more. Rabbi Shmuel replied, "I know, but at least I can yearn to go." This story illustrates the central role of yearning as an act in itself in Breslov Hasidism. I first heard this story from Rabbi Ariel Burger.

9. Deutermony 30.

10. I first heard this idea from Rabbi Yitz Greenberg in the name of Rabbi Joseph B. Soloveitchik. Rabbi Soloveitchik's idea of *shlichut*, or "life purpose," was composed of these elements.

11. The human propensity for greed, hate, and harmful behavior is certainly part of our makeup, which we will explore in chapter 2, but this destructive drive is not associated with the essence of an individual.

12. I first learned about the relationship between solidarity, empathy, sympathy, and pity from the American Jewish World Service.

13. Founded in 1934, the Jewish Labor Committee is the voice of labor in the Jewish community and the voice of the Jewish community to organized labor. The JLC mobilizes Jewish support for worker's rights around the world. New England JLC executive director Marya Axner supported me with advice and counsel during the "ethical contractor" campaign.

14. Jack Canfield, *The Success Principles* (New York: HarperCollins, 2005), 54–55.

15. See Rabbi Gedalia Fleer, *Against All Odds* (Jerusalem: Breslov Research Institute, 2005), for the full story of his travels to Rabbi Nachman's gravesite.

16. 1 Samuel 1:10–13.

17. See Rabbi Ozer Bergman, *Where Heaven and Earth Kiss* (Jerusalem: Breslov Research Institute, 2006), for a book-length description of hitbodedut practice.

18. According to Rabbi Nachman, hitbodedut is the primary vehicle for developing desire. Rabbi Nachman also advocated turning Torah into *tefila* (prayer), as follows: Immediately after hearing or reading an inspiring teaching, turn that teaching into a prayer. You can write the prayer or just speak it out loud. The key is to articulate in your own words your desire to internalize what you

learned or for that teaching to become a reality. The more emotion you can put into the prayer the better. The prayer doesn't need to use formal prayer language, like "Blessed are you . . ." Rather, it is simply an expression of your desire to acquire that particular teaching. Like with hitbodedut, ideally this prayer is said outdoors in a place where you will not be disturbed. However, a room, car, or private corner is also good (based on Rabbi Nachman of Breslov, "Turning Torah into Prayer," in *Outpouring of the Soul*, Rabbi Aryeh Kaplan, trans. [Jerusalem: Breslov Research Institute, 1980], pp. 22–3).

## Chapter 2: Serving with Our Full Selves: The Yetzer Harah

1. Anthony Wright, "Limbic System: Amygdala," in *Neuroscience Online* (Houston: University of Texas Medical School), section 4, chapter 6, http://nba.uth.tmc.edu/neuroscience/s4/chapter06.html (accessed June 2015).

2. Rabbi Israel Salanter, "Letter 30," in *Ohr Yisrael*, Zvi Miller, trans. (Southfield, MI: Targum Press, 2004), 320–21.

3. Genesis 1:31: "God looked at all that God had done and behold, it was very good."

4. Genesis Rabbah 9:7. Genesis Rabbah is an ancient collection of homilies based on verses from the book of Genesis.

5. Babylonian Talmud Sanhedrin 91b.

6. Babylonian Talmud Yoma 69b.

7. Genesis Rabbah 9:7.

8. Nachmanides commentary on Genesis 1:12. Nachmanides, also known by the acronym of his name, Ramban, was one of the great Torah commentators and Talmudists of thirteenth-century Spain.

9. Wolbe, *Essays on the Days of Desire*, 2.

10. Babylonian Talmud Shabbat 105b.

11. Genesis 6:5.

12. Genesis 4:7. I am going after the interpretation of the word *chatat* as the yetzer harah. Literally this word means "sin," or "missing the mark." This verse is also the proof text that Rabbi Yehuda Hanassi brings to support Antinonus's point that the yetzer comes in at birth and not at conception. The word for "door" in our verse is the same word used to mean, "opening of the womb." See Babylonian Talmud Sanhedrin 91b.

13. This section, "Transforming the Yetzer," is a paraphrase of Rabbi Salanter, "Letter 30," in *Ohr Yisrael*, and Rabbi Shlomo Wolbe, "Intellect, Emotion and Enthusiasm," in *Aley Shur*, 2:165–69.

14. These practices are alternately referred to in Hasidic and Mussar traditions as *tikkun hayetzer* (transformation of the yetzer), *tikkun hamiddot* (transformation of the soul traits), and *ha'alat hamiddot* (raising up of the soul traits).

15. Rabbi Salanter, "Letter 7," *Ohr Yisrael*, 190.

16. Soul-accounting narrative journaling is a practice developed by Alan Morinis, founder of the Mussar Institute.

17. Babylonian Talmud Shabbat 156a.

18. Greg Kaufmann, "The Wall Comes Tumbling Down," *Nation*, October 18, 2010, http://www.thenation.com/blog/155437/wall-comes-tumbling-down#.

19. Policy Link, "Tomato Workers in Florida Remake an Industry," May 26, 2014, http://www.policylink.org/blog/tomato-workers-fl-remake-industry.

20. Evan Perez, "Major Grower to Join Wage Plan," *Wall Street Journal*, October 13, 2010, http://www.wsj.com/articles/SB10001424052748704763904575550550086511426.

## Part Two: Signposts

## Chapter 3. A Little Light Overcomes Much Darkness: Seeking Good Points

1. Rabbi Natan Sternhartz, "Orech Chayyim," in *Lekutei Halachot* (Jerusalem: Meshech HaNachal, 1999), vol. 1, lesson 1, parts 1–2. *Lekutei Halachot* is Rabbi Sternhartz's collected teachings about Jewish law based on the teachings of Rabbi Nachman of Breslov. "Orech Chayyim," meaning "The Way of Daily Life," is the first of four sections in one of the classic organizational systems of Jewish law. The other sections are "Holidays," "Marital Relations," and "Civil Law."

2. "Incarceration in the United States," Wikipedia, http://en.wikipedia.org/wiki/Incarceration_in_the_United_States#Race, accessed October 28, 2015.

3. Harriet Sherwood, "Global Refugee Figure Passes 50 Million for First Time since World War II," *Guardian*, June 20, 2014, http://www.theguardian.com/world/2014/jun/20/global-refugee-figure-passes-50-million-unhcr-report.

4. "Hate Crimes Statistics," the website of the Federal Bureau of Investigation, December 8, 2014, http://www.fbi.gov/news/stories/2014/december/latest-hate-crime-statistics-report-released/latest-hate-crime-statistics-report-released.

5. Much of the Jewish wisdom in this chapter is taken from Breslov teachings about good points. For further study see Rabbi Nachman, *Lekutei Moharan* (Jerusalem: Torat HaNetzach, 1997), 1:282; Rabbi Natan Sternhartz, *Lekutei Tefilot* (Jerusalem: Rabbi Odesser Foundation, n.d.), 513–20 (prayer 90). *Lekutei Tefilot* is a collection of Rabbi Sternhartz's personal prayers based on Rabbi Nachman's teachings. There is an English language version of *Lekutei Tefilot* by the Breslov Research Institute called *The Fiftieth Gate*, Avraham Greenbaum, trans. (Jerusalem, 1992). See also Rabbi Sternhartz, *Lekutei Halachot*, 1:1:1–2 ("The Way of Daily Life"), and *Advice*, 88 ("Encouragement").

6. Rabbi Nachman, *Lekutei Moharan*, 1:282. See the Breslov Research Institute

edition for an English translation.

7. Meir Lakein, senior organizer for JOIN for Justice, interview, February 2015.

8. Pirkei Avot 1:6.

9. Ibid.

10. Rabbi Wolbe, *Aley Shur*, vol. 2.

11. Babylonian Talmud Shabbat 127b.

12. Rabbi Aaron Leibowitz, Jerusalem city councilor with the Yerushalmim Party, interview, January 2015.

13. For example, see Sara Rimer and Madeline Drexler, "Happiness and Health," *Harvard Public Health*, winter 2011, http://www.hsph.harvard.edu/news/magazine/happiness-stress-heart-disease/ .

14. Rabbi Nachman, *Lekutei Moharan*, 2:24.

15. I heard this description from Rabbi Natan Greenberg, February 2015.

16. Rabbi Nachman, *Lekutei Moharan*, 1:282.

17. Rabbi Sternhartz, *Lekutei Halachot*, 1:1:1–2 ("The Way of Daily Life").

18. See chapter 1, note 6.

19. The IFS model, developed by Richard Schwartz, is a form of psychotherapy that sees different parts of the psyche (the wounded-child part, the defender part, the creative part, etc.) as members of a family that can be organized by the Self. The more the Self asserts primacy rather than any individual part, the happier and better functioning is the individual. Mastering the use of self-energy is one the goals of IFS therapy. See https://www.selfleadership.org/ for more information about IFS.

20. Rabbi Nachman, *Lekutei Moharan*, 1:282.

21. Rabbi Eliyahu Touger, trans., *Maimonides Mishneh Torah: Laws of Repentance* (New York: Moznaim, 1990), 3:1.

22. Proverbs 27:19. Also see Tosafot's commentary to Babylonian Talmud Pesachim 113b, "Sh'Ra'ah," for a discussion of how people respond in kind to the way they are thought about and treated. Tosafot is the name of a group of medieval Talmud commentators in France and Germany.

23. "Protest Song," Wikipedia, http://en.wikipedia.org/wiki/Protest_song, accessed February 8, 2016.

24. Stacy Horn, "Singing Changes Your Brain," *Time*, August 16, 2013 , http://ideas.time.com/2013/08/16/singing-changes-your-brain/.

25. Peter Yarrow, live concert, Roots Center, Gush Etzion (West Bank), March 17, 2015.

## Chapter 4: The Power of Choice

1. Rabbi Eliyahu E. Dessler, *Strive for Truth, Part 2*, Aryeh Carmell, trans. (Jerusalem: Feldheim, 1978), 49–50. *Strive for Truth* is the English-language translation of the first volume of Rabbi Dessler's five-volume *Miktav M'Eliyahu*.

2. Rabbi Dessler, *Strive for Truth*, 53.

3. Ibid., 54.

4. Ibid.

5. I first heard this idea from Rabbi David Lapin at the Mussar Institute Kallah, October 2010.

6. I am thankful to Timi Gerson, the advocacy director at American Jewish World Service, for making me aware of this process.

7. Ziesl Maayan, interview, February 2015.

8. David Schwarz, interview, April 2015.

9. Rabbi Shmuly Yanklowitz, interview, June 2015.

10. Martin Luther King Jr., "Letter from Birmingham Jail," in *I Have a Dream: Writings and Speeches That Changed the World*, James Melvin Washington, ed. (San Francisco: HarperCollins, 1992), 86–87.

11. Lakein, interview, February 2015.

### Part Three: Walking the Path

1. Mussar classics, like Rabbi Moshe Chaim Luzzatto, *The Paths of the Just/Mesillat Yesharim*, Shraga Silverstein, trans. (Jerusalem: Feldheim, 1966), and *The Ways of the Righteous/Orchot Tzaddikim*, Shraga Silverstein, trans. (Jerusalem: Feldheim, 1995), are organized specifically by middot. Hasidic works, such as Rabbi Nachman of Breslov, *The Alef-Bet Book*, Moshe Mykoff, trans. (Jerusalem: Breslov Research Institute, 1986), are also structured according to middot.

2. Maimonides, *The Eight Chapters*, Yaakov Feldman, trans. (Southfield, MI: Targum Press, 2008) 121–22.

3. Maimonides, *Mishneh Torah: Laws of Character Development* (Jerusalem: Wagshal, 1984), 1:4.

4. Salanter, *Ohr Yisrael*, 318–19.

5. David Lapin, *Lead by Greatness* (Charleston, SC: Avoda Books, 2012), 15–16. The version of this analogy I use in this book is closer to the description I heard from Rabbi Lapin at the Mussar Institute Kallah in New York City, November 2009.

### Chapter 5: Practice

1. Rabbi Moshe Chaim Luzzatto, *The Path of the Just*, Shraga Silverstein, trans. (Feldheim: New York 1966), 3

2. Quoted in Alan Morinis, *Everyday Holiness* (Trumpeter: Boston 2007), 30.

3. Rabbi Wolbe, *Aley Shur*, 2:186–8, 192–4

4. The following story, which I heard from Rabbi Aryeh Wolbe, Rabbi Shlomo Wolbe's grandson, illustrates the centrality of the learning mindset to Mussar. The elder Rabbi Wolbe was in the United States at a gathering of his students in this country. He asked them, "What did you learn from me?" One said, "Humility,"

and another, "Honor," and another, "Faith." Frustrated, the master said, "You didn't learn anything from me. My main thing is hitlamdut [a learning mindset]!"

5. Proverbs 18:21.

## Chapter 6: Responding to the Call: *Anavah*/Humility

1. Rashi quoting *Midrash Tanhuma* (an ancient Torah commentary) to Genesis 22:1. Rashi (d. 1104, France) is one of the great medieval Torah commentators and Talmudists. His commentary accompanies almost all versions of the Talmud. Rashi is the acronym for Rabbi Shlomo, son of Yitzchak.

2. Exodus Rabbah 1:13. Exodus Rabbah is an ancient collection of homilies based on the verses in the book of Exodus.

3. Exodus Rabba.

4. Commentary to Numbers 12:3.

5. Ruth Messinger, interview, May 2013.

6. Ibid.

7. Ibid.

8. Stosh Cotler, interview, August 2015.

9. Ibid.

10. Rabbi Bahya ibn Pequda, *The Duties of the Heart*, Daniel Haberman, trans. (New York: Feldheim, 1996), 43.

11. Rabbeinu Yonah, *Gates of Service*, as quoted in Wolbe, *Aley Shur*, 2:227.

12. Rabbi Ari Hart, interview, March 2013.

13. Ibid.

14. Ibid.

15. Ibid.

16. Ibid.

17. Morinis, *Everyday Holiness*, 49.

18. Ibid.

19. Rabbi Avi Fertig, *Bridging the Gap* (Jerusalem: Feldheim, 2007), 97–98, quoting Salanter, *Ohr Yisrael*, "Letter 30."

20. Rabbi Yosef Yuzel Horowitz, *Madregat Ha'Adam/The Stature of Man* (Bnei Brak, Israel: Elisha Stein, 1976), 245.

21. Alan Morinis, *Every Day, Holy Day* (Boston: Trumpeter Books, 2010), 57.

22. 1 Kings 19:11–12.

## Chapter 7: Creative Discomfort : *Savlanut*/Patience

1. "Black Lives Matter," Wikipedia, https://en.wikipedia.org/wiki/Black_Lives_Matter, accessed February 10, 2016, and Todd Seelie, "The Fight for the Soul of the Black Lives Matter Movement," *Gothamist*, April 7, 2015, http://gothamist.com/2015/04/07/black_lives_matter_movement.php.

2. The IAF is a national congregation-based community-organizing network

founded in the 1940s by Saul Alinsky. Alinsky is often regarded as the father of community organizing. His *Rules for Radicals* (New York: Random House, 1971) influenced generations of organizers and activists around the world.

3. Edward T. Chambers, *Roots for Radicals: Organizing for Power, Action, and Justice* (New York: Bloomsbury Academic, 2003), 108.

4. Maimonides, *Mishneh Torah*, 1:4. See also 2:3 where Maimonides seems to say that it is never a good thing to get angry. Many commentators try to work out this apparent contradiction.

5. Numbers 12:3.

6. There are contrasting midrashim about Moses's emotional state at this moment. At least one midrash claims this behavior was all for educational purposes and Moses was indeed not angry. This may have been a manifestation of cold anger.

7. Numbers 21.

8. Exodus 32–33 and Numbers 13–14. In the latter story, Moses sends twelve spies to scout out the land before the Israelites entered. They returned after forty days, and ten of them convinced the people not to try entering the land because it would be too difficult. This refusal to trust and enter the land "angered" God.

9. It is worth noting that we do not know how God experiences emotion. In fact, there is nothing we can say definitively about God's emotions. References to God's emotions both in the Torah and in our commentary should be taken as metaphor, written in the human idiom, so we can make sense of these stories. References to God's anger or God's heart are not meant to limit God in any way.

10. Exodus 32:9. Some commentators claim that God deliberately created an opening for Moses to petition for God to back down.

11. Exodus 32:9.

12. Exodus 32:9–13.

13. Stephanie Pell, interview, May 2015.

14. Rabbi Nachman, *Advice*, 128. This can also be found in the Hebrew version as Ka'as 1.

15. Michael Oshman, interview, March 2015.

16. Ibid.

17. Rabbi Shaul Judelman, interview, February 2015.

18. Ibid.

19. David Schwartz, interview, March 2015.

20. Ibid.

21. Ibid.

22. Rabbi Jill Jacobs, interview, March 2015.

23. Babylonian Talmud Shabbat 105.

24. King, *I Have a Dream*, 100.

25. Rabbi Moshe Cordevero, *Tomer Devorah/The Date Palm of Devorah*, author's translation (Jerusalem: Dov HaKohen Fink, 2004), 8–9.

26. Gary Rosenblatt, "Unlikely Partners for Peace," *Jewish Week*, July 1, 2015, http://thejewishweek.com/editorial-opinion/gary-rosenblatt/unlikely-partners-peace.

27. Rabbi Nachman, *Advice*, Avraham Greenbaum, trans. (New York: Breslov Research Institute, 1983), 128–30.

## Chapter 8: Created in the Divine Image: *Kavod*/Dignity and Honor

1. David Bornstein, "A Living Wage for Caregivers," *New York Times*, July 10, 2015, http://opinionator.blogs.nytimes.com/2015/07/10/organizing-for-the-right-to-care/.

2. The reason for this exclusion was political, "a concession to Southern lawmakers," says Bornstein in the *New York Times*. Bornstein quotes Sheila Bapat: "In the south, the majority of domestic workers and agricultural workers were African-Americans," Bapat writes in her study *Part of the Family? Nannies, Housekeepers, Caregivers, and the Battle for Domestic Workers' Rights* (New York: Ig Publishing, 2015). "Many were children of former slaves, some had been slaves themselves, and there was opposition to them receiving the same economic protections as white workers and being seen to be on the same economic footing."

3. National Domestic Workers Alliance, "Home Economics," http://www.domesticworkers.org/homeeconomics/summary (accessed February 8, 2016).

4. National Domestic Workers Alliance, "Who We Are," http://www.domesticworkers.org/who-we-are (accessed February 8, 2016).142 Wolbe, *Aley Shur*, 2:225–26.

5. Rabbi Wolbe, *Alev Shur*, 2:225–26.

6. Genesis 1:27.

7. Rabbi Irving Greenberg and Shalom Freedman, *Living in the Image of God* (Northvale, NJ: Jason Aronson, 1998) 31.

8. Genesis Rabbah 24.

9. The great Mussar leader Rabbi Nosson Tzvi Finkel (1849–1927) made the divine image of humans a central part of his program. His Slobodka yeshiva was known for emphasizing "the greatness of man." In 1928 Rabbi Isaac Sher and Rabbi Avraham Grodzinski published a collection of Rabbi Finkel's writings under the title, *Ohr Hatzafan*/The Hidden Light. This book is out of publication and difficult to find. For information about Rabbi Nosson Tzvi's teachings and life see http://web.stevens.edu/golem/llevine/SpecialEdition2.pdf.

10. Rabbi Wolbe, *Aley Shur*, 2:225.

11. National Domestic Workers Alliance, "Who We Are." (Emphasis added.)

12. Rabbi Jacobs, interview, March 2015.

13. Rabbi Yanklowitz, interview, May 2015.

14. Pope Francis, "*Laudato Si'*—Care for our Common Home," *Our Sunday Visitor*, 2015, section 2.

15. King, *I Have a Dream*, 7.

16. Pirkei Avot 4:28

17. Rabbi Joshua Lesser, interview, July 30, 2015.

18. Rabbeinu Yonah, Pirkei Avot 4:28 interprets the teaching literally. Loving kavod actually shortens your life. He cites the case of Joseph, who died ten years earlier than his brothers in Egypt because he sought after public office. Others explain that seeking honor makes one vulnerable to attacks from others, which drives one from the world. See Rabbi Nachman, *Lekutei MoHaran*, 1:6:1, and Rashi to Pirkei Avot 4:28.

19. Po Bronson, "How Not to Talk to Your Kids: The Inverse Power of Praise," *New York Magazine*, August 3, 2007, http://nymag.com/news/features/27840/.

20. Rabbi Avraham Yitzchak HaKohen Kook, *The Lights of Penitence, The Moral Principles, Lights of Holiness, Essays, Letters, and Poems*, Ben Zion Bokser, trans. (Mahwah, NJ: Paulist Press, 1978), 171–72. For the Hebrew version, see Rabbi Kook, *Orot HaTorah, Orot Hateshuva, Orot HaRaya, Mussar Avicha, Rosh Milin* (Jerusalem: Mossad HaRav Kook, 2006), Middot HaRayah Kavod 4.

21. Pirkei Avot 4:1.

22. Rabbi Shalom Noach Berezofsky, *Netivot Shalom on Pirkei Avot* (Jerusalem: Machon Emunah V'Daat, 1995), 83.

23. Rabbi Yitz Greenberg, interview, September 2015.

24. David Schwartz, interview, April 2015. Marshal Ganz is a senior lecturer in public policy at the Ash Center for Democratic Governance and Innovation, Kennedy School of Government, Harvard University.

25. Rabbi Nachman, *Lekutei Moharan*, 1:282.

26. Ibid., 1:6:1–2.

27. Nancy Kaufman, interview, March 2013

28. Ibid.

29. Rabbi Nachman, *Lekutei Moharan*, 6:2.

30. Rabbi Nachman attributes inner kavod to the mastery it took to respond to provocation with stillness. Another way inner dignity could grow from non-reactivity is by gaining the ability to hear the still, small voice within us that is often drowned out by our own defensiveness. Meriting hearing this voice, like Elijah the prophet heard the *kol demamah dakah*, "the still, small voice in the desert" (2 Kings 19), is a great honor and affirmation of inner dignity. Hearing this voice affirms our essential connection and goodness, which is the basis of our dignity. This is a dignity that no one can take away because it is so deeply imbedded within us.

31. Ariel Burger, "Hasidic Nonviolence: R. Noson of Bratzlav's Hermeneutics of Conflict Transformation" (PhD diss., Boston University, 2008), 139–41.

32. Caroline M. Clements, Caryn M. Sabourin, and Lorinda Spiby, "Dysphoria and Hopelessness Following Battering: The Role of Perceived Control, Coping, and Self-Esteem," *Journal of Family Violence* 19, no. 1 (2004): 25–36.

## Chapter 9: Balancing Trust with Effort: *Bitachon*/Trust

1. I heard this story from Janette Hillis-Jaffe, who was working with the organization as a consultant. The names have been changed to maintain anonymity.

2. Exodus 1–15.

3. Exodus 3:10.

4. For example, see Wolbe, *Aley Shur*, 2:596, and Rabbi Avraham Yeshayahu Karelitz, *Emunah u'Bitachon* [Book of Faith and Trust] (Tel Aviv: Gitler, 1944).

5. The following well-known story demonstrates the absurdity of living life only with bitachon: A man was traveling by boat, and the boat crashed into a rock and sunk. He treaded water and prayed to God for help. A large piece of wood floated by, but he refused to grab it because he had complete trust in God and was waiting for God to help him. Then a raft floated by, but he refused to grab it for the same reason. Then a helicopter came to rescue him. When the pilot called out for him to grab the rope ladder and climb aboard, he refused, saying that he trusted in God and was waiting for God to save him. He drowned. When he got to heaven, he was angry. "God, I trusted in you and you let me drown!" God said, "I sent you a board, a raft, and a helicopter, and you didn't take any of my help." The message of the story is clear. Trust in God does not mean that we do not have to do anything. There always needs to be a balance of hishtadlut (human initiative) and bitachon (trusting and letting go of control).

6. Exodus 16:4–20.

7. Genesis 3:17–19.

8. Deuteronomy 8:17.

9. Lucy Westcott, "At the U.N., Pope Condemns Thirst for Greed and Power," *Newsweek*, September 25, 2015, http://www.newsweek.com/un-pope-condemns-greed-and-lust-power-376776.

10. Wolbe, *Aley Shur*, 2:573–626.

11. Dessler, *Strive for Truth*, 2:280. A traditional Jewish perspective is to maximize trust in God and minimize effort at making a living regarding one's own well-being. Regarding someone else's well-being, it is not appropriate to rely on trusting God. We are to do the maximum we can to help the other. That said, there is still room for some bitachon for the reasons explained above, even when our efforts are in service of others.

12. Lakein, interview, February 2015.

13. Zeisel Maayan, interview, February 2015.

14. Rose Sadler, interview, March 2015.

15. Rabbi Daniel Roth, interview, March 2015.

16. Jeremiah 2:13.

17. Jeremiah 17:17–18.

18. In this way bitachon is similar to another middah, *emunah*/trustworthiness. They have in common the trait of reliability.

19. Wolbe, *Aley Shur*, 2:576.

20. In 2004 the Supreme Judicial Court of Massachusetts ruled denying marriage licenses to same-sex couples was unconstitutional. Massachusetts was the first state to legalize gay marriage.

21. Rabbi Jonah Pesner, interview, April 2013.

22. The Industrial Areas Foundation was founded by Saul Alinsky in the 1930s. It uses a model of community organizing sometimes referred to as "relational organizing" and "congregation-based community organizing."

23. Jonah Pesner and Hurman Hamilton, "A Community, Not Simply a Coalition," in *My Neighbor's Faith: Stories of Interreligious Encounter, Growth and Transformation,* Jennifer Howe Peace, Or N. Rose, and Greg Mobley, eds. (New York: Orbis Books, 2012), 251.

24. Rabbi Dessler, *Strive for Truth,* 2:269.

25. I heard Rabbi Miller use this term at the Mussar Institute Kallah in Miami, Florida, in May 2007.

## Part Four: Rest

## Chapter 10: Shabbat as a Social-Change Ritual

1. Babylonian Talmud Shabbat 54b.

2. Genesis 2:2–3.

3. Marge Piercy, "Wellfleet Shabbat," from *The Art of Blessing the Day: Poems with a Jewish Theme* (New York: Knopf, 1999).

4. Leviticus 18:5.

5. Babylonian Talmud Yoma 85a–b discusses different reasons why saving a life overrides Shabbat observance, including our verse "Live by them," to which the Talmud adds, "And don't die by them."

6. Exodus 25:8.

7. Exodus 25.

8. Exodus 35:2–5 and commentaries.

9. Parker J. Palmer, *The Courage to Teach* (San Francisco: Jossey-Bass, 1998), 63.

10. Rabbi Judelman, interview, March 11, 2015.

11. Rabbi Irving Greenberg, *The Jewish Way* (New York: Summit Books, 1988), 130.

12. Isaiah 6:3.

13. Ibid.

14. Tikkunei Zohar 57.

15. Rabbi Nachman, *Lekutei Moharan*, 1:1; Wolbe, *Aley Shur*, 2:225–26.

16. Exodus 20:9.

17. Deuteronomy 4:12.

18. Rabbi Sternhartz, *Lekutei Halachot* (Jerusalem: Meshech HaNachal, 1999), vol. 8, lesson 4, part 16.

19. Exodus 16:4–29.

20. We did get the condo.

21. Maayan, interview, February 20, 2015.

22. Babylonian Talmud Beitza 16a.

23. Greenberg, *The Jewish Way*, 127–29.

24. See the last stanza of the popular Shabbat song "Mah Yedidut."

# INDEX

Abu Awwad, Ali, 151–52
adversaries, finding good in, 75–78
adversity, developing inner kavod
    and, 173–77
Akiva, Rabbi, 162
American Jewish World Service, 118,
    168
Anan, James Kofi, 168–69, 178
anavah (humility), 112–36
    defined, 113
    flexibility and, 126–30
    as giving and taking space, 129–30
    hineini (here I am) and, 114–16,
        121–24
    humility traps, 121–26
    leadership and, 120
    low self-esteem vs., 124–26
    of not responding, 116–21
    practices for, 131–36
    resources for exploring, 131
    sustainability and, 122
anger
    grief and, 138–40, 152
    hot vs. cold, 137–42, 147–48, 152
    leading to violence, 138–39
    reflection on, 142–43
    tempering with compassion, 141,
        143–45
Antinonus, 42
Ark of the Covenant, 218
Ashkenazi Jewish community, 6,
    8, 9
attacks. *See* criticism and personal
    attacks
Avraham ibn Ezra, 45

Baal Shem Tov, 6, 8
Bahya ibn Pequda, Rabbi, 8, 124–25
barriers (meniya)

focus phrase for engaging, 32
    reflection on, 31–32
    skillfully engaging, 26–32
Bell, Shirah, 106
Ben Azzai, 162, 179
Bend the Arc, 122, 123
Ben Zoma, 170, 179
Besht, the, 6
bitachon (trust), 185–207
    confidence and, 196–202
    defined, 186
    facing fears and, 201
    hishtadlut (effort) and, 186–88, 202
    hishtadlut (effort) without, 190–94
    making a living and, 188–90, 194
    practices for, 203–7
    reflections on, 193, 196, 202
    resources for exploring, 203
    Shabbat and, 222–23
    social activism and, 192–94
    as source of renewal, 195–96
#BlackLivesMatter, 137–38
Boesky, Ivan, 53–54
Boston Law Collaborative, 73
Breslov Hasidism, 6–7, 10, 79, 177
Breslov Research Institute, 63, 64
brokenheartedness (lev shavor), 69
brokenness of the world, seeing, 10,
    20, 61, 80, 81, 146
Berezofsky, Rabbi Shalom Noach, 170
Burger King, 53
Burstein, Rabbi Nachman, 7

Cain and Abel, 45–46
campaigns
    choice points for, 92–95
    finding good points in, 78–79
    *See also* social-change activism
capitalism, 53–54, 161

National Domestic Workers Alliance, 158–60
Nazi regime, 163
needs
    hierarchy of, 19–20
    unmet, and yetzer energy, 42–43, 46
New England Jewish Labor Committee, 30
nonviolent direct action, 96
not responding, wisdom of, 116–21
Novardok Mussar, 171, 201

Obama, Barack, 90, 189–90
Occupy movements, 165–66
oppression
    choice points and, 98–99
    despair and, 69–70
    inner kavod and, 178
    pity as, 21–23
    role of yetzer in, 52–57
    within social-change movement, 56–57
    spiritual anatomy of, 54
organizations, choice points for, 92–95
Oshman, Michael, 15–16, 17, 18, 56, 144–45
otherness
    cruelty and, 5, 18, 45
    dehumanization and, 162–63
    as essential to existence, 5
others
    finding good in, 75–79, 172–73
    judging favorably, 66–68
    treating with dignity, 170, 172–73

Pacific Tomato Growers, 55–56
Palmer, Dr. Parker J., 217
Path of the Just, The (Luzzatto), 106
patience. See savlanut (patience)
Pell, Stephanie, 143–44
Penzner, Rabbi Barbara, 27–28
people in power
    seeing good points of, 65, 77
    transformation of yetzer and, 55

Pesner, Rabbi Jonah, 197–99
Piercy, Marge, 213–14
pity
    as oppression, 21–23
    solidarity vs., 28
police brutality, 137–38
Pope Francis, 164, 189, 229
practices, 105–11
    for anavah (humility), 131–36
    for bitachon (trust), 203–7
    for choice points, 87–88, 94–95, 97–98
    contemplation, 110–11
    for creating a Shabbat, 224–25
    cultivating sensitivity, 48
    facilitator's guide to group, 233–36
    finding good points, 78–79, 81
    focus phrases, 108
    guided meditation, 111
    hitbodedut (speaking our desire), 36–37, 109–10
    kabbalot, 108
    for kavod (dignity and honor), 178–84
    learning mindset, 107
    power of decision, 49–50
    for savlanut (patience), 153–57
    soul accounting (cheshbon hanefesh), 108–10
    spiritual check-in (sichat chaverim), 110, 239–40
    Torah learning, 107–8
    transforming yetzer harah, 51–52
    va'ad group, 234–35, 237–38
    visualization practice, 110
prayer
    model for authentic, 35
    speaking our desire as, 32–37

racism, 99
    despair and, 69–70
    police brutality toward blacks, 137–38
    social-justice movement and, 21–23, 57